Fashion Technology
for
Supervisor's

Akhil Jk

ISBN-10: 1505995078
ISBN-13: 978-15-5995077

DEDICATION

I would like to dedicate this book to my beloved Mom

CONTENTS

ACKNOWLEDGMENTS

I would like to express my gratitude to the many people who saw me through this book; to all those who provided support, talked things over, read, wrote, offered comments, those who have helped me to do this. Also I like to dedicate this to my beloved mom who supported me a lot to be alive in this world after many failures .
This book is made after the advice from my friend " You should share what you have learned" which made me awake and creating this .

1 THE STEP BY STEP PROCESS IN RMG

The Indian textile industry occupies a unique and important place, being one of the earliest industries in existence of with a trade linkage to foreign countries from the second century BC. A hoard (mass stored) of block printed materials in calico fabric with Guajarati designs, discovered in the "Tombs of Fostat" Egypt, are the proof of large scale Indian exports of cotton textiles in historical period

Indian sub-continent is the second largest manufacturer of garments after china being the global leader in garment production. India is known for its high quality garments. Indian garment industry is well organized with small and medium scale industries.

1. History of Garment Industry

Industrial revolution started in the 19th century, garment industry also began to evolve but it was in its immaturity and had no developed system for garment manufacturing. The Indian clothing and apparel industry had its origin during the Second World War mainly for mass production of military uniforms. Technology has been gradually upgraded from the ancient pedal sewing machineries to most modern automatic sewing machines now a days. Now India is emerged as a strong destination of all types of apparel products with wide product and quantity range.

The apparel industry grew from these tailors/businessmen, as they built manufacturing factories for production, which pattern engineering accommodated. Pattern making was first taught to "designers". Paris was center of the developments in style and creation in garments, many other countries copied from them. Garment industry has developed many new and time saving techniques, processes and machinery for the effective production today. The most important is the CAD/CAM which enables the designer, pattern maker, marker and grader to do their jobs precisely and effectively.

2. Definitions

- **Fibre: -** It is defined as one of the delicate, hair portions of the tissues of a plant or animal or other substances that are very small in diameter in relation to their length. A fiber is a material which is several hundred times as long as its thickness.

- **Textile Fibre: -** The essential requirements for Textile fibers to be spun into yarn include a length of at least 5 millimeters, flexibility, cohesiveness, and sufficient strength. Other important properties include elasticity, fineness, uniformity, durability, and luster will make a fiber into textile fiber

- **Yarn: -** Yarn is a long continuous length of twisted or interlocked fibers, suitable for use in the production of textiles, sewing, crocheting, knitting, weaving, embroidery, and rope making.

- **Thread** is a type of yarn intended for sewing by hand or machine. Sewing threads may be finished with wax or other lubricants to withstand the stresses involved in sewing. Embroidery threads are yarns specifically designed for hand or machine embroidery.

- **Fabric: -** Fabric is a flexible two dimensional material that is made by a network of natural or artificial fibers. The formation of fabric maybe interlacing (Weaving), interloping (Knitting), or inter meshing (as in knotting, punching etc.)

- **Cloth :-** Cloth is a fabric which is wearable without doing any stitches or seams in it. Example sarees, dhotis, shawls etc.

- **Garment: -** Garment is a three dimensional form made with fabrics, sewing is the major method used to construct the garments. Apparel is any clothing material made using any textile fabric/ material. Hence all garments are apparels but all apparels are not garments (e.g. CAPS, shoes etc. are apparels, shirts, trousers, etc. are garments)

There are many more definitions used, but these are some basic ideas to identify the term and it distinguish the differences between each. The other definitions are explained in the respective sessions itself.

3. Conversion chain from Fiber to Garment

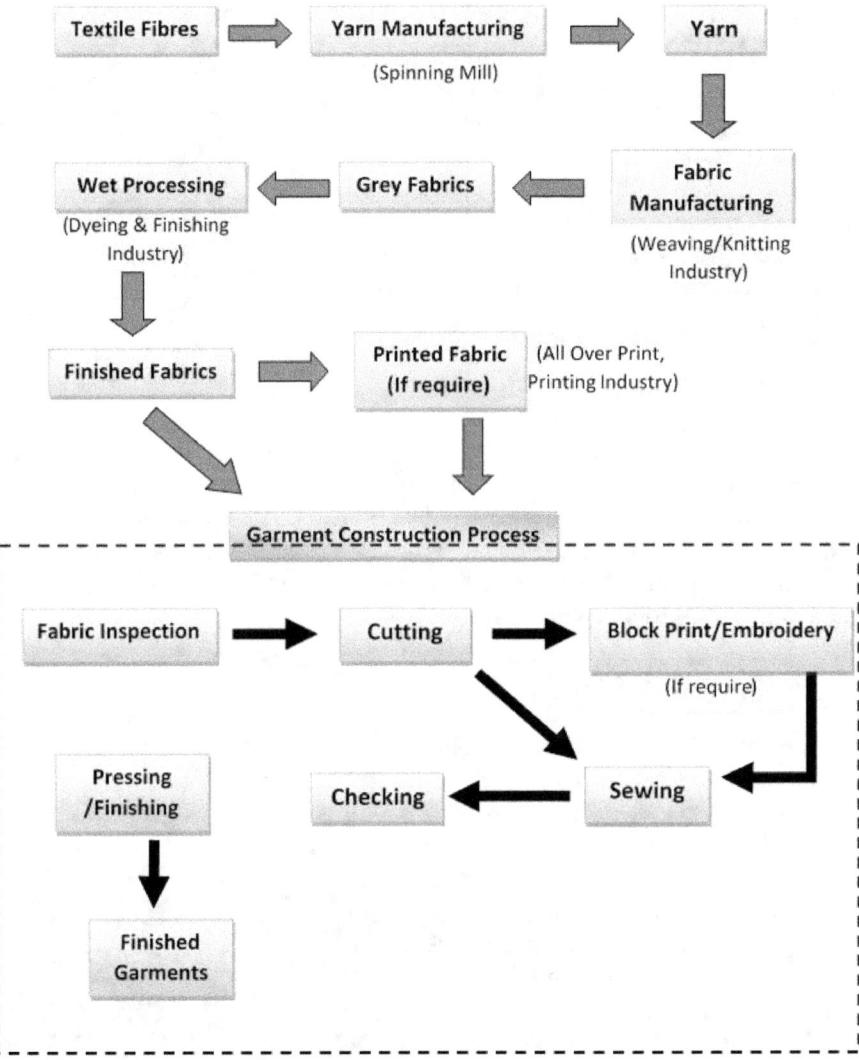

The illustration shows how a fiber is converted to a garment in basic ideas, there are many other methods available for garment manufacturing and fabric manufacturing such as braiding, looping, knitting, knotting etc. for the fabric production. The most used method is illustrated above

4. Step by Step Garment Production

Design / Sketch

The first step in garment Manufacturing is designing the sketch for the dresses that have to be prepared. For this purpose the designer first draw sketches. The designer also draws working drawings along with the sketch. Working drawings are flat drawing of the sketch and it help pattern maker in understanding the pattern details involved in the construction

Sample Making:

The first patterns are sent to the sewing unit for assembling them into garment. This is usually stitched on calico or muslin which is an inferior quality of fabric and it reduces cost. This sample is constructed to analyse the pattern fit and design too. After the sample garment is stitched it is reviewed by a panel of designers, pattern makers and sewing specialists. If any changes have to be made they are made at this time.

Production Pattern

The pattern design is now taken for creating the production patterns. The production pattern is one which will be used for bulk production of garments. The pattern maker makes the patterns on standard pattern making paper. These papers are made-up of various grades.

Garment patterns can be constructed by two means: manual method, CAD/CAM method. Today many companies have developed CAD/CAM because of the ease of designing patterns, fluency and precision involved which cannot be guaranteed with the manual method and the economy in duplication and correction. Investing once into the CAD/CAM unit is worth in itself.

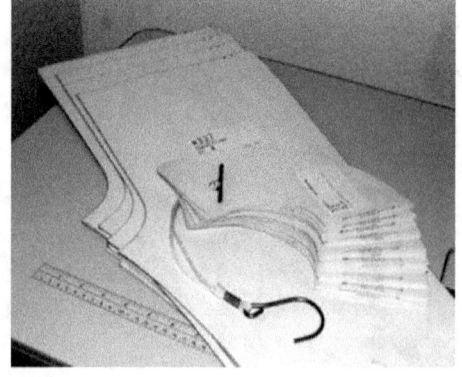

Grading

The purpose of grading is to create patterns in different sizes. Grading a pattern is really scaling a pattern up or down in order to adjust it for multiple sizes. Pattern grading by manual method is a cumbersome task because the grader has to alter the pattern on each and every point from armhole, to neckline, sleeve cap and wrist etc. by using CAD it is much easier and faster.

Marker Making:

The measuring department determines the fabric yardage needed for each style and size of garment. Computer software helps the technicians create the optimum fabric layout to suggest so that fabric can be utilized maximum. Markers, made in accordance to the patterns are attached to the fabric with the help of adhesive stripping or staples.

Markers are laid in such a way so that minimum possible fabric gets wasted during cutting operation. After marking the manufacturer will get the idea of how much fabric he has to order in advance for the construction of garments.

Computer marking is done on specialized software's. In computerized marking there is no need of large paper sheets for calculating the yardage, in fact, mathematical calculations are made instead to know how much fabric is required.

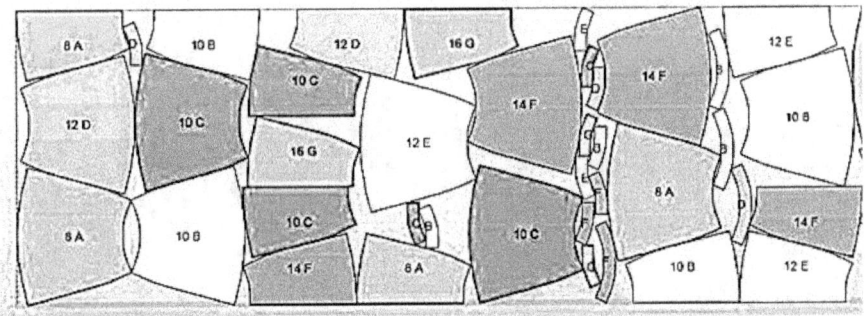

Spreading

Spreading is the layering of fabric ready for cutting, the lay length will be calculated according to the marker and the lay height (number of lays) will be according to the cut order plan of the specific order. Marker is placed on top of the lay to guide for cutting. The lays are put on One-way or Two-way direction methods

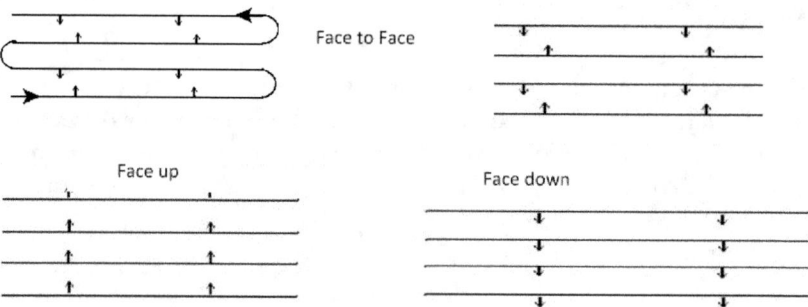

Face to Face

Face up

Face down

Two-way:- two way spreading is done on the symmetrical fabrics such as poplin. The fabric are laid continuously from left to right and right to left without cutting at the end. This method the fastest and efficient method of spreading but cannot be used for grain restrictions and one directional or most of the printed fabric. In this condition the fabric is placed as *face to face.*

One-Way:- the fabric is laid from onside to other side and the fabric has to cut in length of the marker to put the second lay, fabrics such as corduroy, velvet etc. are laid in this method. According to the fabric used the face side of the fabric may face upward or downward direction for example the corduroy is placed face down and printed fabrics are *faced up*

Cutting

The fabric is then cut with the help of cloth cutting machines suitable for the type of the cloth. These can be a straight knife, band knife, Round knife, die clickers similar to die or punch press; or computerized cutting machines that use either blades or laser beams to cut the fabric in desired shapes.

Sorting/Bundling:

The sorter sorts the patterns according to size and design and makes bundles of them. This step requires much precision because making bundles of mismatched patterns can create severe problems. On each bundle there are specifications of the style size and the marker too is attached with it. Each part is numbered for later matching.

Sewing/Assembling

The sorted bundles of fabrics are now ready to be stitched. In this workplace, there are many operators who perform a single operation (generally for product which have more than 5 operations).

Various industrial sewing machines too have different types of stitches that they can make. These machines also have different configuration of the frame. Some machines work sequentially and feed their finished step directly into the next machine, while the gang machines have multiple machines performing the same operation supervised by a single operator. All these factors decide what parts of a garment can be sewn at that station. Finally, the sewn parts of the garment, such as sleeves or pant legs, are assembled together to give the final form to the clothing.

Inspection

Open seams, wrong stitching techniques, non- matching threads, and missing stitches, improper creasing of the garment, erroneous thread tension and raw edges are some of the sewing defects which can affect the garment quality adversely. During processing the quality control section needs to check each prepared article against these defects. There are inline, end line, and final audits to control the defects and to separate critical defected garments from the lot.

Pressing/ Finishing

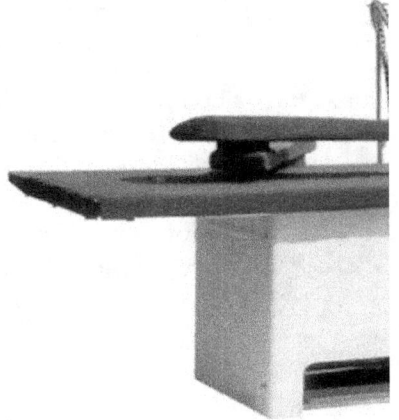

The next operations are those of finishing and/or decorating. Molding may be done to change the finished surface of the garment by applying pressure, heat, moisture, or certain other combination. Pressing, pleating and creasing are the basic molding processes. Creasing is mostly done before other finishing processes like that of stitching a cuff, decorating the garment with something like a pocket, appliqués, embroidered emblems etc. There are lot of machineries used in finishing the garment. Pressing machine, steam presses, form press, etc. Are examples

Final Inspection

For the textile and apparel industry, product quality is calculated in terms of quality and standard of fibres, yarns, fabric construction, colour fastness, designs and the final finished garments. Quality control in terms of garment manufacturing, pre-sales and posts sales service, delivery, pricing, etc are essential for any garment manufacturer, trader or exporter. Certain quality related problems, often seen in garment manufacturing like sewing, colour, sizing, or garment defects should never be over looked.

- **Sewing defects:** - Open seams, wrong stitching techniques, non-matching threads, and missing stitches, improper creasing of the garment, mistaken thread tension and raw edges are some of the sewing defects which can affect the garment quality adversely.

- **Colour defects:-** Variation of colour between the sample and the final garment, wrong colour combinations and mismatching dyes should always be avoided.

- **Size mixing:-** Wrong gradation of sizes, difference in measurement of various parts of a garment like sleeves of XL size for body of L size garment can deteriorate the garments beyond repair.

- **Garment defects:-** Broken or defective buttons, snaps, stitches, different shades within the same garment, dropped stitches, exposed notches and raw edges, fabric defects, holes, faulty zippers, loose or hanging sewing threads, misaligned buttons and holes, missing buttons, needle cuts or chews, pulled or loose yarn, stains, unfinished buttonhole, short zippers, inappropriate trimmings etc. all can lead to the end of a brand name even before its establishment.

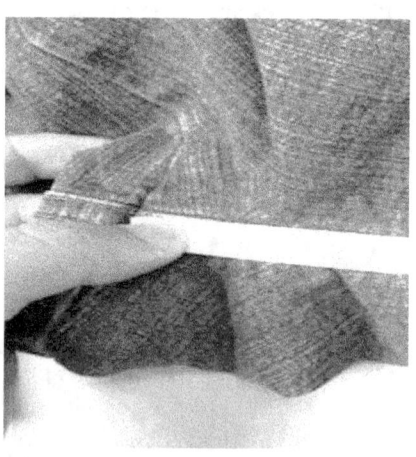

Packing

The finished garments are finally sorted on the basis of design and size and packed to send for distribution to the retail outlets. Basically packaging acts as a consumer guide which is meant to create Attraction, Interest, Desire and Sale, hence most care is taken when doing the packaging.

2 GARMENT CLASSIFICATION AND PARTS

The garments produced in the garment industry are classified based on the two parameters,

1. **Style variation: -** The extent, by which the design, fabric and makeup of the basic garment produced, varies from style to style.

2. **Frequency: -** The rate by which the change take place i.e. twice a week or twice a year.

Garment classification

1. Staple Product: - It has continuous production and design unchanged, except minor changes in Fabric, and some shapes only. As for production staple products are having continuous production as these categories are fashion. E.g. Men's under wear, Industrial work dress, etc.

2. Semi Styled Product: - A basic type of garment but with minor variations from style to style. Fabric and closures changes frequently. Production amount per fabric and style are considerably shorter than staple product. E.g. Men's classic shirt.

3. Styled Product: - This is based on one type of garment but with frequent style changes. The fabric and colour changes from style to style. The product amount somewhat shorter than for semi styled. E.g. Ladies skirt, Dress, coats etc.

4. Fashion Product: - This has extreme and abrupt change in design and cloth from one style to another style. The product amount is very less. Time is the most important factor

The garments are generally classified according to the basic method as shirt, T shirt, skirt, trouser and dress.

SHIRT

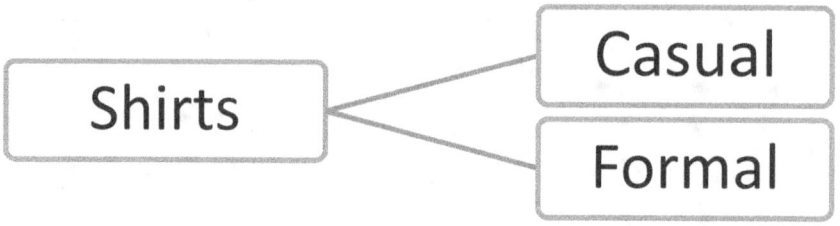

Formals Shirt

As the name indicates, it is meant for formal occasions. Formals usually seen in dark or light colour, the design is not necessary and usually used a single colour. In majorly used with ties and blazers, formals generally made of cotton, linen etc.

Casual Shirt

These types of shirts usually seen in vibrant and excessive designs, Bright colours and funny patterns may also use. Casuals generally made of denim, cotton, silk or any almost all materials are used

Formal Shirt

Casual Shirt

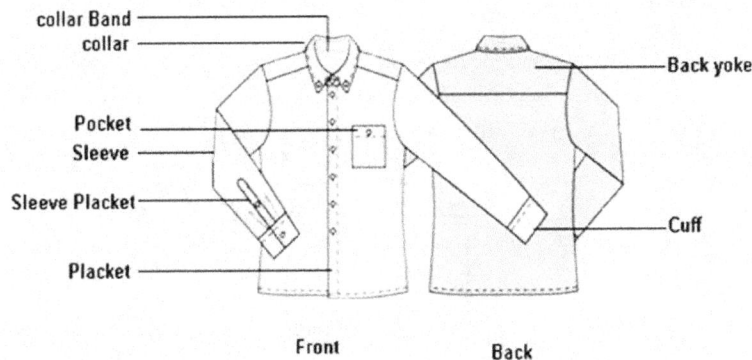

collar Band
collar

Pocket
Sleeve

Sleeve Placket

Placket

Back yoke

Cuff

Front   **Back**

T shirts can also include in this category .But it's having so much of specification to consider as a separate category.

POLO SHIRTS /T-SHIRT TYPES

Polo Shirt    T Shirt

Henley Shirts

Components of a T Shirt

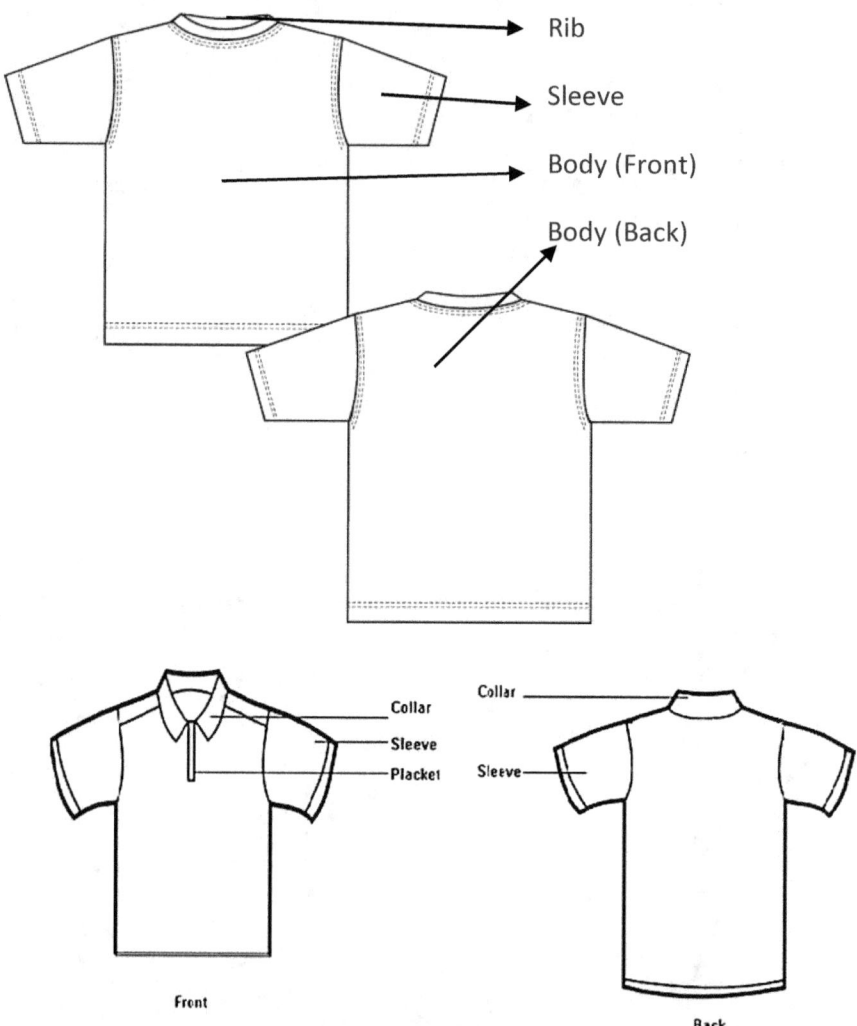

TROUSER

Trouser can be categorized into formal trousers, casual trousers.

Formal trousers are used for the formal events like, in offices, in official meetings, weddings etc.

Casual trousers include jeans, khakis, and sports trousers. It can be worn in sports, shopping, jogging, picnic, aerobics and home etc. Casual trousers can be worn by any age group. In men's fashion clothing the use of casual trousers is more than formal trousers because it is more comfortable than formal trouser.

Semiformal is a grouping of dress codes indicating the sort of clothes worn to events with level of protocol between informal and formal.

Tracksuit bottoms or Sweatpants are a casual variety of soft trousers intended for comfort or athletic purposes

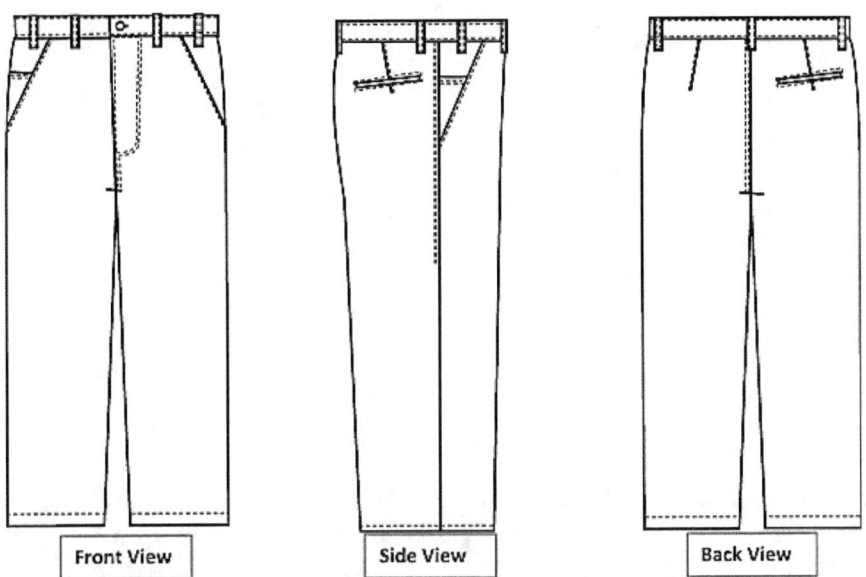

| Front View | Side View | Back View |

The components of a basic Trouser are, Front panel (2 No.), Back Panel (2 No.), Waist band (2 No.), Fly piece (3 No.), Pocket facing (2 No.), Welt facing (4 No.), Pocket bag (3 No.), Belt loop (7 No) etc.

BASIC SKORT / A LINE SKIRT

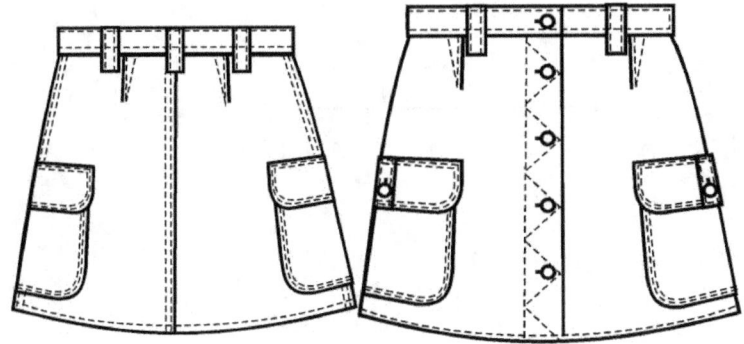

The components of a basic Skirt are, Front (2), Back (2), Waist band (2), Belt loop (5), Pocket (2), Pocket flap (4), Flap (2) etc.

DRESS

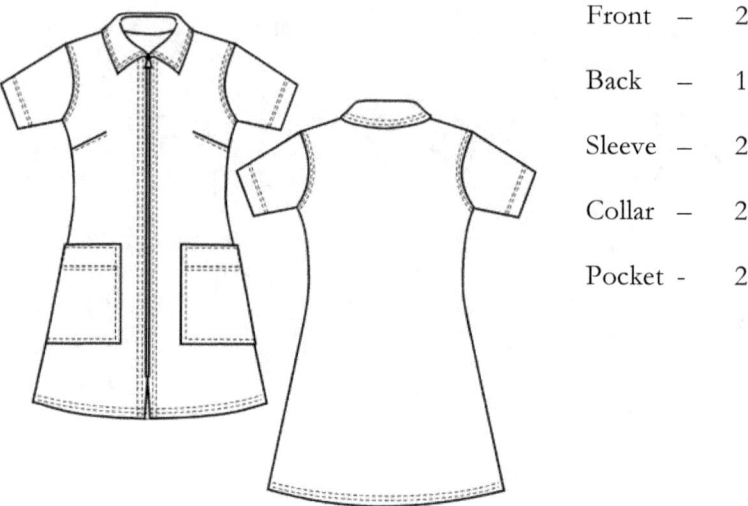

Front   –   2

Back   –   1

Sleeve   –   2

Collar   –   2

Pocket -   2

Apart from these there are many modified garments and accessories like Innerwear, sports garments, SPT garments etc. all kind of garments are modifications from the base garment according to the style, mode of usage requirements. Most of the garments are having different parts but the major similarity is most are the modifications from this basic categories

3 TRIMS AND ACCESSORIES

TRIMS are the items used in garments for

- Decoration
- Utility
- To make it functional

Anything other than Fabric & being used in Garment is called a trim or accessory. The materials used for some functional use such as closing, etc. are known as trims, and all other materials are accessories.

All Trims are accessories but all accessories are not trims.

1. ZIPPER

A zip is a popular device for temporarily joining two edges of fabric.

The components of a zipper are:

1. Top tape extension
2. Top stop
3. Slider
4. Pull tab
5. Tape
6. Chain width
7. Bottom stop
8. Bottom tape extension
9. Single tape width
10. Insertion pin
11. Retainer box

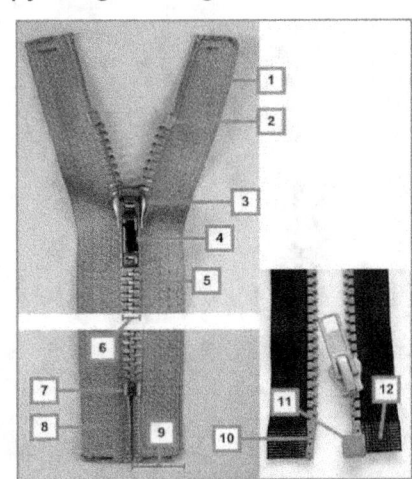

12. Reinforcement film

Zippers may:
- Increase or decrease the size of an opening to allow or restrict the passage of objects, as in the fly of trousers or in a pocket.

- Join or separate two ends or sides of a single garment, as in the front of a jacket, dress or skirt.

- Attach or detach a separable part of the garment to or from another, as in the conversion between trousers and shorts or the connection / disconnection of a hood and a coat.

- Decorate an item.

2. THREAD

Thread is a type of yarn intended for sewing by hand or machine. Modern manufactured sewing threads may be finished with wax or other lubricants to withstand the stresses involved in sewing,

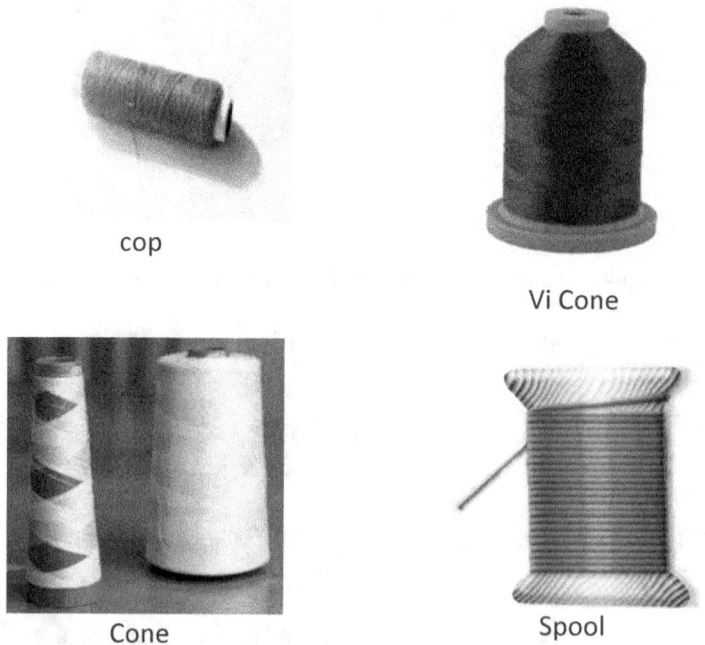

cop

Vi Cone

Cone

Spool

3 BIAS AND TWILL TAPE

Bias tape or bias binding is a narrow strip of fabric, cut on the cross-grain. The strip's fibres, being at 45 degrees to the length of the strip, make it stretcher as well as more fluid and more drape able compared to a strip that is cut on grain. Many strips can be pieced together into a long "tape." The tape's width varies from about 1/2" to about 3" depending on applications. Bias tape is used in making piping, binding seams, finishing raw edges, etc. It is often used on the edges of quilts, placemats, and bibs, around armhole and neckline edges instead of a facing, and as a simple strap or tie for casual bags or clothing.

4 LINING

Lining is a material layer that enhance

- Overall Look
- Strength

By supporting the interiors of the garment or garment part

5 HANG TAG

These items are used to display the information of respective product & Brand. Generally hangtags are placed after the packing or just before packing. There are variety of tags used.

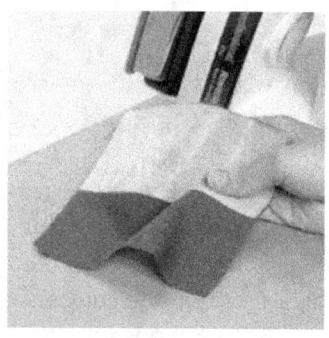  

6 EMBROIDERY

Embroidery is the art or handicraft of decorating fabric or other materials with needle and thread or yarn. Embroidery may also incorporate other materials such as metal strips, pearls, beads, quills, and sequins.

 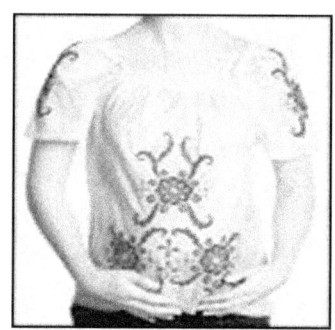

7 PIPING

In sewing, piping is a type of trim or embellishment consisting of a strip of folded fabric inserted into a seam to define the edges or style lines of a garment or other textile object. Usually the fabric strip is cut on the bias, and often it is folded over a cord. It may be made from either self-fabric (the same fabric as the object to be ornamented) or contrasting fabric, or of leather

8 APPLIQUÉS

Appliqué is a smaller ornament or device applied to another surface. Example - Various fabrics shapes, Motifs etc.

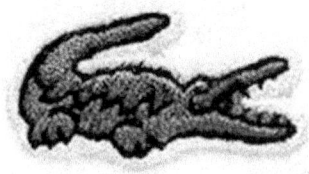

9 LACE

Lace is an ornamental openwork fabric or trim made into variety of designs by intricate Manipulation of fibre or yarn.

10 LABELS

A label is a piece of paper, polymer, cloth, or other material affixed to a container or article, on which is a legend, information concerning the product and consumer.

Examples

*   Size label

*   Fit Label

*   Show Label etc.

11 BUTTONS

A button is small fastener, which secures two pieces of fabric together or Join two edges temporarily. Measuring Unit of button is Ligne. There are 12 lignes to one inch. The standardized conversion for a ligne is 2.2558291 mm (1 mm = 0.443296 ligne), and it is abbreviated with the letter L.

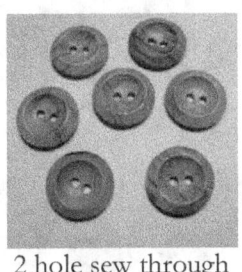

2 hole sew through

4 hole sew through

Shank

fancy decorative

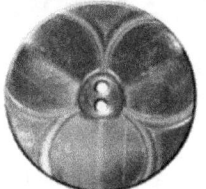

Shell

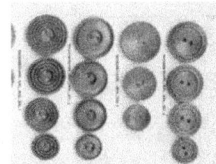

Wooden

12 SNAP BUTTON

Snap button (also called stud) is a pair of interlocking discs commonly used in place of buttons to fasten clothing. A circular lip under one disc fits into a groove on the top of the other, holding them fast until a certain amount of force is applied. Snap fasteners are often used in children's clothing, as they are relatively easy for children to use.

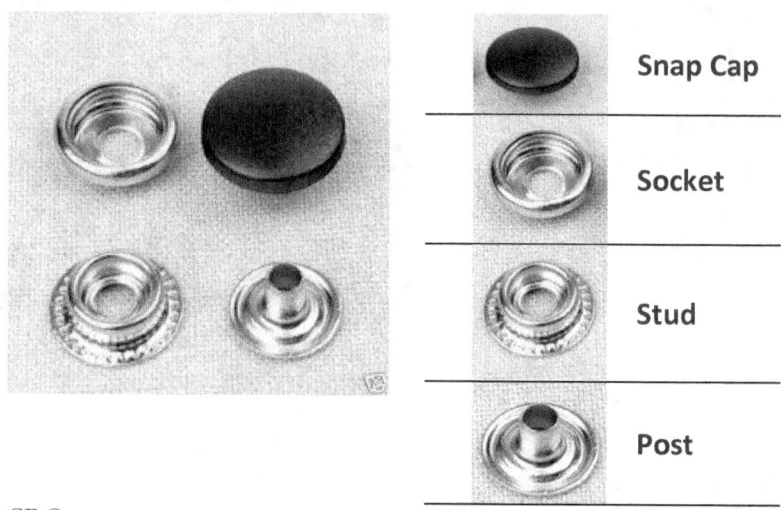

13 VELCRO

Velcro is a snap fastener, locks with its hooks and loops

It consists of two layers:

- A "hook" side, which is a piece of fabric covered with tiny hooks
- And a "loop" side, which is covered with even smaller and "hairier" loops. When the two sides are pressed together, the hooks catch in the loops and hold the pieces together when the layers are separated, the strips make a characteristic "ripping" sound.

14 ELASTIC

A band capable of resuming original shape after stretching or compression, mostly used in kids wear as kids are the rapidly growing bodies.

 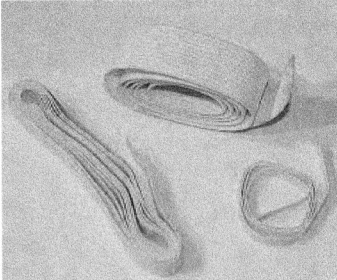

There are many more accessories used in garment production, all are according to developed according to its use and designed according to the design of the garment and function of the part to do.

+++++

4 MEASURING

1. MEASURING TAPE

A tape measure or measuring tape is a flexible form of ruler. It consists of a ribbon of cloth, plastic, fiber glass, or metal strip with linear-measurement markings. It is a common measuring tool. Its flexibility allows for a measure of great length to be easily carried in pocket or toolkit and permits one to measure around curves or corners. Fiber made measuring tape is used in the garment industry which has Inches on 1 side and Centimeters on the other side.

An 1/16th of an inch is the smallest measurement on a tape measure. The distance between every line on the tape measure is 1/16 of an inch.

A 1/8 of an inch is twice as big as the 1/16 of an inch. It is every other mark.

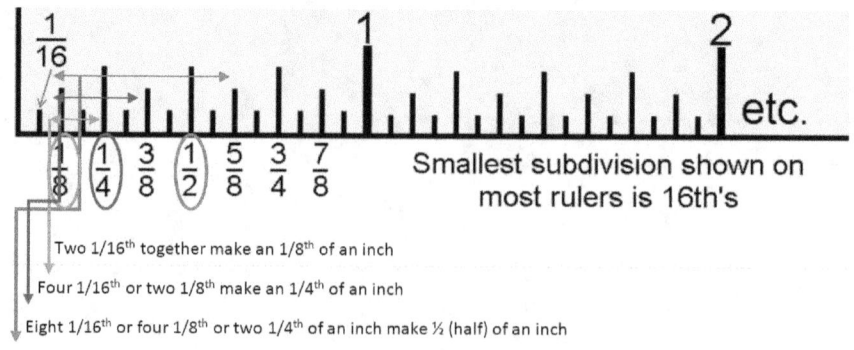

HOW TO USE A MEASURING TAPE

1.   Hold the front of the tape at the point you wish to start the measurement from, and extend it to the point where you want to stop.

2.   The correct way to read a measurement in measuring tape is shown in the figure below. The eye must be positioned vertically above the mark to avoid error

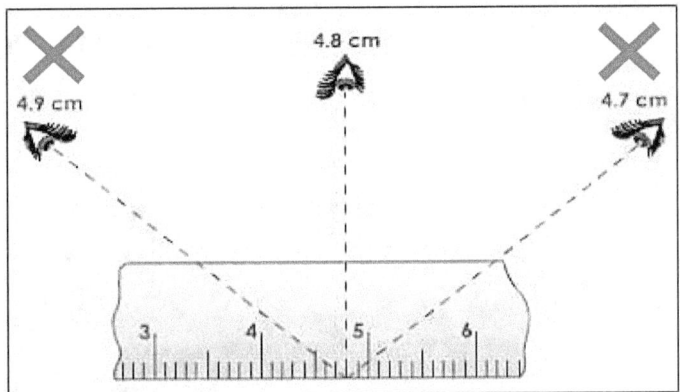

3.   Read the first large number before your stop point - this will tell you the number of inches

4.   Read the smaller lines of various sizes (remembering what the various sizes mean) up until your stop point. This will tell you you're fraction of an inch.

Precautions while using tape

1.   Line up the 1-inch mark with one end of the object being measured. Sometimes the metal hook becomes loose and can cause your measurement to be off by up to 1/16 of an inch. Be sure to deduct 1 inch from the measurement.

2.   Freeze the starting point of the measuring tape before starting the measurement so that it doesn't slide from initial point of measurement

5 SEWING TOOLS

Tailor's chalk: -

Tailor's chalk is a type of chalk which is designed to make temporary markings on cloth. Using tailor's chalk, an operator can make markings where fabric needs to be cut or garments need to be sewn or altered, and the chalk can also be used to mark out cutting, hemming, and darting lines on garments as they are constructed. Once the markings are no longer useful, they can be easily brushed off or washed out, leaving no residue behind.

Measuring Tape

A tape measure or measuring tape is a flexible form of ruler. It consists of a ribbon of cloth, plastic, fiber glass, or metal strip with linear-measurement markings generally inches on one side and centimeters on another

Scissors

Scissors are hand-operated shearing instruments. They consist of a pair of metal blades pivoted so that the sharpened edges slide against each other when the handles (bows) opposite to the pivot are closed. Scissors are used for cutting various thin materials, such as paper, cardboard, metal foil, thin plastic, cloth, rope, and wire. Scissors can also be used to cut hair. Hair-cutting scissors have a specific blade angle ideal for cutting hair. Using the incorrect scissors to cut hair will result in increased damage and or split ends by breaking the hair. Food scissors, also known as kitchen scissors, are for cutting and trimming foods such as meats. Hair-cutting scissors and shears are functionally equivalent, but the larger implements tend to be called shears.

A large variety of scissors and shears exist for different specialized purposes.

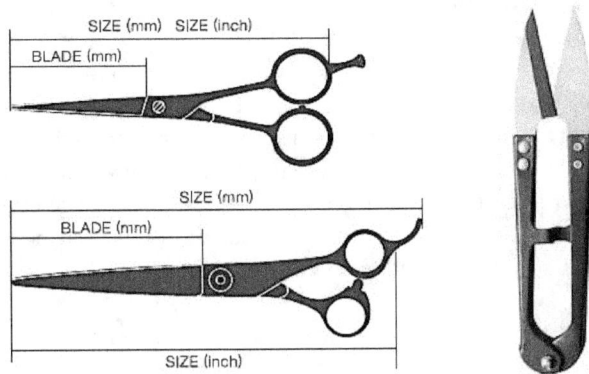

Modern scissors are often designed ergonomically with composite thermoplastic and rubber handles which enable the user to exert either a power grip or a precision grip.

Seam Ripper

Seam ripper is a specialty notion that features a curved blade ending in a sharp point on one side and a small ball on the opposite edge, to help protect against damaging adjacent fabric. Seam rippers are available in sizes to fit different hands, ranging from 2¾ inches to 6 inches (7–12.7 cm). They also come in a variety of colors and handle styles.

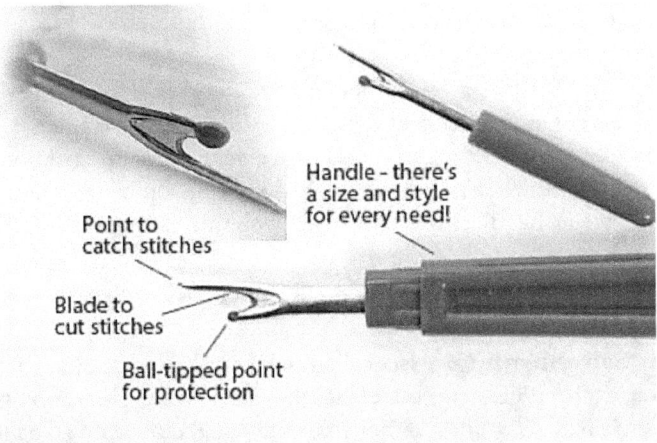

Point to catch stitches

Blade to cut stitches

Ball-tipped point for protection

Handle - there's a size and style for every need!

A Marking pencil is another marking tool apart from tailor's chalk. They are available in different colours light colours are used for marking on dark fabrics and vice versa.

Hand Sewing Needle

A sewing needle is a long slender tool with a pointed tip. The first needles were made of bone or wood; modern ones are manufactured from high carbon steel wire, nickel- or 18K gold plated for corrosion resistance. The highest quality embroidery needles are plated with two-thirds platinum and one-thirds titanium alloy. Traditionally, needles have been kept in needle books or needle cases which have become an object of adornment. Sewing needles can also be kept in an etui, a small box that held needles and other items such as scissors, pencils and tweezers.

A needle for hand-sewing has an eye, at the blunt end to carry thread or cord through the fabric after the pointed end pierces it.

Types of hand sewing needles

Hand sewing needles come in a variety of types/ classes designed according to their intended use and in a variety of sizes within each type.

- **Sharp Needles**: used for general hand sewing; built with a sharp point, a round eye, and are of medium length. Those with a double-eyes are able to carry two strands of thread while minimizing fabric friction.
- **Appliqué**: These are considered another all-purpose needle for sewing, appliqué, and patch work.
- **Embroidery**: Also known as crewel needles; identical to sharps but have a longer eye to enable easier threading of multiple embroidery threads and thicker yarns.
- **Betweens or Quilting:** These needles are shorter than sharps, with a small rounded eye and are used for making fine stitches on heavy fabrics such as in tailoring, quilt making and other detailed handwork; note that some manufacturers also distinguish between quilting needles and quilting between needles, the latter being slightly shorter and narrower than the former.
- **Milliners**: A class of needles generally longer than sharps, useful for basting and pleating, normally used in millinery work
- **Easy- or Self-threading:** Also called calyxeyed sharps, side threading, and spiral eye needles, these needles have an open slot into which a thread may easily be guided rather than the usual closed eye design.

- **Beading**: These needles are very fine, with a narrow eye to enable them to fit through the centre of beads and sequins along with a long shaft to thread and hold a number of beads at a time.
- **Bodkin**: Also called ballpoints, this is a long, thick needle with a ballpoint end and a large, elongated eye. They can be flat or round and are generally used for threading elastic, ribbon or tape through casings and lace openings.
- **Chenille**: These are similar to tapestry needles but with large, long eyes and a very sharp point to penetrate closely woven fabrics. Useful for ribbon embroidery.
- **Darning**: Sometimes called finishing needles, these are designed with a blunt tip and large eye making them similar to tapestry needles but longer; yarn darners are the heaviest sub-variety.
- **Doll**: Not designed for hand sewing at all, these needles are made long and thin and are used for soft sculpturing on dolls, particularly facial details.
- **Leather**: Also known as glovers and as wedge needles, these have a triangular point designed to pierce leather without tearing it; often used on leather-like materials such as vinyl and plastic.
- **Sailmaker**: Similar to leather needles, but the triangular point extends further up the shaft; designed for sewing thick canvas or heavy leather.
- **Tapestry**: The large eye on these needles lets them to carry a heavier weight yarn than other needles, and their blunt tip—usually bent at a slight angle from the rest of the needle—allows them to pass through loosely woven fabric such as embroidery canvas or even-weave material without catching or tearing it; comes in a double-eyed version for use on a mounted frame and with two colors of thread.

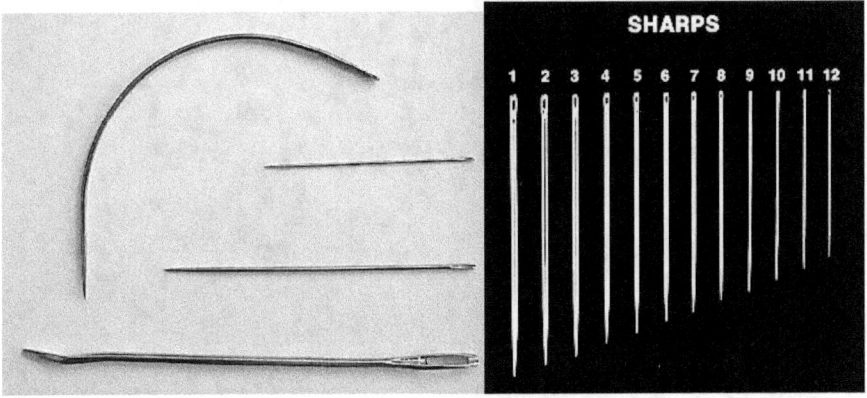

- **Tatting**: These are built long with an even thickness for their entire length, including at the eye, to enable thread to be pulled through the double stitches used in tatting.
- **Upholstery**: These needles are heavy, long needles that may be straight or curved and are used for sewing heavy fabrics, upholstery work, tufting and for tying quilts; the curved variety is practical for difficult situations on furniture where a straight needle will not work Heavy duty 12" needles are used for repairing mattresses. Straight sizes: 3"-12" long, curved: 1.5"-6" long.

Machine Sewing Needle

Needles are the most important and frequently changeable part of the sewing machine and they can change how the sewing machine forms stitches, the correct size and type of the sewing needle is necessary to produce a good quality sewing. The selection of the needle is based on the fabric type & seam. The below are the major extracts of the classification

Needle classification based on sewing needle point are, Universal needle, Sharp point needle, set point needle, ball point needle etc. [a detailed chapter is following]

Bobbin and Case

A bobbin case is used in sewing and it is locked into the hook using latch mechanism. It is round .It is used to hold the bobbin into the machine and apply time tension to the machine.

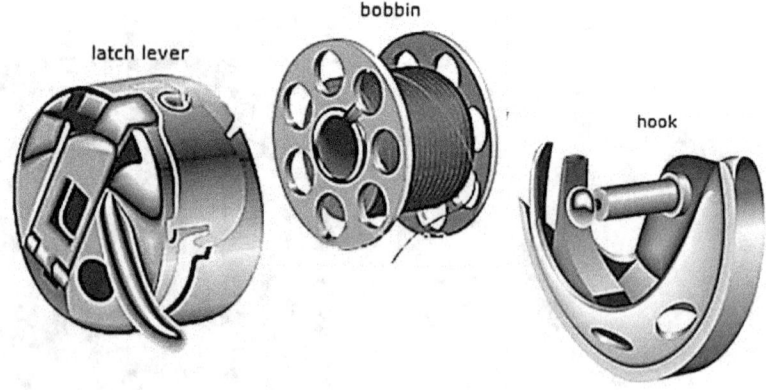

Apart from these basic tools there are other tools like Thimble, pins etc are also in use and most are based on the application of those tools.

6 BASICS OF TEXTILES

A supervisor should have basic knowledge about textiles, how the fabrics are made etc. this chapter will contain such key areas, prepared according to the necessary knowledge to a supervisor.

Fiber

A fiber is an individual hair like substance, with comparatively high ratio of length to width, a textile fiber only can be spun into yarn or made into a fabric. The essential properties like at least 5 mm of length, flexibility, cohesiveness and sufficient strength makes the textile fibers

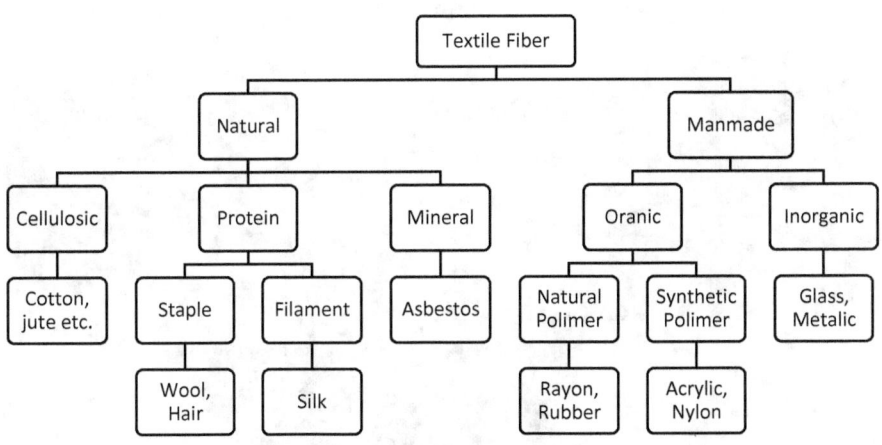

Yarn

Yarns are defined as group of fibers twisted together to form a continuous strand. All textile fabrics (except for a few like felt) and non-woven fabrics are produced from yarns.

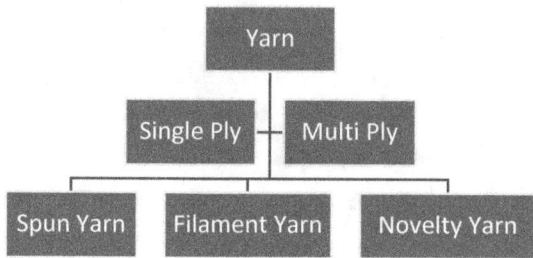

Spun yarns are composed of relatively short length of fiber twisted or spun so that they hold together.

Filament Yarns are composed of continuous strands of fiber that may be kilometers long. These yarns are produced directly from spinnerette or from a silk cocoon. Because filament yarns, unlike spun yarns, contains fibers of infinite length, they do not need to be highly twisted. Most filament yarns are of low twist (enough to hold the fibers together) to provide a smooth, lustrous surface.

Novelty Yarns, also called as fancy yarns, are not of uniform thickness throughout their length, but have deliberate irregularities on their surface, these irregularities may be knots, bumps, curls, or similar effects.

Filament Yarn

Spun Yarn

Novelty

Yarn Twist.

Yarns are made by twisting together parallel or nearly parallel fibers. The amount of twist in the yarn is defines as TPI (Twist per Inch) of the yarn. The TPI in the yarn has important bearing on the appearance and durability of yarn and the fabric which will be made from it.

Yarn Twist Direction

There are two type of yarn twist 'S' and 'Z' In an S twist yarn, the spirals run upward to the left corresponding to the direction of the central part of the letter S. In an Z twist yarn the spirals run upward to the right similar to the center part of the letter Z. yarn twist direction will not have effect on properties such as strength or abrasion resistance. And it effect the surface appearance of fabric

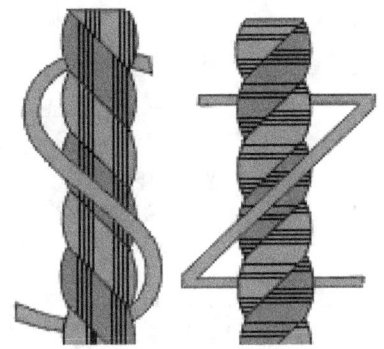

Yarn Count:

Count is a numerical value, which express the coarseness or fineness (diameter) of the yarn and also indicate the relationship between length and weight (the mass per unit length or the length per unit mass) of that yarn. Therefore, the concept of yarn count has been introduced which specifies a certain ratio of length to weight.

The cotton count system is based on the number of 840 yard hanks you get from one pound of thread. You get 8,400 yards of size 10 (coarse) or 84,000 yards of size 100 (extremely fine) from one pound of cotton yard in this system. The size is measured for an individual yarn or strand. Most threads are made from multiple strands or plies. In the cotton count system, 50/2 designates a two-ply thread made from two size 50 yarns. That has the same fiber content as one size 25 yarn.

The Hong Kong ticket system is the same as the cotton count system, just written without the slash. So a cotton count 50/2 thread is a Hong Kong ticket 502 thread.

Singles equivalent gives the single yarn size (1-ply) with the same weight as the thread being measured. For example,

30/3 is singles equivalent size 10, while 30/2 is singles equivalent size 15

Thread weight gives the yarn size of the 2-ply thread with the same weight as the thread being measured. For example,

> 30/3 is thread weight 20 (20/2 = 30/3), while 30/2 is thread weight 30. Thread weight is used commonly for embroidery threads.

Cotton ticket gives the yarn size of the 3-ply thread with the same weight as the thread being measured. For example,

> 30/3 is cotton ticket 30, while 30/2 is cotton ticket 45 (45/3 = 30/2). You have to know which of these systems is being used, or your thread sizes can be off by a factor of three!

The Tex system is based on the weight in grams of a thread 1 kilometer long. A kilometer of tex 10 (very fine) thread weighs 10 grams, while a kilometer of tex 100 (very coarse) weighs 100 grams. The Tex system measures the entire thread, no matter how many strands or plies it has. While a thread can have any actual weight, the Tex system has official ranges of sizes that get the same Tex number. For example,

> all threads weighing between 24.0 and 26.9 grams per kilometer are designated T-24.

Ticket Numbering

Ticket number is a system to give easy approximations of the specific size of finished thread and is different for different thread types even if the Tex no is same.

> To convert Tex into ticket (1000/Tex No) x 3 Lower the Ticket, thicker the thread

Direct count (Fixed-length) systems: the thicker the yarn, the higher the count. (eg. Tex, Denier etc.)

Count   = number of weight units for a fixed length unit

              = weight / length unit

10 Tex   = 10 grams / 1 km (1000 Mtr.)

10 Denier   = 10 grams / 1 Dn. (900 Mtr.)

Indirect Count (Fixed-weight) systems: the thicker the yarn, the lower the count.

Count   = number of length units for a fixed weight unit

              = length unit / weight unit

10s cotton   = 10 hanks of 840 yards / 1 pound

Sewing threads.

Sewing threads are special kind of yarns that are engineered and designed to pass through a sewing machine rapidly, to form a stitch efficiently, and to function while in a sewn product without breaking for the least useful life of the product.

Fibers and Finishing used for Threads

Cotton, nylon, polyester, and rayon are the commonly used fibers to manufacture sewing threads. Cotton-covered polyester is the most used sewing thread. All sewing threads whether spun, filament, or core spun are highly twisted ply yarns, and are often finished with mercerizing, soft, glace and bonded finishing may be done. Some special finishes like flame-resistance, heat – resistance are applied for high speed sewing threads.

Thread Selection

The type of thread used will determine the durability, appearance, and satisfaction of the product.

- Thread size should be fine as possible, consider the strength also

- The breaking strength of the seam should be less than that of the fabric sewn. (min 60% of fabric strength)

- For a synthetic thread. The shrinkage rate should be same as of the fabric.

- Heavy weight thread should be used for the heavy weight fabrics to reduce puckering.

Comparison of Sewing Thread Types.		
Spun Thread	Filament Thread	Core spun thread.
Lower strength	Higher strength than spun, Finer threads can be used	Combines the best features of both
Versatile for all type on machines	Produce neat seams, machine settings are cautious	Especially useful in durable-press garments
Less amount of seam pucker	Greater possibility of puckering	Same puckering as spun thread
Least cost	Costlier, texturisation required, Good for knits	Most costly

Fabric

A fabric is a two dimensional substance made using yarn, which can be used for manufacturing of garments, or can be used as clothes. Cloth is a fabric which can be wearable. The term fabric denotes fibers or yarns that can be made to fabric by means of a variety of methods as follows.

- Weaving
- Knitting
- Braiding
- Felting   etc…

Woven fabrics are composed of longitudinal warp threads and transverse weft threads which are interlaced each one another; according to the class of structure and form of design that are designed. A warp thread individually produced with definite twist and strength and is known as end. While the terms pick and filling are applied to the weft threads but in order to distinguish one series from the other the warp threads are mostly described as ends and the weft threads as picks.

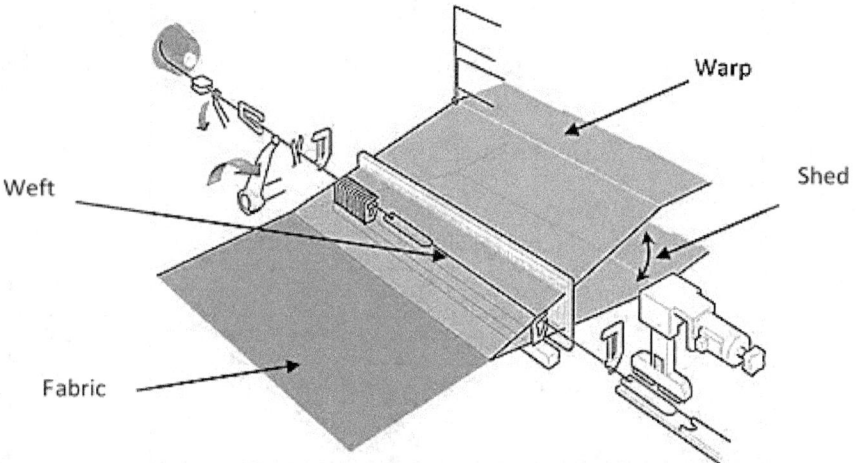

Fabric Features.

- **Selvedge**: - is a lengthwise edge of the fabric usually between ¼ "to ½ inch wide and exist on both the edge of the fabric. The purpose being the edge of the fabric will not tear when the cloth is undergoing stress and strain of the finishing process

- **Warp and Weft:** - the warp yarns are those running throughout the length of the fabric and the Weft of filings are the cross threads. The interlacement of the warp and weft makes the fabric construction.

- **Face and Back:** - the face side has the better appearance and usually forms the outside of the garment. The two sides may be different because of the weave, finish.

- **Yarns per inch:** - the yarns per inch or density in a fabric is given by two numbers with and "x" mark between them. For example 80 x 70 (pronounced as eighty by seventy) means eighty yarns per inch in the warp and seventy yarns per inch in the weft

- **Weave:** - weave is the order in which the yarns are interlaced.

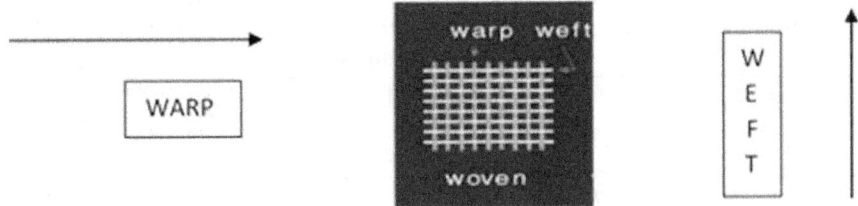

Knitting

Knitting the a method of making the yarn into a fabric by interloping the yarn or yarns together or on a specific design or method,

Knit fabrics are classified as,

1. Weft Knit e.g.:- Single Jersey, Rib, Interlock, Pique etc.

2. Warp Knit e.g.:- Rachel, Tricot, Milanese etc

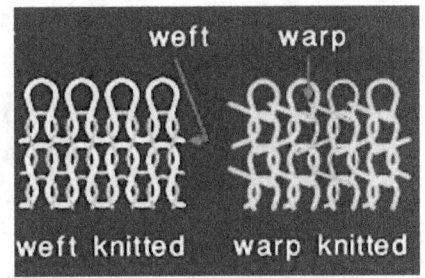

Fabric Differences Woven and Knitted Fabric

Sl	Woven Fabric	Knit Fabric
1	Fabric is made by interlacing of yarns.	Fabric is made by inter-looping.
2	Two sets of threads-Warp and Weft are used in making the fabrics.	One or one set of threads is used in making the fabric.
3	Weaving requires more number of preparatory processes.	Knitting requires less number of preparatory processes.
4	Machines are mostly Flat.	Machines are flat as well as circular.

5	Fabric is comparatively more rigid.	Fabric is comparatively less rigid.
6	Fabric is less stretchable.	Fabric is more stretchable.
7	Fabric does not bend easily and results less comfort and form fitting properly.	Fabric bends easily and results good comfort and form fitting properly.
8	It is easy to tear the fabric.	It is difficult to tear the fabric.
9	Fabric has low wrinkle (crease) resistance.	Fabric has high wrinkle (crease) resistance.
10	Lesser inherent tensions cause minimum shrinkage and loss of size.	During conversion of yarn into loop tension development is high which results higher shrinkage.
11	Moisture absorption power is less due to compact structure.	Moisture absorption is more because of comparatively loose and voluminous construction.
12	Fabrics are more dimensional stable due to tighter construction and intersecting of warp and weft at right angles.	Because of loop structure and inability of yarns to return to original position the dimensional stability is poor.
14	Woven Fabric	Knit Fabric

There are many more features like dyeing, printing, finishing etc. but these included here are the just basics of a fabric that a supervisor must understood and identify.

7 SIZE AND SPEC' CHART

Spec' Sheet

Specification sheets provide important details to ensure the correct execution of your patterns into finished garments. Spec sheets help to produce accurate samples, which improves turnaround time and simplifies communication during all stages of manufacturing and quality control.

Spec sheets include detailed technical diagrams, construction notes, finished garment measurements, fabric yields and material and trim details.

A spec sheet for an overseas manufacturer of shirt might have the following information's in the spec sheet:

1. Photo of the approved sample.
2. Size of approved sample – this size is used as the basis for your grading (sizing).
3. Style number of the shirt
4. Details of the required Stitches and Seams – cover stitch, baby hem, overlock etc...
5. Fabric swatches and specifications – if more than one, then specify where they go on the shirt
6. Trim card and placement details – buttons, bows, ribbons, embroidery etc.
7. Component sewing instructions - Pockets, placket, collar etc...
8. Garment / fabric Dyeing and finishing details
9. Fabric & Garment Shrinkage details like post wash shrinkage
10. Fusing details such as temperature, pressure etc.
11. Grading instructions – Grade is 1", 2", 2 14" etc...
12. Label placement position details

13. Care label placement position

14. Size label placement

15. Made in label placement

16. Hang tag placement.

17. Type of packaging (Hanger with poly bag or folded in a poly bag etc)

18. Package Printing instructions

19. Carton box packing ratio etc.

Or any additional information and requirement

The Spec Sheet is also known as Tech pack once it comes with the full details and is in a Booklet form,

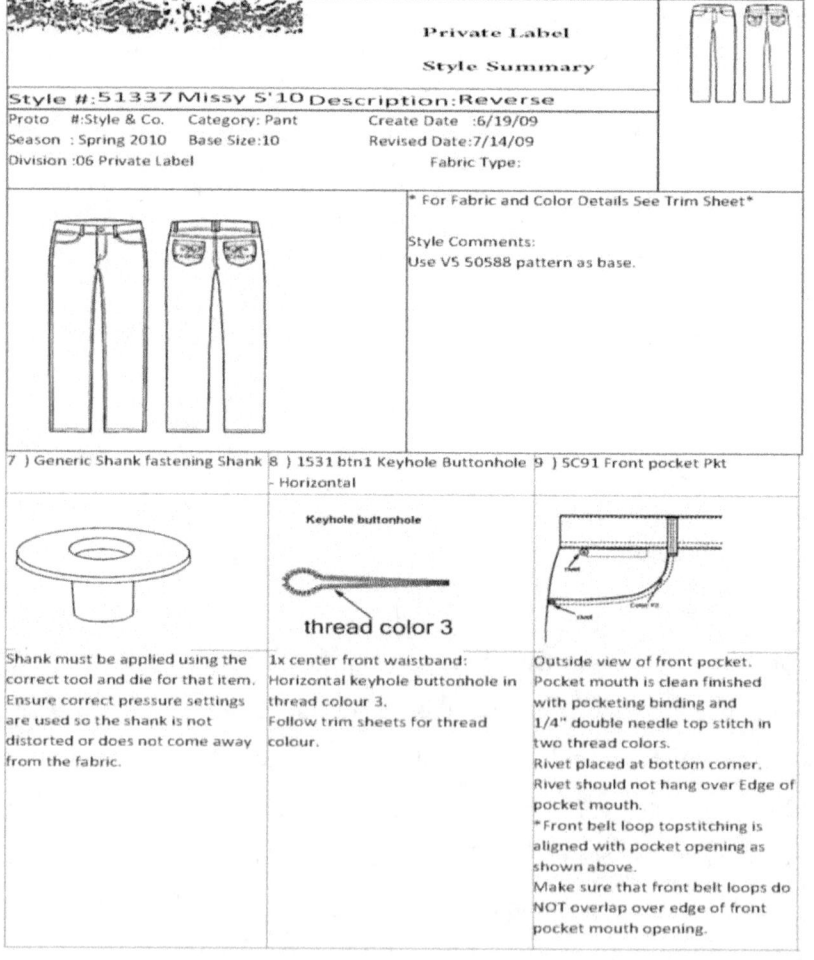

	Private Label Measurement		

Style #:51337 Missy S'10 Description:Reverse

Proto #:Style & Co.	Category: Pant	Create Date:6/19/09
Season: Spring 2010	Base Size:10	Revised Date:7/14/09
Division:06 Private Label		Fabric Type:

Ref. #	Measurement Point	Position	10		Tol+/-
B-1B	Waist relaxed at top of band		32 1/2		1/2
B-1C	Waist relaxed at bottom of band		35 1/4		1/2
B-5B	Low hip from top of waist	6"	40		1/2
B-8A	Thigh width at crotch		26		3/8
B-9	Knee Width	12" below crotch	17 3/4		3/8
B-10C	Leg opening pants		17 1/2		1/4
B-11	Inseam	average	32 1/2		1/2
B-12A	Out seam below waistband (Pant)	average	40 1/2		3/4
B-6B	Front rise from top of waist		10 1/4		1/4
B-7B	Back rise from top of waist		15 1/2		1/4
B-3A	Waistband height		1 3/4		1/8
B-13A	Front pocket from Side Seam@ waist		4		1/8
B-14A	Front pocket below waistband		2 1/4		1/4
B-15A	Inside pocket bag length below waistband		7		1/2
B-16	Coin pocket from side seam		5/8		1/8
B-18	Coin pocket width		3/8		1/8
B-18A	Coin pocket length		2 1/2		1/8
B-19A	Yoke height at center below waistband		2		1/8
B-20A	Yoke height at side seam below		1		1/8
	Back Pocket below yoke	at CB	1		1/8
	Back pocket below yoke	at SS	1 1/4		1/8
B-21	Back pocket length	at center	5 1/2		1/8
B-21	Back pocket length	at side	4 3/4		1/8
B-22	Back pocket width	at top	5 3/4		1/8
B-22	Back pocket width	at bottom	4 1/2		1/8
B-25	Distance between back pocket at top		3		1/4
B-27A	Fly length below waistband	to bottom of J	5		1/4
B-28	Fly width	to outer stitch	1 3/8		1/8
B-29	Zipper length @ fly		4		1/4
B-80	Belt loop length		2 1/2		1/8
B-81	Belt loop Width		1/2		1/8
B-82	Hem width		1/2		1/8
	Out seam stitch length		6		1/4

US Standard clothing size

Women's sizes

Women's sizes are divided into various types, depending on height. There are multiple size types, designed to fit somewhat different body shapes.

Variations include the height of the person's torso (known as back length), whether the bust, waist, and hips are straighter (characteristic of teenagers) or curvier (like many adult women), and whether the bust is higher or lower (characteristic of younger and older women, respectively). These categories are,

- **Misses** sizes:-The most common size category. For women of about average height (5'4") with an average bust height and an hourglass figure.

- **Junior** sizes: - For short women with higher busts and fairly straight bodies.

- **Women's** sizes or plus sizes: - For larger, curvier women of average height, sometimes with lower bust lines. Like misses' sizes

- **Misses petite**: - For short women with average busts and more hourglass body shapes.

- **Junior petite**: - For very short women with average busts and fairly straight bodies.

- **Women's petite**: - For larger, curvier, shorter women, sometimes with lower bust lines.

- **Young junior**: - For short women with high busts and fairly straight bodies.

- **Tall sizes**: - For taller women (usually 5'8" or above), usually with a proportionately average bust height and an hourglass figure.

- **Half sizes**: - For short women with lower busts and more hourglass body shapes.

Women's sizes								
5'5"–5'6" (165–168 cm) tall, average bust, average back								
size	34	36	38	40	42	44	46	48	50
Bust	38	40	42	44	46	48	50	52	54
Waist	30	32	34	35.5	37.5	39.5	41.5	43.5	45.5
Hip	39	41	43	46	48	50	52	54	56
Back-waist length	$17\frac{1}{4}$	$17\frac{3}{8}$	$17\frac{1}{2}$	$17\frac{5}{8}$	$17\frac{3}{4}$	$17\frac{7}{8}$	18		

Men's Size Chart

size	S		M		L		XL		2XL		3XL		4XL	
Chest	34	36	38	41	42	44	46	48	50	52	54	56	58	60
Waist	28	30	32	34	36	38	40	42	44	46	48	50	52	54
Seat/Hips	33	35	37	39	41	43	45	47	49	51	53	55	57	59
Neck band	14	14½	15	15½	16	16½	17	17½	18	18½	19	19½	20	20½
Shirt sleeve	32	33	33	34	34	35	35	36	36	37	37	37½	38	38½
Inseam	30		31		32		32		34		34		34	

Girls' sizes

Dimension/size	7	8	10	12	14	16
Chest	25.5	26	28	30	32	
Waist	22.5	23	24	25	26	
Hip	26.5	27	29	31	33	
Height	52	54	57	60	64	

Boys' sizes

Dimension/size	7	8	10	12	14	16	18	20
Chest	26	27	28	30	32	33½	35	40
Waist	23	24	25	26	27	28	29	30
Hip	27	28	29½	31	32½	34	35½	37
Neckband	11¾	12	12½	13	13½	14	14½	15
Height	48	50	54	58	61	64	66	68

Children's sizes

Dimension/size	1	2	3	4	5	6	6X
Chest	18.5	20	20.5	21.5	22	23	
Waist	17	18.5	19	20	20.5	21	21.5
Hip	19	20	21	22	23	24	24½
Height	31	34	37	40	43	46	48
Back-waist length	8¼	8½	9	9½	10	10½	10¾
Finished dress length	17	18	19	20	22	24	25

Size Chart Men/Unisex Shirts								
	XXS	**XS**	**S**	**M**	**L**	**XL**	**2XL**	**3XL**
Chest (inches)	29-31	30-32	34-36	38-40	42-44	46-48	48-50	50-52
Waist (inches)	27-29	28-30	30-32	32-33	33-34	36-38	40-42	44-48

Chest:

Measure under arms around the fullest part of the chest. Be sure to keep tape level across back and comfortably loose.

Waist:

Measure around natural waist with a measuring tape. This sizing chart is approximate. For more detailed information, please see garment specifications or contact a customer service representative.

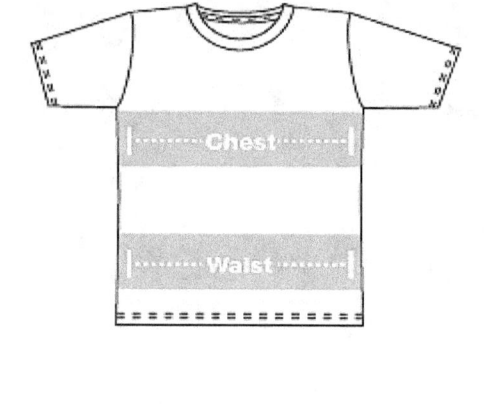

8 GARMENT MEASURING

There are two methods in use for getting the measurements for a garment,

1. Taking measurements from Body or from a Mannequin are same
2. Getting measurements from a Garment

Steps for taking Measurements from Body

1. Get a flexible measuring tape.
2. **Neck**:- The neck measurement is taken around the neck with the tape resting on your shoulders. You should put one finger between the tape and the neck if you want to allow for some extra room
3. **Chest**:- The chest measurement is taken as a circumference measurement around your chest at the widest point. Stand in a relaxed posture and breathe out.
4. **Waist**:- The waist measurement is taken as a circumference measurement around your waist just above your belly button. Stand in a relaxed posture and breathe out.
5. **Hips**:- Stand with legs about 6 inches apart and measure around the fullest part of your hips.
6. **Seat** :-The seat measurement is taken as a circumference measurement around your seat at the widest part.
7. **Shirt Length** :- The shirt length measurement is taken from the top of the shoulder, close to the mid side of your neck, following your body down to the point where you want your shirt to end.
8. **Shoulder width** :- Think of a line going from your armpit straight upwards to your shoulder. Measure between those two points and hold the tape measure straight.
9. **Arm length** :- The sleeve length measurement is taken from the point of your shoulder (where you took the shoulder width measurement), following your bent arm down to where you want the sleeve to end.

NOTE 1! Bend your arm slightly when taking this measurement.

NOTE 2! This measurement is always the full length of the arm. For short sleeve and 3/4 sleeve you should still measure the full length of the arm.

10. **Short sleeve length :-** The short sleeve length measurement is taken from the point of your shoulder (where you took the shoulder width measurement), down to where you want the short sleeve to end.

11. **Wrist :-** The wrist measurement is taken as a circumference measurement around your wrist.

12. **Biceps** :- The biceps measurement is taken as a circumference measurement around your biceps. Relax the muscle and measure at the widest part of your upper arm.

13. **Inseam** :- The inseam is measured from the crotch along the inner side of the leg to a point where you want the hem of the trousers to end. Stand upright, do not bend the leg and ask someone to help you take the measurement.

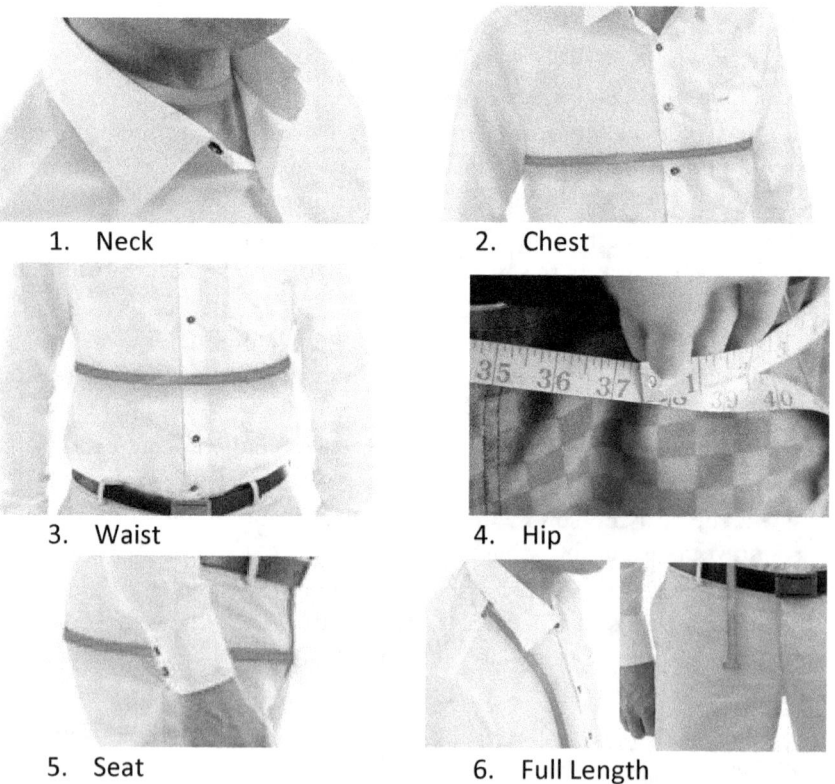

1. Neck 2. Chest

3. Waist 4. Hip

5. Seat 6. Full Length

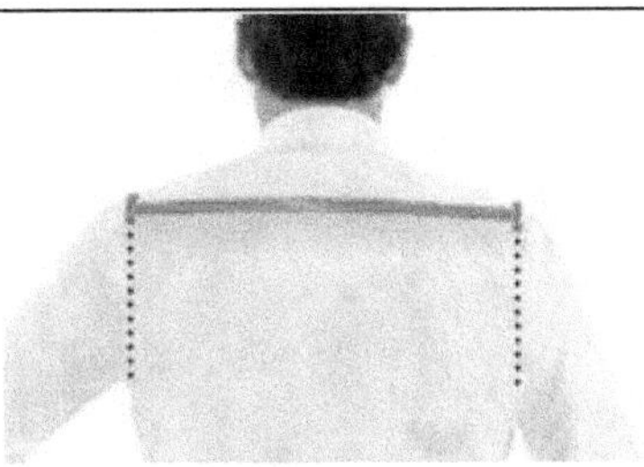 7. Shoulder	 8. Arm
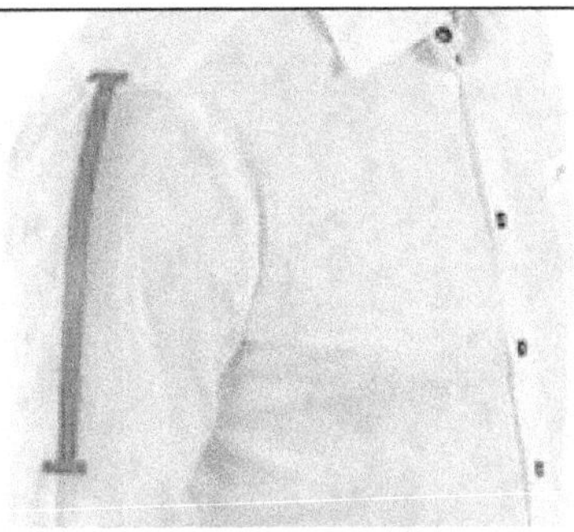 9. Short Sleeve	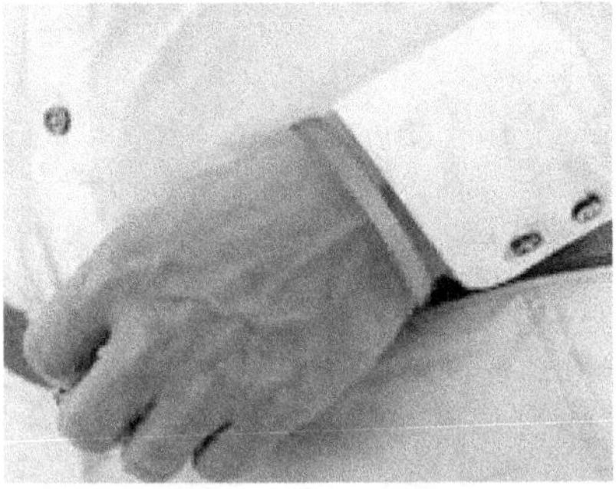 10. Wrist
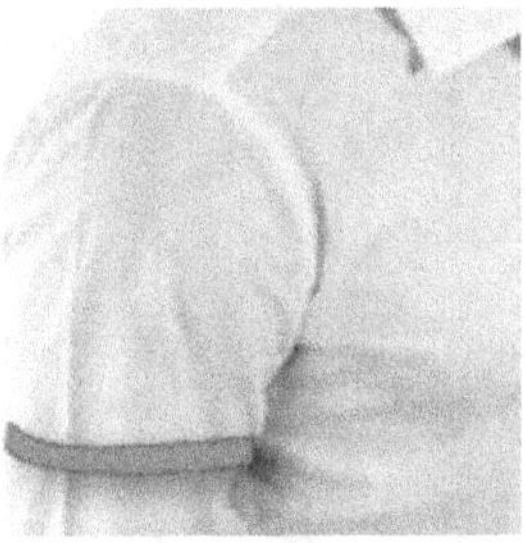 11. Biceps	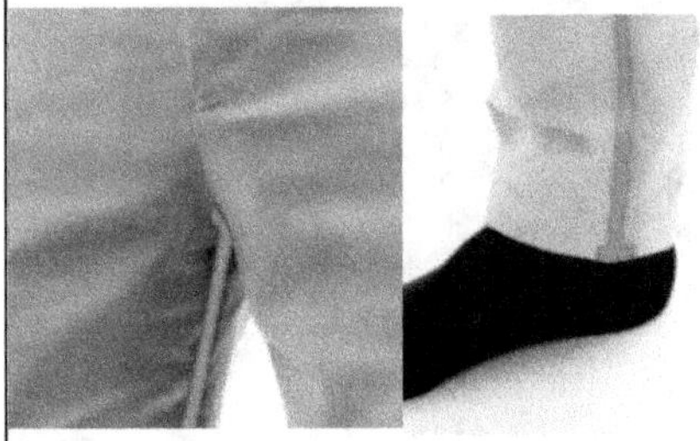 12. Inseam

Additional measurements for Women

Bust:- Wrap tape measure under the armpits, around the fullest part of the bust.

Measuring from Garments

COLLAR

The collar measurement should be taken from the middle of the button hole to the center of the collar button when the collar is spread flat

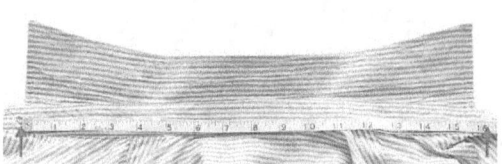

HALF CHEST

Button the shirt and lay it flat. Then measure from left seam to right seam just below the armpit

HALF WAIST

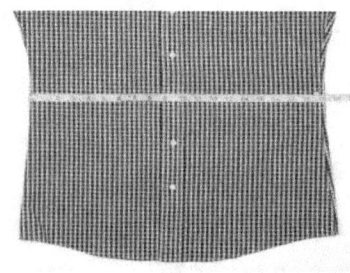

With the shirt laid flat, measure from left seam to right seam at the waistline.

HALF HIPS

With the shirt laid flat, measure from left seam to right seam at the base of the shirt.

SLEEVE LENGTH

Lay a sleeve flat and measure along the outside edge (opposite to the sleeve seam) from the top of the shoulder (starting at the seam) to the end of the cuff.

ELBOW

When you require a width for the elbow, provide us with the "Elbow reference point" and "Elbow width".

Elbow reference point: Measure from top shoulder seam (point A) as seen on image above to where your elbow normally sits when you wear a shirt

Elbow width: Measure from points D to Y as shown in the image above.

FOREARM

When you require width for the forearm, provide us with the "Forearm reference point" and "Forearm width".

Forearm reference point: Measure from top shoulder seam (point A) as seen on image above to where your forearm normally sits when you wear a shirt (point C).

Forearm width: Measure from points C to X as shown in the image above

CUFF

Spread the cuff on flat surface. Place the measuring tape on the center of the buttonhole and measure across to center of the button.

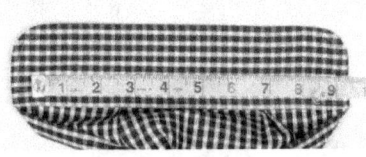

YOKE

Measure the distance between the sleeves, from one edge of the shoulder to the other, across the back.

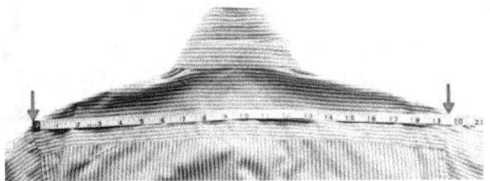

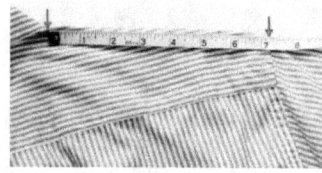
from well-fitting shirt

SHOULDER

Measure the distance between sleeve and collar along the shoulder seam. This is a secondary reference. Yoke is primarily considered when submitting measurements

SHIRT LENGTH

Measure at the back from the base of the collar seam at the middle to a point where the shirt ends.

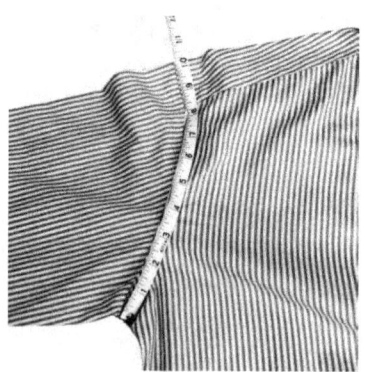

HALF ARMHOLE

Place the shirt on a large flat surface so the front of the shirt is facing you. Place the measuring tape at the top of the armhole seam and follow it along its edge to the point where the armhole meets the sleeve seam. (Note: this is a curved measurement, so please measure carefully.)

HALF WAIST

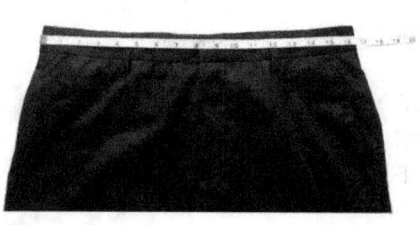

1. Button up the pants.
2. Lay the garment out on a flat surface.
3. Measure from one side of the waist to the other.

FRONT RISE

The Front Rise is the vertical measurement from crotch seam to the top of the waistband.

HALF HIPS

1. Button up the pants.

2. Lay the garment out on a flat surface. Take care to pull any wrinkles and fullness from the back panels.

3. Measure the distance between the two hip points

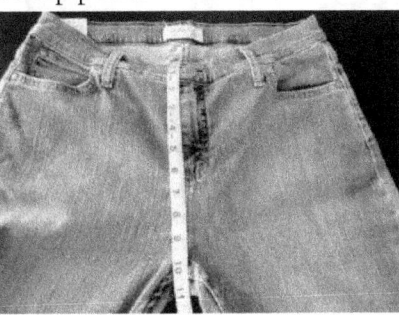

BACK RISE

The Back Rise is the measurement from crotch seam to top of waistband at back center

IN SEAM

Inseam is the distance between the seam of the crotch area and the lower part of the jeans leg opening.

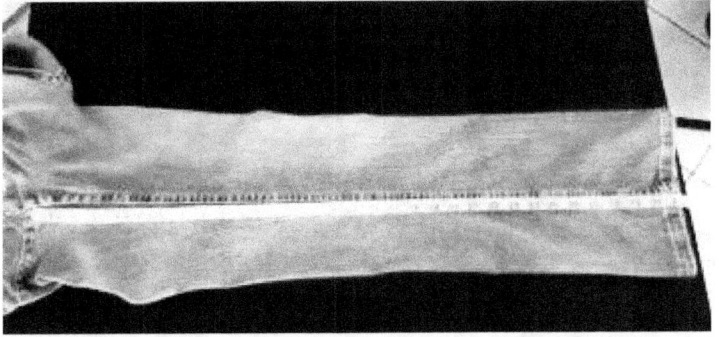

OUT SEAM

The out seam is the length of a jean from top to bottom. Take a look on the picture how it was measured

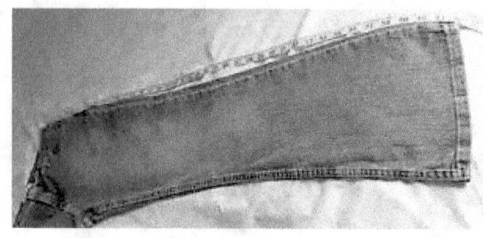

HALF THIGH

1. Button up the pants.
2. Lay the garment out on a flat surface.
3. Measure at the crotch seam line – from point "E" as shown on the left image to the outside of the leg, point "F", parallel to the waist band.

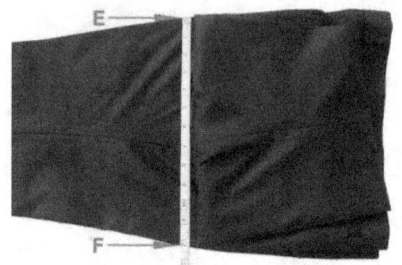

KNEE

The Knee measured 13 inches down from crotch seam. Then edge to edge of that area of the jean.

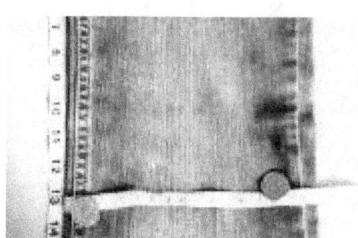

THE LEG OPENING

The bottom opening of the trouser

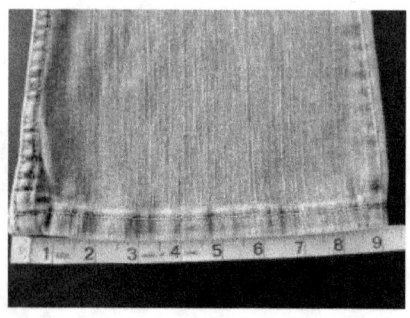

There are certain other measurements like inner seam, zip opening etc. are specified according to style to style.

9 ROLES AND RESPONSIBILITIES OF SUPERVISOR

The supervisors are the next step above the shop floor workers or operator level employees in the organization pyramid. A supervisor is the key man who interprets management to the workers and at the same time responsible for production. The task of the supervisor is the make sure that the factory works well, workers are kept in line, assure that the workers are meeting the targets in time.

Roles and responsibilities if Supervisor

All departments in apparel industry such as patternmaking or sewing requires supervisors to manage and motivate workers. Supervisors keep track of daily duties and make sure the workers meet the company targets a supervisor generally has to take care of the following

1. Selecting and training of workers
2. Managing workers and production
3. Control of quality and reduction in cost of quality
4. Discipline, motivation and moral of worker
5. Work method improvement
6. Accident prevention
7. Maintaining machinery and supplies
8. Record keeping etc.

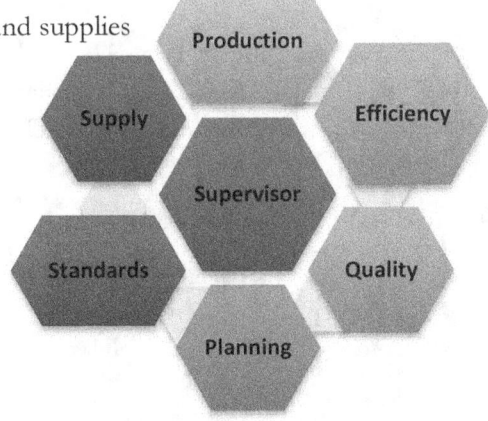

The skill requirements for the Supervisor.

1. **Technical Skills**

   a) Should have sufficient knowledge to operate the machineries used in the production department.

   b) Should know the quality parameters of the product to control its quality and to reduce cost to quality

   c) Utilization of proper machine and attachments and its operation methods should be known to supervisor

2. **Human Resource Skill**

   Supervisor must understand the need of manpower and utilize them properly without conflicts. This can be achieved through proper communication. The operators are to be utilized in such a way that the productivity should improve day by day.

3. **Management Skills**

   The supervisor have to manage the workers in proper manner so that there should be no chaos between the management and workers.

4. **Cost Control Skills**

   The supervisor should be known with the cost control aspects of the production department, and he has to manage the work flow without any bottle necks and properly utilize the operators so that there should be no unutilized operators in the floor. Supervisor has to ensure that the production of each and every operator in right quality to reduce the rework.

Duties and responsibilities

Depending on the particular company the duties of the supervisor may varies, the supervisor may plan, direct or coordinate activities and obtain resources necessary for production success. The below are the main expectations and responsibilities of a supervisor.

Towards the Management

❖ To convey management policies to workers
❖ To accept full responsibility for all work in the department
❖ To convey the workers feedbacks to management

- ❖ To achieve required production done in time
- ❖ To boost productive efficiency and product quality
- ❖ To minimize the wastage rate and rework done due quality issues
- ❖ To keep records for the further actions and references.

Towards the workers

- ❖ Has to educate workers about the company policies and procedures
- ❖ Has listen patiently to the worker to their suggestions and complaints
- ❖ Has to maintain discipline
- ❖ Has to develop a sense of belongings to the workers
- ❖ Has to maintain neat, clean and safety working condition.
- ❖ Has to divide the work among the workers in accordance with their capacity and skills
- ❖ Has to represent workers to the management
- ❖ Has to train the workers on the job
- ❖ Has to set good example in punctuality, leadership, efficiency and rational to all

Towards the fellow worker

- ❖ To cooperate with them in making policies in success
- ❖ To give respect to the suggestions of fellow supervisor
- ❖ To corporate work with other department
- ❖ Sitting together with the other colleague to solve the problem
- ❖ Avoid the creation of harsh feeling among the fellow supervisor

Towards Work

- ❖ Well plan the work
- ❖ Make sure that the materials are available in sufficient quantity to do the work
- ❖ To make sure that the necessary equipment's and tools are available in good condition
- ❖ To make sure that the work is accomplished as per schedule
- ❖ To ensure proper material handling
- ❖ To ensure smooth flow of work
- ❖ To coordinate works of different sessions
- ❖ To confirm the work is as per required quality and quantity
- ❖ To update the modernization and advanced knowledge in his field

Major qualities of a Supervisor

- ❖ Diplomatic leadership
- ❖ Judgment and decision making in an existing situation
- ❖ Full knowledge of man material and machine
- ❖ Helpful and cooperative, sympathetic attitude towards others,
- ❖ Ability to develop the organization
- ❖ Ability to plan and control the work done
- ❖ Constructive and independent thinking
- ❖ Ability to handle workers properly
- ❖ Self-control and firmness
- ❖ Self-discipline and motivate others.

Training

Supervisors often do not require any formal education on how they are to perform their duties but are most often given on-the-job training or attend company sponsored courses. Many employers have supervisor handbooks that need to be followed. Supervisors must be aware of their legal responsibilities to ensure that their employees work safely and that the workplace that they are responsible for meets government standards.

Key.

Effective supervisors are person-centered. They rate higher in the consideration function than do unsuccessful supervisors.

Effective supervisors are supportive. They are more helpful to employees and more willing to defend them against criticism from higher management than are less effective supervisors.

Effective supervisors are democratic. They hold frequent meetings with employees to solicit their views and encourage participation. Less effective supervisors are more autocratic.

Effective supervisors are flexible. They allow employees to accomplish their goals in their own way whenever possible, consistent with the goals of the organization. Less effective supervisors dictate how a job is to be performed and permit no deviation.

Effective supervisors describe themselves as coaches rather than directors. They emphasize quality, provide clear directions, and give timely feedback to their workers.

10 SEAMS

Seam is the result of joining together two or more pieces of fabric by means of stitching or bonding. Seams are functional and may be used for decorative purpose. A seam line is the designated line along which the seam is to be joined. A seam allowance is the distance from the fabric edge to the stitching line.

The basic function of a seam is to hold pieces of fabric together. A seam is a joint between two pieces of fabric. To perform its function correctly the seam should have properties closely allied to those of the fabric being sewn. Most seams are constructed on the inside, or wrong side of the garment

The characteristic of a properly constructed seam are,

1. Strength
2. Extensibility
3. Durability
4. Security
5. Appearance

1. Strength

A seam must be strong so that it should not open or break the joint when applied stretch of force, the standard being maximum thickness and economy of sewing thread strength is usually measured in two directions

- Lateral or Transverse - Across the seam
- Longitudinal   - along the seam

2. Extensibility

This is required in all seams although the degree varies according to the fabric being sewn. The characteristic of the seam must confirm to those of the fabric as closely as possible. For example the seam must be capable of stretching at least as much as to the fabric to be used.

3.   Durability

A seam must be durable, long lasting and not abrade (scrape) or wear easily during everyday use of the garment including all necessary laundering. By proper selection of fabric, thread, and the type of seams used, the seam should make the strengthen the garment itself

4.   Security

Security is closely connected with durability. A seam need to be secure and not to unravel or broke during everyday use of the garment.

5.   Appearance

The ideal seam should join pieces of fabric in an unobtrusive and efficient manner with no discontinuity in physical properties or appearance as the grains in the garment are traversed. This is of course an ideal but it does provide a target at which to aim.

Classification of Seams

The British standards divide the stitched seams into eight classes according to the minimum number of parts that make up the seams. The part can be main fabric of the garment or some additional items such as lace, elastic etc.

o   Class 1 :- Super Imposed Seam

o   Class 2 :- Lapped seam

o   Class 3 :- Bound seam

o   Class 4 :- Flat seam

o   Class 5 :- Decorative seam

o   Class 6 :- Edge neatening

o   Class 7 :- Application of edge stitches

o   Class 8 :- Seams with one piece of fabric

CLASS 1 : SUPER IMPOSED SEAM

This type of seam is formed by superimposing the edges of one piece of material on another. A variety of stitches can be used on this type of seam both for joining the fabric and neatening the edges. This type of seams can be constructed in one step or several or by inserting additional component on piping. This is the commonest construction seam on garments.

Application:-,

- Main seaming in dresses, blouses, shirts, skirts, jeans, trousers, pants, shorts, jackets, coats, etc.
- Garment containing a lining, to attach lining.
- Cut and sew sweaters and knit garments
- Outer edges of collars, cuffs, neckline, waistbands, and waistlines.
- Attach button hole strips

Common seams in super imposed seam category are plain seams, piped seam, Taped seams, French seams, edge stitches etc.

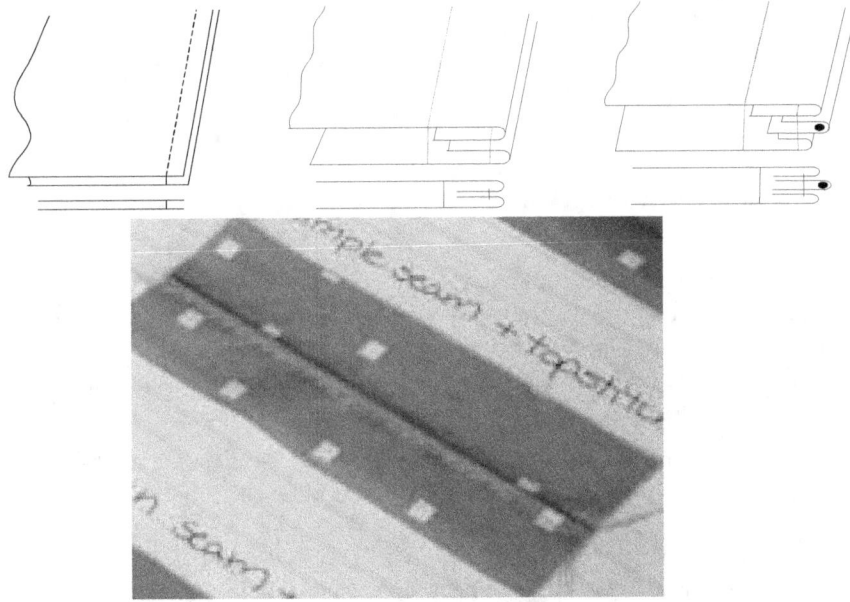

CLASS 2: LAPPED SEAMS

This type of seam is formed with two or more plies of fabric are overlapped with raw edges exposed (for fabrics resistant to raveling) or the seam allowance is folded under and stitched with one or more row of stitching.

It is almost commonly used in making of sails and the joining is done using a zigzag machine. Another type of this seam is the lap felled seam used in jeans and shirts sewn with two rows of two rows of stitches on a twin folding device this provides a very strong seam in garments. Another type of lapped seam is the welted seam used in down skirt panels or tier skirts. Though it looked like a superimposed seam it is also other vice called as top stitch seam.

Applications

- Used mainly in denim jeans, jackets etc.
- Used for fabrics that will not easily ravel, eg. Leather, lace etc.
- Side seams of shirts
- Joining lace to another fabric
- Joining yoke, patches, patch pocket etc.

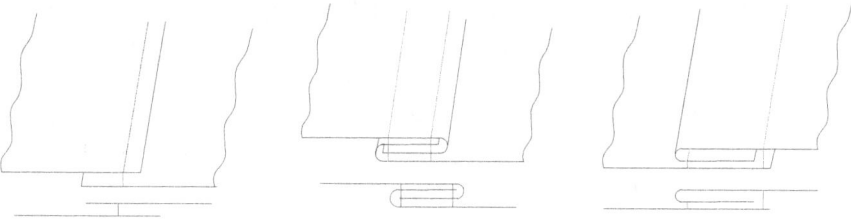

CLASS 3 : BOUND SEAMS

In this class the edge on the material is bound by another fabric. But again the fraying material used for binding becomes a problem unless a tape is used with finished edges. To avoid this, the material used in binds is folded on both the sides. A folder is normally used and the fabric is bias in many cases and a contrast colour is given for a decorative effect if required for it.

Most of the bound seams are used in underwear, T-shirt, extended plackets in men's shirt, cuff plackets, and also the waist band of trouser.

Applications,

- Used mainly finishing of neck lines, sleeve hems, inside waist bands of trousers and pants
- Finishing raw edges
- Setting collar and sleeve bindings on knits

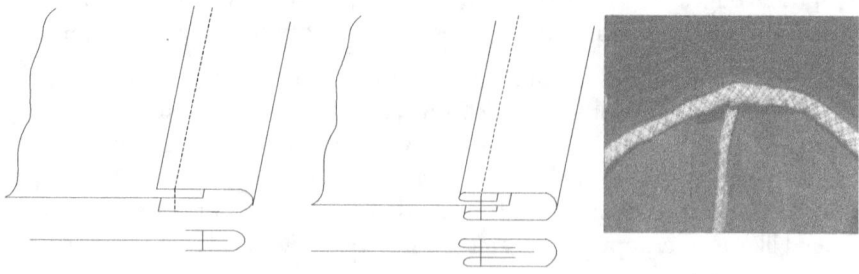

CLASS 4: FLAT SEAMS

This class is referred to as flat seams because the fabric edge doesn't overlap. They are put close together and joined across by a stitch which has two needle sewing into each fabric and covering threads passing back and front between needles on both sides of the fabric. This kind of seam is mostly used in knitted under wears the advantage of this seam is that it provides a join that is free from bulk I garments worn close to the skins such as swim suits etc.

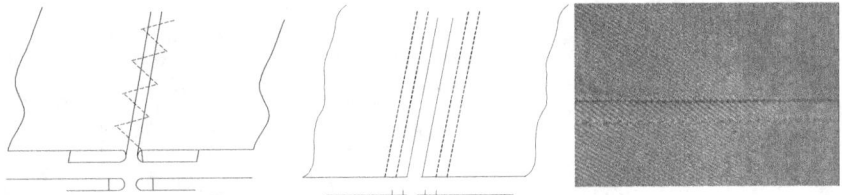

Application

- Close fitting garments where the seam allowance may put pressure on the body e.g. swim suits
- Seams in High stretch fabrics, athletic apparel, shape wear, under garments

CLASS 5: DECORATIVE SEAMS OR ORNAMENTAL STITCHING

A category of seam that add ornamentation to one or more plies of fabric by creating straight or curved lines in a designated design. Example of ornamented stiches are Pin tucks, channel seams, attachment of laces etc.

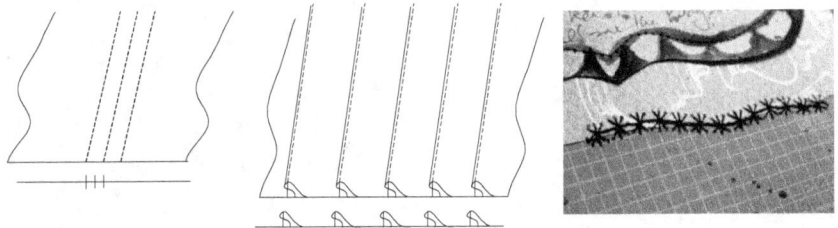

Application

- Adding a design detail
- Cording, piping, tucking, welting etc. are created
- Box or inverted pleating

CLASS 6: EDGE NEATENING

Seam constructed with one or two plies of fabric used to finish the edge of a garment or item. There are three finishing types in this classification. The first secures the folded edge to the shell fabric by stitching, either on the face or back. For the second type stitch is used in edge or to cover the edges and may or may not be folded. The third type applies the binding on a single ply of a seam allowance to finish.

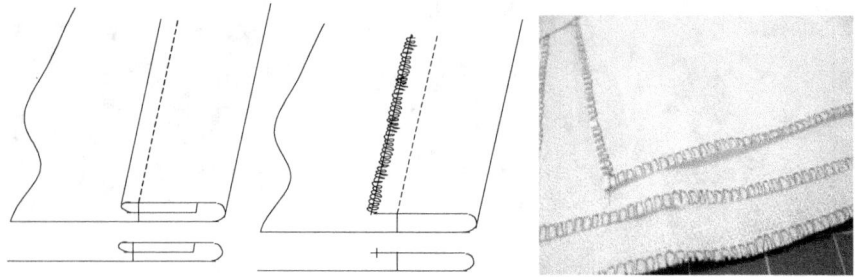

Application

- Hemming of woven and knit fabrics
- Blind hemming in knit garments
- Belt loops, facing etc. are in the category

CLASS 7: APPLICATION OF ADDITION OF SEPARATE ITEMS

The seams in this class relate to the addition of separate items to the edge of a garment part. They are similar to the lapped seam except that the added component has a definite edge on both sides.

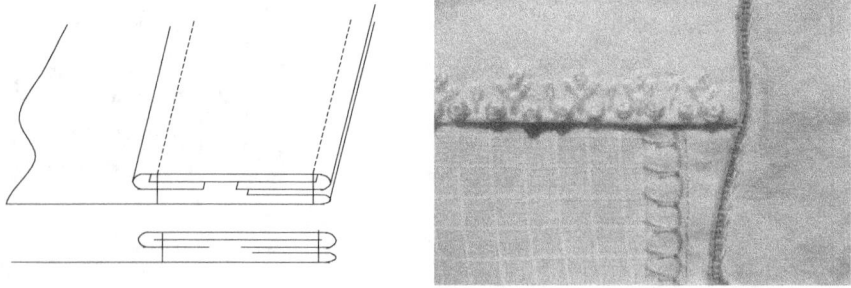

Application

- Attaching laces to the edge of a slip, inserting elastic on a swim suit.
- Elastic braids on the inner wears.
- Invisible tapes attached in single piece garments. Etc.

CLASS 8: SPECIALIST SEAMS

The final seam class in the British standard where only one piece of material need to be involved in constructing the seam. The commonest seam in this class is the belt loop as used on jeans. Rain coats etc. Also included in this seam class is belt itself.

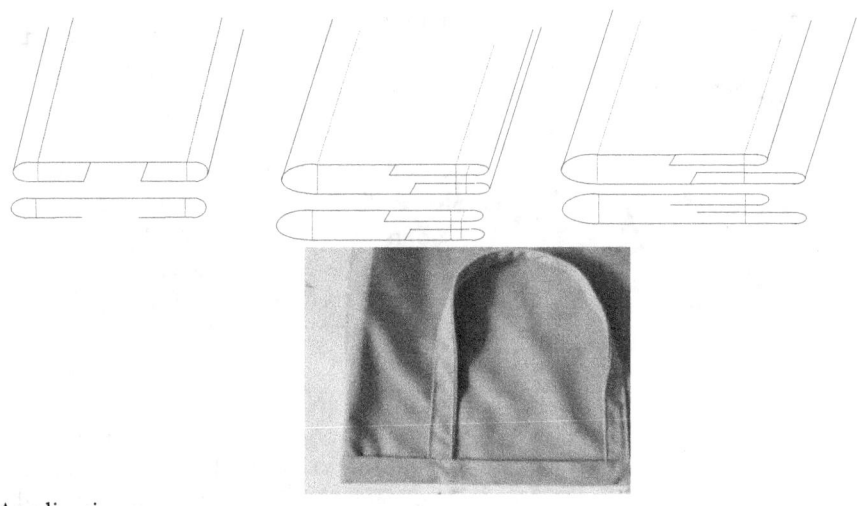

Application

- Attaching Belt Loops and Straps
- Other decorative specified seams

Summary

Seam Type	Uses
Super Imposed	Main seams in dress, blouses, shirts, lining attachment, button hole strips
Lapped Seams	Main seams in denim garments, leather, shirt side seams, patch pocket
Bound Seams	Neckline finishing, decorative seams, raw edge finishing, waist bands
Flat Seams	Seams in close fitting garments like swim suits, athletic apparels, thin fabrics
Ornamental Stitching	Designs, cording, piping, box pleats etc.
Edge Finishes	Hemming woven & knits, blind hemming, shoulder straps etc.
Addition of separate items	Attaching laces, elastic, invisible tapes, etc.
Specialist Seams	Belt loops and straps attaching

Seam Drawing	ISO 4916	Application	Requirement
	3.01.01	Binding Carpets, etc. with selvedge edge binding	Specify the Binding finished width.
	3.01.01	Setting collarets & Sleeve Binding on Undershirts, etc. Usually sewn with a 602 or 605 cover stitch	1) Specify the needle spacing if 602 or 605 stitch is used; 2) Binding finished width.
	3.03.01	Setting collarets on T-Shirts; binding legs and fly on knit briefs, etc. Usually sewn with a 406 bottom cover stitch	1) Specify the needle spacing if 406 stitch is used (Ex: 1/8", 3/16");
	3.05.01	For setting sleeve facings to shirts, piping edges of outerwear, etc. Can be sewn with a 301 lockstitch or 401 Chainstitch	1) Specify the width of the binding. Example: 1/2" Binding. 2) Requires a binding folder.
	3.01.02	Seaming with selvedge edge binding on Outerwear	1) Specify the needle spacing; 2) Width binding. Example: 3/8" needle spacing and 1/4" Binding. 3) Requires a binding folder.

	6.02.01	Hemming Selvedge Edge Shirt Front	1) Specify width of hem.
	6.02.07	Hemming Tee Shirts, Polo Shirts, etc. Generally sewn with a 406 stitch.	1) Specify width of hem; and 2) Needle Spacing. (Ex. 1" hem with 1/4" needle spacing).
Clean Finish Hem	**6.03.01**	Hemming Shirts, Jeans, Shorts, etc.	1) Specify width of hem. 2) Generally a hemming folder is required or a hemming PF.
Blind hemming	**6.06.01**	Hemming bottoms of Tee Shirts, Undershirts, etc. Usually sewn with a 503 Stitch.	1) Specify width Hem. (Ex. 1" hem); 2) Generally a hemming guide is required.
Topstitch hidden in seam line		"Stitch in a Ditch" - Topstitching waistband with stitch line on top of Previous seam line.	1) May require special PF with Guide so stitch is totally hidden
Sewn in 2 Operations	**3.14.01**	Mock Clean Finish Binding	1) Specify width of Binding

Sewn in two operations	**3.05.06**	Mock Clean Finish Binding	1) Specify the width of the binding. Example: 1/2" Binding.
Waistbanding on Jeans	**3.05.01**	Waistbands to jeans, etc. Can be sewn with a 401 Chainstitch or 301 lockstitch	1) Specify needle spacing; 2) Specify the width of the binding. (Example: 1- 3/8" and 1- 5/8" Binding.) 3) Requires a binding
Seaming and binding on Outerwear	**3.05.05**	Seaming and binding on Outerwear	1) Specify the needle spacing; and 2) Width binding. (Example: 3/8" needle spacing and 1/4" Binding.) 3) Requires a binding folder.
Blindstitch Hem		Hemming Dresses, Slacks, Coats, bedspreads. Generally sewn with103 blind stitch	1) Specify Width Hem
Belt Loops		Making Belt Loops for Jeans and Casual Pants, Shorts, Etc. Usually sewn with 406 stitch.	1) Specify needle Spacing & 2) Width of Belt Loop. (Ex. 1/4" needle Spacing and 3/8" width belt loops) 3) Requires belt loop folder.

11 STITCHES

Stitch is one unit of conformation resulting from one or more strands or loops or groups of threads by interloping or passing into or through the material. Stitch is the formation of thread for the purpose of making a seam.

The art of stitching have many new stitches. These different types are referred to by names or terms which vary widely throughout the industry. To avoid the confusion caused by this multiplicity of names it is proposed to refer stitches according to British Standard System, Set out in BS: 3870: 1965,

Classification   of Stitches :- According to Stitch Formation Method

INTRA LOOPING

Intra looping is the passing of one loop of thread through another loop of the same thread supply. An example of this is the single thread chain stitch

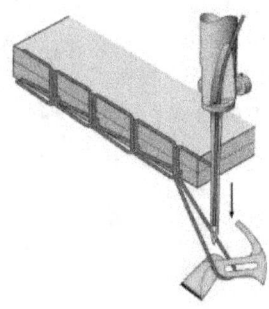

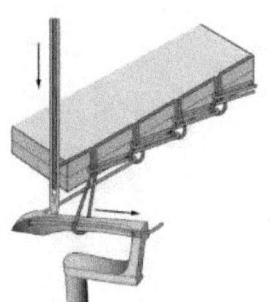

INTER LOOPING

When one loop of thread is passed through a loop formed by a separate thread supply, this is called inter looping: an example of this is double lock chain stitch

INTERLACING

Interlacing occurs when a thread is passed around or over a separate thread supply or a loop of that supply, for example in lockstitch

Classification According To British Standard System

A numerical system is used to classify stitches according to their formation.

- Class 100 : Chain stitches
- Class 200 : Hand stitches
- Class 300 : Lockstitches
- Class 400 : Multi thread chain stitches
- Class 500 : Over edge chain stitches
- Class 600 : Cover seam chain stitches

CLASS 100: CHAIN STITCH

This class of stitch (100) is formed by the intra looping of a needle thread supply through or around the fabric. The loop of one needle thread is passed through the material from the needle side and intra looped on the other side

Single thread chain stitch is often used in temporary applications, as it is easy to remove. This is because each successive loop is dependent upon the previous loop for security

Applications:

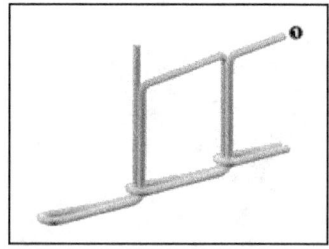

- It is ideal for temporary basting; attaching buttons or press-studs;
- Blind stitching edges; spot tacking (cuffs, vents and socks etc.
- Securing product labels to garments and socks

CLASS 200: HAND STITCHES

A category of stitches created by hand or by machine to imitate hand work. One of more needle threads pass through a ply or plies of fabric as a single line of thread that interlopes on itself or is secured by passing in and out of the material to show alternately on the face and back of the fabric.

Applications:

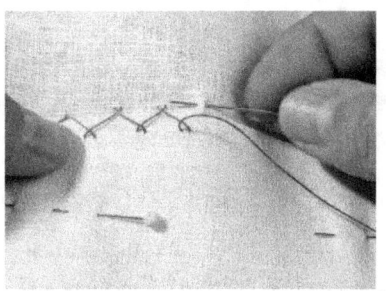

- Hand stitches are highly expensive are more common in decorative purpose.
- Saddle stitches, running stitches etc

CLASS 300: LOCK STITCH

Lockstitch is the most widely used stitch formation. These stitches are extremely secure, as a break in one stitch will not cause the seam to unravel completely although it will compromise the overall seam performance Lockstitch 301 is often referred to as 'double lockstitch'. It is formed by interlacing a needle thread with a bobbin thread underneath the material being sewn

Advantages:

There are several advantages in using this stitch. Lockstitch has a neat appearance and is useful in applications where the stitching should not be obvious; alternatively it can be used as a decorative stitching feature.

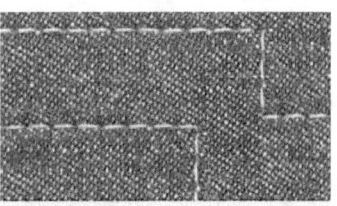

It is reversible (as the seam has the same appearance on both sides), it is strong (when the tension is correct and the load is equal on both threads) and it is secure (the seam does not unravel or runback easily if the threads are cut or damaged). Finally is it versatile and can be used in a wide range of applications, from stitching cotton blouses to leather upholstery.

Disadvantages: main disadvantage of using this stitch is the production stoppages required to change the bobbins.

Applications:

Most common stitches used in all types of garments.

- SNLS (Single Needle lock stitch), Button Stitch machine produce this class of stitches.
- Most used in those seam where same appearance is required on both sides of the seam.
- Mostly suitable for topstitching collars and cuffs etc

CLASS 400: MULTI THREAD CHAIN STITCHES

Chain stitch 400 is often referred to as 'double lock chain stitch' because each needle thread loop is interconnected with two loops of the same, single under thread. This stitch type is formed by interloping the needle thread supply with a separate looper thread supply on the underside of the fabric.

Advantages:

The large cones of thread that continuously supply the chain stitch machine make it perfect for continuous, long seaming applications. Another advantage is its strength and extensibility. Chainstitch uses almost twice as much thread as lockstitch, making the stitches extensible and stronger, and allowing the use of much finer thread. It also reduces seam pucker as the stitch is set underneath the fabric rather than between the fabric layers. All these factors contribute to increased production.

Disadvantages:

Its disadvantages lie in runback: the seams can unravel or runback easily if the threads are cut or one of them is damaged. The seam can also runback from the finished end. To reduce this problem the seam should be over-sewn or bar-tacked.

Applications:

- Most often used to sew leg seams on jeans and trousers.
- Also used to sew inside seam of shirts and sleeve.
- Feed of Arm machine produce this class of stitches

CLASS 500: OVER EDGE CHAIN STITCH

This class of chainstitch is formed by interloping the needle thread supply with one or more looper threads supplied on the side and underside of the fabric. This stitch type is often referred to as 'over locking' and, as the name implies, it is formed when at least one or more threads are passed around the fabric edge. This type of chainstitch is the most widely used stitch formation for neatening continuous seaming applications.

Advantages:

These chainstitch machines are used where it is important to prevent.

They are generally used to seam and neaten the cut edge of the fabric plies.

This class of stitch is excellent for long seam applications because the thread is supplied from large cones. The seams produced are highly extensible and strong as this chainstitch uses almost five times as much thread as lockstitch, making it possible to use much finer thread.

Disadvantages:

There are, however, some disadvantages. This stitch type is prone to seam grinning (the threads are exposed when the seam is pulled at right angles to the line of sewing) and the finish may be somewhat bulky due to the complexity of the seam construction.

Application of 504 over edge Chainstitch

- This stitch formation uses one needle and three threads (one needle thread and two Looper threads) to secure a seam.
- It is predominately used in the knitted garment industry for seaming, joining and neatening the edges of cut and sew knitwear, lingerie, underwear, sportswear, ski wear, Lycra cycle and dancewear products, t-shirts, polo shirts, tights, stockinet and children's wear.
- It is useful where seam extensibility is required in stretch materials.

CLASS 600: COVER SEAM CHAIN STITCHES

Covering Chainstitch utilizes between two and four needle threads but predominantly one looper thread and one cover thread. The cover thread lies on the top surface of the stitch line and is secured by the needle threads. The looper threads interloop with all of the needle threads on the underside of the stitch line.

Applications:

- This stitch type is used to reduce seam impression on the wearer's skin or on outer garments.
- It is used in underwear, foundation wear and fashion sportswear.

Stitch Dimensions

The Dimension of stitches are as below,

STITCH LENGTH:-

It is specified as the number of stitches per inch (SPI) and it is an indicator of quality. High SPI means short-stitches and low SPI means long-stitches.

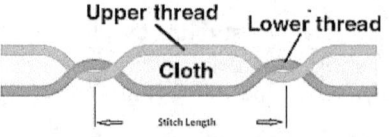

Generally the greater SPI holds greater holding power and seam strength.

STITCH WIDTH:-

Stitch width refers to the horizontal span covered in the formation of one stitch or single line of stitching. Stitch having width dimensions require multiple needles or lateral movement of thread carriers. Stich width is often termed as needle gauge as for a double

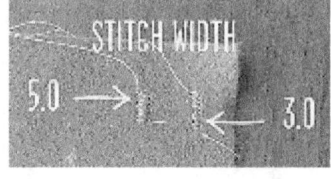

needle machine the distance between two needle is called as needle gauge.

STITCH DEPTH:-

Stitch depth means the distance between upper and lower surface of the stitch. Stitch depth should be sufficient to catch all fabric plies, yet not deep enough to show through on the face of fabric. Curved needles are used for this purpose.

STITCH CONSISTENCY:-

Stitch consistency is the uniformity with which each stitch is formed in a row of stitches. Stitches are divided into six classes, within each of which are several types of stitch. The characteristics of each class are indicated below, followed by

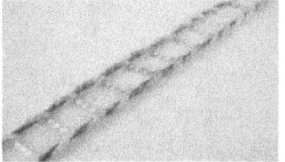

illustrations of common stitch types and details of their properties and applications

Stitch Type	Uses
Single Thread Chain	Blind hems on skirts, pants, and dress
Hand Stitches	Decorative stitching that show on the face of the garment, saddle stitch, run stitch
Lock Stitches	Straight sewing, trim attaching, top stitching, bar tacking, button holes etc.
Multi thread Chain stitch	Straight sewing (knits), hems on knit garment, embroidery, elastic attaching
Over edge stitches	Knit sewing, edge finishing, decorative hems, preventing fraying, rolling, ravelling etc.
Cover Stitches	Main sewing on knits, decorative stitching, seams in tight fitting garments, flat seams

12 THREAD CONSUMPTION

Thread is a major component of the trim   that plays a major role in sewing. If the thread found excess or shortage it can affect the final costing. Shortage of thread can even lead to shipment delays. Thread cost are less than 1% of total material cost, but thread performance has a direct bearing on labor cost and productivity. In today's competitive market place there is a need for tight cost control. The quantity of thread required for a particular garment varies according to the stitch and seams used. This can be determined by unravelling several inches of stitches of each stitch type and measure the thread consumption.

The amount of thread consumption in a sewn product must be calculated to

1.   To estimate the number of cones needed for that production.

2.   Calculate the cost of thread needed to manufacture the garment.

Actual thread consumption of unit length of seam depends on the following factors,

1.Stitch Classes

2.Stitches per inches (SPI)

3.Thickness of the seam (fabric thickness)

4.Thread tension Thread count (thickness of sewing thread

It is easier to calculate the thread consumption by using the thread consumption ratio of various stitch types

Stitch	Description	thread usages per cm	No of needle	% of needle thread	%Looper/U nder (Including cover threads
301	Lock stitch	2.5	1	50	50
101	Chain stitch	4.0	1	100	0
401	Two thread chain stitch	5.5	1	25	75
304	Zigzag lockstitch	7.0	1	50	50
503	2 thread over edge stitch	12.0	1	55	45
504	3 thread over edge stitch	14.0	1	20	80
512	4 thread mock Safety stitch	18.0	2	25	75
516	5 thread mock Safety stitch	20.0	2	20	80
406	3 thread covering stitch	18.0	2	30	70
602	4 thread covering stitch	25.0	2	20	80
605	5 thread covering stitch	28.0	3	30	70

Note:
- Above ratios are obtained with a stitch density of 18 stitches per inch. 10% to 15% of waste should be added as per shop floor condition.
- To calculate the thread consumption of a particular seam, multiply the seam length with thread consumption ratio of that seam type and frequency (no. of times that particular seam in a garment).

THREAD CONSUMPTION METHODS

1. By measuring the actual amount of thread consumed
2. By calculation using thread consumption ratios

MEASURING ACTUAL THREAD CONSUMED

A specified length of a given seam is measured and then the thread is pulled out of this length. We can use the amount pulled out of this specified length to calculate the ratio of thread consumed in the entire seam. By dividing the amount of thread by the seam length, we get the ratio of thread consumed. If we multiply this factor times the total length of seam, we can determine the total thread consumed for that seam.

Example:

Stitch class -401s-2 thread chain stitch

Length of seam		=100 cm
Length of seam which thread is removed for		=15 cm
Needle thread removed		=19.5 cm
Needle thread factor -19.5/15		=1.3
Looper thread removed		= 62.0 cm
Looper thread factor = 62.0/15		=4.1
Total needle thread	=100 cm x1.3	=130 cm
Total looper thread	=100 cm x 4.1	=410 cm
Total thread consumed	= 130 + 410	= 540 cm
Add 15% wastage*	= 540 cm x 1.15	= **621 cm**

*Generally, 10% to 15% wastage of thread is added to the consumption derived. This wastage occurs due to shop-floor conditions like machine running, thread breakage, repairs, etc. The above example shows the total thread consumed for one type of stitch class in a garment. By following a similar procedure, you can calculate the thread consumed for different stitching operations in a garment.

THREAD CONSUMPTION RATIOS

The easier method is to use the generally applicable Thread Consumption Ratios for the various stitch types that are listed in the table below. By relating these ratios to the length of seams using each stitch type, total thread consumption can be calculated.

Note:

1. The above ratios are arrived at with a stitch density of 7 stitches per cm (18 stitches per inch).
2. These ratios are the prescribed minimum in regular conditions and marginally vary with the factors affecting thread consumption.
3. A certain percentage of wastage is to be added to the above ratios as per shop floor conditions. It may vary from 10% to 15%.

Example:

Length of seam	=100 cm	
Stitch class -401s-2 thread chain stitch		
Total thread usage per cm of seam		=5.5 cm
Total Thread consumption =100 cm x5.5		=550 cm
Estimated needle thread	=550 x0.25	=138 cm
Estimated Looper thread	=550 x 0.74	=412 cm

Add 15 % wastage   = 550 cm x 1.15   = 633 cm of thread per seam

By applying thread consumption ratios in a manner similar to the calculation in the above example, a sample consumption working for an average sized knitted t-shirt is shown in the table below.

Example
Thread consumption for an average-sized knitted t-shirt

Stitch	Type	Seam length	Thread ratio	Total Consumption	NT	LT
301	Lock stitch	4.0	2.50	10.0	5.0	5.0
504	3threaover edge stitch	3.0	14.0	42.0	8.5	33.6
401	2 thread chain stitch	0.75	5.50	4.0	1.0	3.0
503	2 thread over edge stitch	0.95	12.0	11.4	6.3	5.1
101	1 thread chain stitch	0.10	4.0	0.4	0.4	0.0
Total Thread consumed				67.8	21.1	46.7
Wastage- 15%				10.0	3.0	7.0
Total after considering wastage				77.8	24.1	53.7

Note: Stitch density, stitch / seam choice, variations in style, fabric thickness and number of plies are factors that can affect thread consumption. It is also necessary to make provision for possible thread wastage (usually 15%) while calculating thread consumption.

13 SEWING MACHINE CLASSIFICATION

In 1834 Sir Isaac Singer of U. K. invented the domestic sewing machine and in 1900 the Singer Company developed industrial sewing machines.

Difference between domestic and industrial sewing machines:

Industrial Sewing Machine	Domestic Sewing Machine
1. Low Speed (up to 500 rpm)	1. Higher Speed (up to 700 rpm)
2. Less Productive	2. High Productive
3. Manual Operation	3. Power operated
4. Poor quality	4. Good Quality
5. Health issues of operator is high	5. Health issues are low

Sewing machines are the main tool used in Apparel Industry. The sewing machines are designed in different ways depending on the kind of material, finish and seam.

The major classification starts according to the Material used, (light weight, medium weight and heavy duty machines) the second classification according to the bed of the sewing machine head. And the third according to the type of stitch

ACCORDING TO MACHINE BED

Bed is the portion of sewing machine where the sewing is effecting in the fabric, i.e. the area is with needle plate, thought plate, and nearer areas. This will vary in position and shape according to the requirement of the machine for its application in sewing.

1 FLAT BED MACHINES

The flat bed is used in the majority of sewing where a large and open garment part can easily be stitched or handled under the needle. It provide suitable surface for each flat stitches and also facilitates the use of marker to control the position of garment parts. e.g. DDL 8300 SNLS

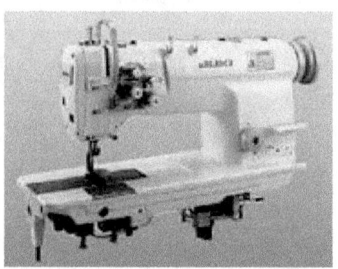

Application:

Sewing flat pieces of fabric together, straight stitches

2 RAISED BED SEWING MACHINE

This type of machine are having the feed portion as raised from the table to enable easy handling e.g. Over lock machines

Application:- Surging knit garments, over locking in knit and woven,

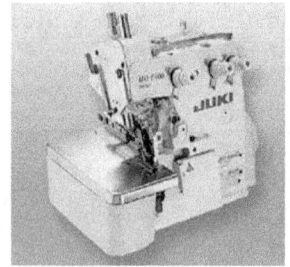 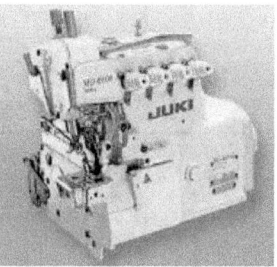 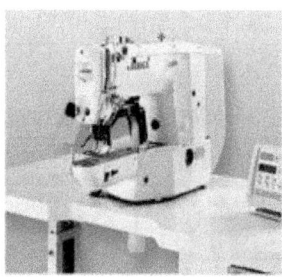

Raised Bed   Cvlinder bed   Cvlinder bed

3 CYLINDER

These machines feature a narrow, horizontal column as opposed to a flat base. This allows fabric to pass around and under the column. The diameter of the cylinder-bed varies from 5 cm to 16 cm

Application: - attaching cuffs, doing hems Sleeves of a Knit T shirt, button sewing, bar tacking etc.

4 FEED OF ARM

The least common group, these machines require workers to feed material along the axis of a horizontal column. The design limits the length of the seam sewn to the length of the column, but is useful for applications such as sleeve and shoulder seams

Application: -

Sleeve attaching, Jeans side seams, fabric pipes stitching etc

5. POST BED

Post bed sewing machines have a vertical rectangular or round post rising up from the bed of the machine to where the needle and presser foot meet (where the sewing occurs). Post bed machines are used for a wide variety of applications where products cannot fit on the regular flat bed. Shown below is a high post bed sewing machine, called "high" because it has a longer than normal post. The height of the post may vary from 10cm to 45cm

Application:-

Attaching emblems in caps, boot making, leather shoe making, glove making etc.

ACCORDING TO STITCH FORMATION

1. LOCKSTITCH

Lockstitch is the familiar stitch performed by most household sewing machines and most industrial "single needle" sewing machines from two threads, one passed through a needle and one coming from a bobbin or shuttle. Each thread stays on the same side of the material being sewn, interlacing with the other thread at each needle hole by means of a bobbin driver. As a result, a lockstitch can be formed anywhere on the material being sewn; it does not need to be near an edge

2. CHAIN STITCH

Chain stitch is a sewing and embroidery technique in which a series of looped stitches form a chain-like pattern. Chain stitch is an ancient craft.

Chainstitch was used by early sewing machines and has two major drawbacks are,

• The stitch is not self-locking, and if the thread breaks at any point or is not tied at both ends, the whole length of stitching comes out. It is also easily ripped out.

- The direction of sewing cannot be changed much from one stitch to the next, or the stitching process fails.

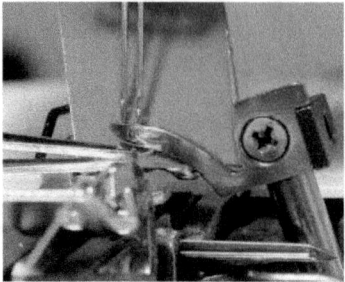 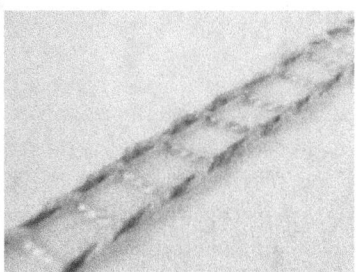

A better stitch was found in the lockstitch. The chainstitch is still used today in clothing manufacture, though due to its major drawback it is generally paired with an overlock stitch along the same seam.

3. OVERLOCK

Overlock, also known as "serging" or "serger stitch", can be formed with one to four threads, one or two needles, and one or two loopers. Overlock sewing machines are usually equipped with knives that trim or create the edge immediately in front of the stitch formation. Machines using two to four threads are most common, and frequently one machine can be configured for several varieties of overlock stitch.

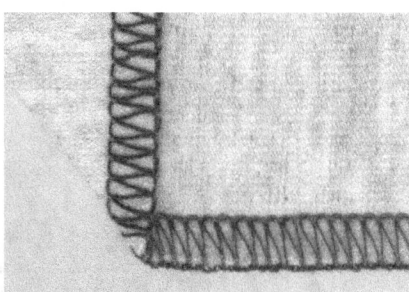 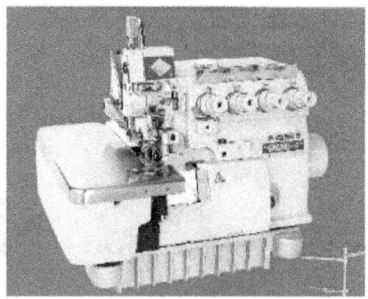

Overlock machines with five or more threads usually make both a chainstitch with one needle and one looper, and an overlock stitch with the remaining needles and loopers. This combination is known as a "safety stitch".

4. ZIGZAG STITCH

A zigzag stitch is variant geometry of the lockstitch. It is a back-and-forth stitch used where a straight stitch will not suffice, such as in preventing ravelling of a fabric, in stitching stretchable fabrics, and in temporarily joining two work pieces edge-to-edge.

5. COVER STITCH

Cover stitch is formed by two or more needles and one or two loopers, coverstitch can be formed anywhere on the material being sewn. One looper manipulates a thread below the material being sewn, forming a bottom cover stitch against the needle threads. An additional looper above the material can form a top cover stitch simultaneously. The needle threads form parallel rows, while the looper threads cross back and forth all the needle rows. Cover stitch is so-called because the grid of crossing needle and looper threads covers raw seam edges, much as the overlock stitch does.

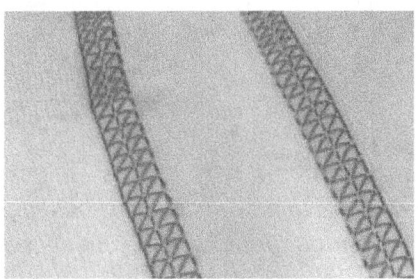 

It is widely used in garment construction, particularly for attaching trims and flat seaming where the raw edges can be finished in the same operation as forming the seam.

ACCORDING TO FEED MECHANISMS

Besides the basic motion of needles, loopers and bobbins, the material being sewn must move so that each cycle of needle motion involves a different part of the material. This motion is known as feed, and sewing machines have almost as many ways of feeding material as they do of forming stitches.

For general categories, there are: drop feed, needle feed, walking foot, puller, and manual. Often, multiple types of feed are used on the same machine. Besides these general categories, there are also uncommon feed mechanisms used in specific applications like edge joining fur, making seams on caps, and blind stitching.

1. DROP FEED

The drop feed mechanism is used by almost all household machines and involves a mechanism below the sewing surface of the machine. When the needle is withdrawn from the material being sewn, a set of "feed dogs" is pushed up through slots in the machine surface, then dragged horizontally past the needle. The dogs are serrated to grip the material, and a "presser foot" is used to keep the material in contact with the

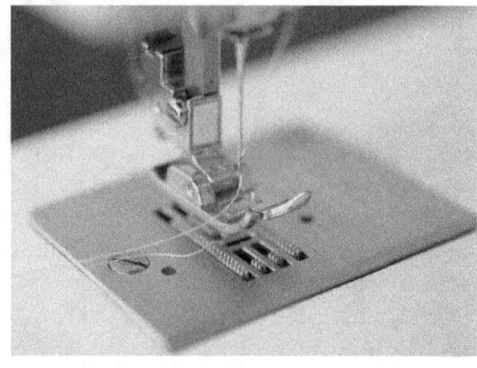

dogs. At the end of their horizontal motion, the dogs are lowered again and returned to their original position while the needle makes its next pass through the material.

2. NEEDLE FEED

A needle feed, used only in industrial machines, moves the material while the needle is in the material. In fact, the needle may be the primary feeding force. Some implementations of needle feed rock the axis of needle motion back and forth, while other implementations keep the axis vertical while moving it forward and back. In both cases, there is no feed action while the needle is out of the material. Needle feed is often used in conjunction with a modified drop feed, and is very common on industrial two needle machines. The advantage of needle feed over drop feed is that multiple layers of material, especially slippery material, cannot slide with respect to one another, since the needle holds all layers together while the feed action takes place. Household machines do not use needle feed as a general rule.

3. WALKING FOOT

A walking foot replaces the stationary presser foot with one that moves along with whatever other feed mechanisms the machine already has. As the walking foot moves, it shifts the work piece along with it.

It is most useful for sewing heavy materials where needle feed is mechanically inadequate, for spongy or cushioned materials where lifting the foot out of contact with the material helps in the feeding action, and for sewing many layers together where a drop feed will cause the lower layers to shift out of position with the upper layers.

4. PULLER FEED

Some factory machines and a few household machines are set up with an auxiliary puller feed, which grips the material being sewn (usually from behind the needles) and pulls it with a force and reliability usually not possible with other types of feed. Puller feeds are seldom built directly into the basic sewing machine. Their action must be synchronized with the needle and feed action built into the machine to avoid damaging the machine. Pullers are also limited to straight seams, or very nearly so. Despite their additional cost and limitations, pulling feeds are very useful when making large heavy items like tents and vehicle covers.

5. MANUAL FEED

A manual feed is used primarily in freehand embroidery, quilting, and shoe repair. With manual feed, the stitch length and direction is controlled entirely by the motion of the material being sewn. Frequently some form of hoop or stabilizing material is used with fabric to keep the material under proper tension and aid in moving it around. Most household machines can be set for manual feed by disengaging the drop feed dogs. Most industrial machines cannot be used for manual feed without actually removing the feed dogs.

Apart from this basic classifications the machine are also classified as Clutch , Servo motors, Dry Head, Semi Dry head, oil lubricated, etc. which are according to the type of motor used, lubrication used, thread used, etc.

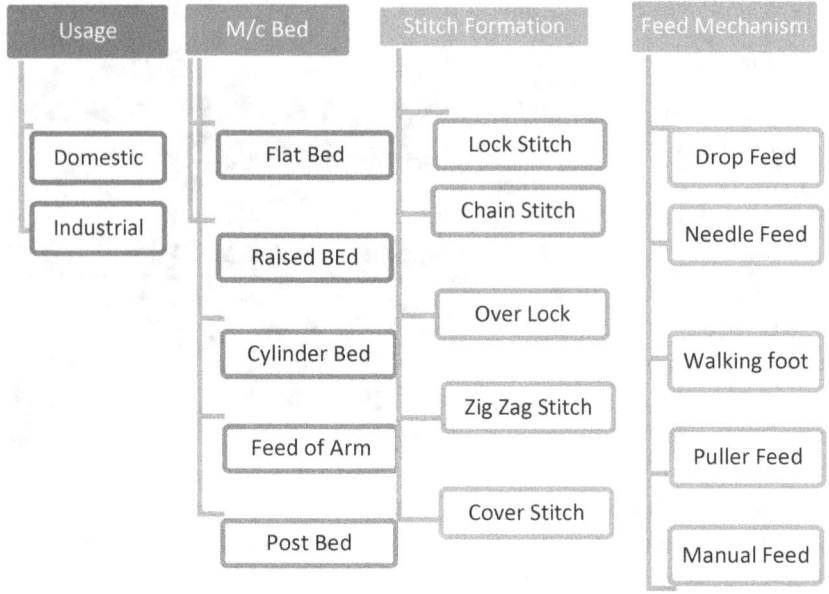

The difference between chain stitch and lock stitch sewing machines are,

Chain Stitch	Lock Stitch
Chain stitch sewing machines are Over lock, Flat lock, blind hem	Lock stitch sewing machines are used in General sewing, Button sewing, bar tacking, zigzag stitches, etc.
Easy to unravel	Strongest and tough to unravel
Stitches are formed using the looper threads	Stitch formed by interlacing of needle and bobbin thread
Clearly visible Looper below the thought plate	Hook set and bobbins are seen
Large package of thread is used	Both large and small packages can be used
Thread consumption is high	Comparatively Low rate of thread consumption
Stitch are stretchable	Stitches are non-stretchable

14 TYEPE OF NEEDLES

NEEDLE

It is a device which helps to stitch the fabric .It is made of stainless steel with carbide coating.

In the apparel industry, there are literally thousands of different machines, each requiring a different needle type. Needles are manufactured with a wide variety of needle points appropriate for the differing properties of materials which have to be sewn.

PARTS OF A SEWING MACHINE NEEDLE

All sewing machine needles have the same basic parts. The variation in needles is caused by the shape of the parts and the length of the parts.

Shank :- The upper thick part of a sewing machine needle is called the shank. This part of the needle is inserted in the machine.

Shaft :- The shaft of a sewing machine needle is the area from the bottom of the shank to the point. The shaft contains the groove, scarf, eye and point of the needle.

Groove :- A groove is in the side of the needle leading to the eye. The groove is a place for the thread to lay into the needle.

Use your fingernail and feel the groove of the needle on various sizes to understand why a different size thread would be needed for heavier thread.

Scarf : - The scarf is a groove out of one side of the needle. The scarf allows the bobbin case hook to intersect with the upper thread and form stitches.

Eye :- The eye of the needle carries the thread so the machine can keep forming stitches.

The size of the eye can vary and works in conjunction with the groove of the needle.

Using a needle with an eye that is too small or too large can cause your thread to shred and break.

Point :- The point of the needle is the first contact with the fabric and responsible for how the needle pierces the fabric.

The most common types of point are sharps, ballpoint and universal.

- Sharp needles are for all woven fabric. The sharp point is especially helpful when sewing straight lines and tasks such as tops stitching.

- Ballpoint needles are designed for knit fabric so that the point glides between the loops of a knit fabric without disturbing the fibers that make up the fabric. Ball point needles do not form as straight stitching as sharp needles. The non-straight stitching is more apt to stretch with the fabric.

- Universal needles can be used with woven or knit fabric. The point of a universal needle is sharp yet very slightly rounded giving it the characteristics of a sharp and a ballpoint needle. If you are not happy with the stitches your machine is forming, try switching the needle to either a ball point or sharp

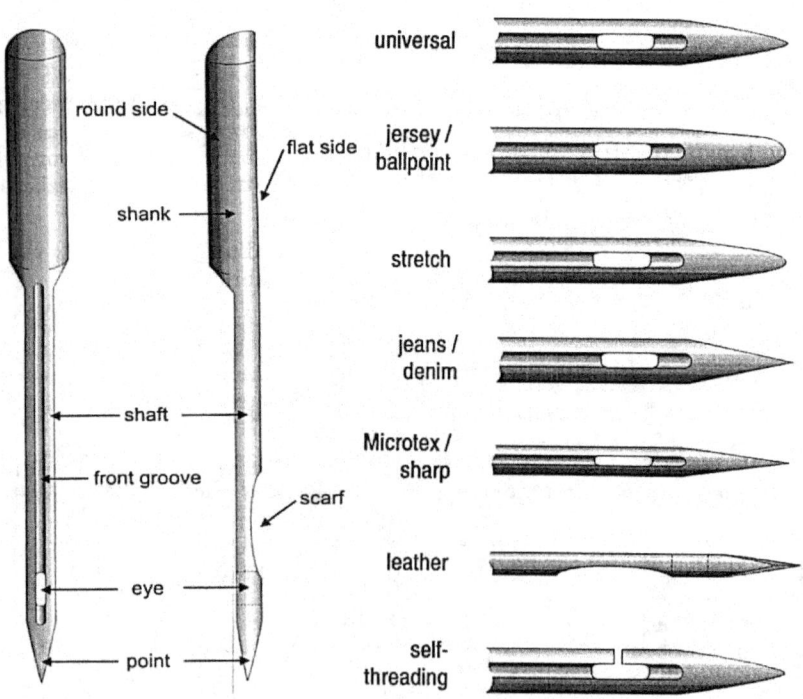

Other Types of Needle points are

- Stretch Needle: - Having the tips rounded are also known as round point needles used in light weight closely woven fabrics, and stretchable fabrics like Lycra etc.

- Denim Needles: - used for sewing in denim fabrics which are heavy weight. The needle have sharp points

- Leather Needles: - leather needles have diamond or chisel shaped tips and sharp points. As the leather is heavy weight and will not stretch during the needle penetration it need to be cut to enter.

- Self-threading needles: - The self-threading needle eyes have a opening to catch the thread. This type of needle are most used in domestic sewing and it the threads can be pulled through the eye opening, the main dis advantage of this needle is its low strength. Hence can use in slow speed sewing and lightweight materials.

NEEDLE NUMBER

Needle number is the identification for the size of a needle it is a direct proportion to the needle diameter in the blade. There are two methods used on representing this needle numbers.

1. Metric system :- The numeric value of needle diameter in Nm is represented directly i.e. if the needle diameter is 90 Nm the needle size is represented as 90, the needle diameter is measured just above the needle scarf

2. Numeric system :- In metric system the value is represented in numerical values like 6, 7, 8, 9, 10 etc. as the number increases the size of the needle also increased

Needle size in Metric system $\quad = 90\,\text{Nm}$

Needle number in Numeric system $= (90 - 20) / 5 = 14$

SELECTION OF NEEDLE.

The selection of proper sewing machine needle is important to avoid defects due to needle such as needle cuts, and frequent needle breaks.

The selection of needle is done in consideration to,

1. Type of fabric – light, medium, heavy or extra duty
2. Fabric density
3. Knit or woven

4.   Thickness or folds in a seam

5.   Type of machine and speed of sewing

For example: for the side seam attachment of a denim jeans we have to use denim needle size 14 or above.

American	8	9	10	11	12	14	16	18	19
European	60	65	70	75	80	90	100	110	120
	Light Weight Materials				Medium Weight Materials			Heavy weight materials	

KNIT SEWING MACHINE NEEDLE AND EFFECT ON FABRIC

The wrong selection of a needle can cause major damages in knit fabric compared to woven fabric, the major defects caused by the wrong selection of needle is Needle cutting.

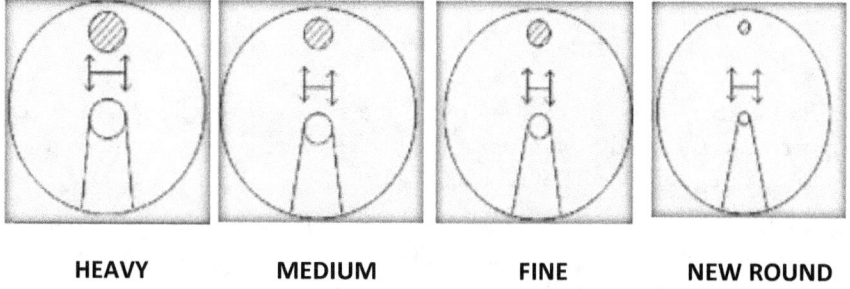

| HEAVY | MEDIUM | FINE | NEW ROUND |

Needle cutting is the breaking of yarns in the fabric as the needle enters the seam. On knit that are made with interloping yarn constructions, a cut yarn will result in a "run" along the seam line. Therefore, when the needle enters the seam, the needle point should not cut the yarns but push them aside as it penetrates the fabric.

Checklist That Will Aid In Reducing Needle Cutting.

- Use a ball pointed needle as well as possible. A ball pointed needle should not cut the yarns in the fabric as the needle penetrates the seam but shift the yarns to one side. This also requires a small diameter thread. On some classes of needles, there are different types of ball points available. Make sure the type of ball point matches the size of the yarn in the fabric. Too large of a ball point will burst the knit fabric made from very fine yarns. Too small of a ball point will pierce and possibly cut or weaken larger yarn sizes used in sweaters, etc

- Use a tapered blade needle with a ball point if it is available. A tapered blade needle allows the use of the smallest possible needle with minimum needle breakage.
- Inspect the needles at regular intervals and replace them if they show signs of having a sharp or burred point. Sometimes the sewing machine can be out of adjustment allowing metal to metal contact that will damage the point. Readjust the sewing machine if necessary to minimize this condition.
- Check for signs of needle heat that may be melting the fibers. If needle heat is identified as the problem by observing melted fibers around the needle hole, reduce the needle heat by one of the following methods:
  - use a double grooved needle if available;
  - make sure the thread has a good lubricant on it; and
  - Use some types of needle cooler.

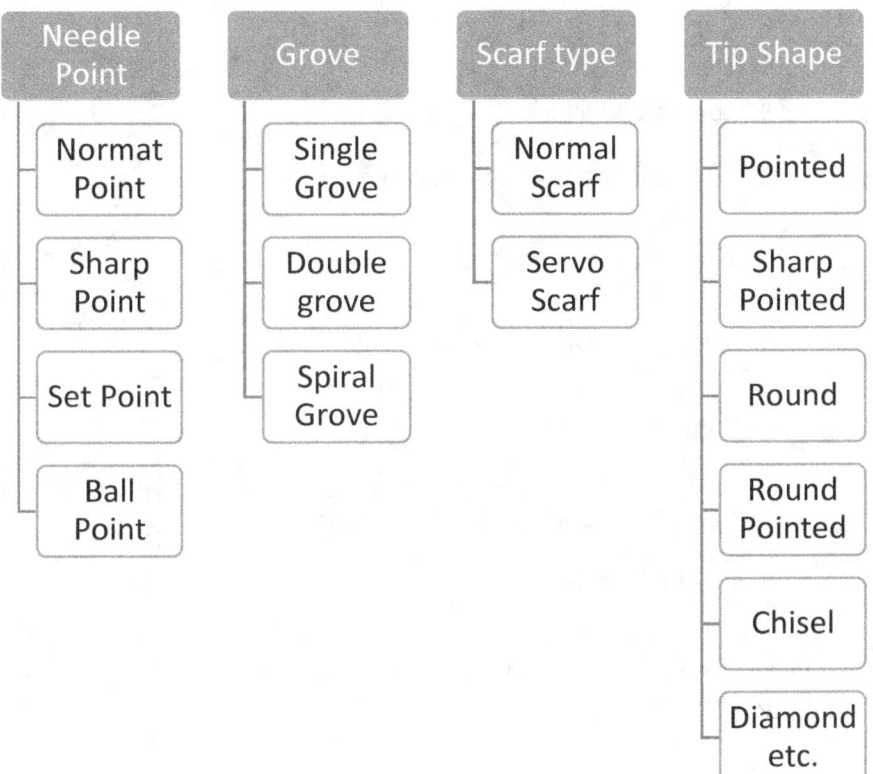

Sl no	Types of Sewing Machines	Needle System
1	Single Needle Lock Stitch Machines	DA X 1 , or DBX 1
2	Single Needle Lock Stitch Machine witch Automatic Thread Trimmer	DA X 1or DB X 1
3	Single Needle Lock Stitch Machine witch Fabric Edge Trimmer	DA X 1or DB X 1
4	Double Needle Lock Stitch Machine	DP X 5
5	Single Needle Lock Stitch Zigzag Machine	DB X 1
6	THREE Thread Over Lock Machine	DC X 1 or DC X 27
7	FIVE thread Over Lock With Safety Stitch Machine	DC X 1 or DC X27
8	Button Hole Machine	DP X 5
9	Chain Stitch Button Stitch Machine	TQ X 1 or TV X 7
10	Lock Stitch Button Stitch Machine	TQ X 1 or TV X 7
11	Inter Lock/Flat Lock Machine	UY X 1 or GAS
12	Feed Of The Arm Machine For Denim	TV X 1 or TV X 7
13	One &Two Needle Chain Stitch Machine	TV X 1 or TV X 7
14	Blind Stitch Machine	LW X5.

Apart from this there are many more types of needles used in garment sewing machineries and the common types are shown here.

15 WORK FLOW OF A FASHION FACTORY

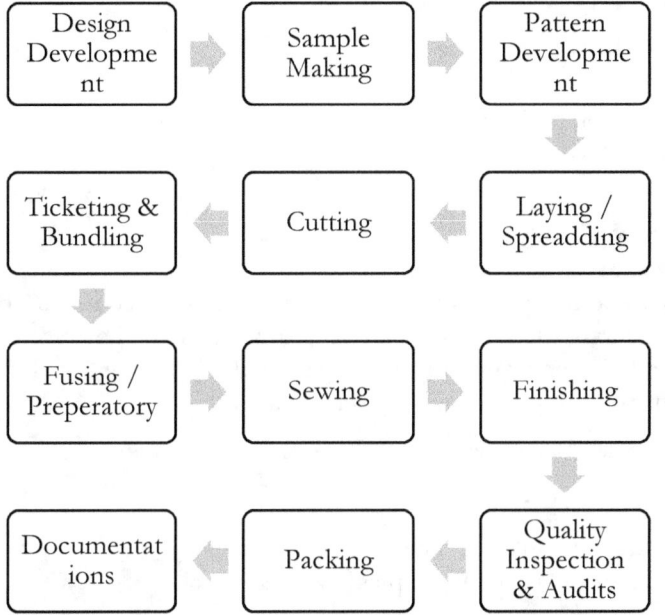

DESIGN / SKETCH

The first step in garment Manufacturing is designing the sketch for the dresses that have to be prepared. For this purpose the designer first draw sketches. The designer also draws working drawings along with the sketch. Working drawings are flat drawing of the sketch and it help pattern maker in understanding the pattern details involved in the construction

SAMPLING

The samples decide the ability of an exporter. The buyer will access the exporter and his organisation only by the samples. By doing sampling the exporter can estimate the yarn consumption for developing the fabric, a clear idea on costing more ever the manufacturing difficulties. Besides by doing sampling only the exporter can optimize the processing parameters for mass production, which helps to avoid all kind of bottlenecks.

The Details Attached to the Garment Sample

After the confirmation of order, each sample sent t 0 the buyer has the following details attached to it, with the help of a tag.

- Ref no.
- Color
- Fabric
- Composition
- Description
- Quantity
- Style n0/ Size
- Store

There may be a separate sampling department in a company. But as the merchandiser is the person who is interacting with the buyers regarding samples and other requirements, this sampling department will work under the supervision of merchandising department.

We have to send many samples to buyers. Some of them are,

1. Proto samples or fit samples
2. Counter samples or reference samples or approval samples
3. Wash test samples
4. Photo samples
5. Pre-production samples
6. Production samples
7. Salesmen samples or promotional samples
8. Shipment samples etc

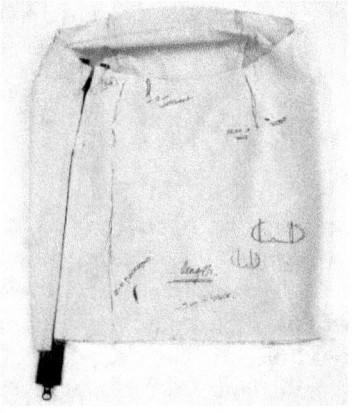

1 Prototype sample:

A sample produced with the available fabrics and trims to check the patterns, measurements and fitness as per the sketch or specification provided by buyer or merchandiser. It is also very important to see whether the particular sample can be prepared or not with the machines available in the particular industry and the operators are skilled enough or not to produce the quality products.

2   Size and fit sample:

These samples are produced with original fabrics and trims after the approval of prototype of samples. Generally graded patterns are used as per required sizes. These are treated as original specimen for bulk production and any mistakes are removed at the stage itself for further solution. Generally more care is taken for the preparation of the samples because they send for buyer's approval.

3   Production sample:

Before going for bulk production these samples are generally produced in production line itself to see the quality can be produced by the operators and type of defects can be taken place during bulk production. The steps are followed or instructions are given to the inspectors or checkers as per the defects taking place in production samples to avoid further problem and to run the production smoothly.

4   Shipment sample:

These samples are collected from the bulk. These are sent to customer once the production is over or online for further comments such as final inspection, shipment details etc.

5   Sample order or salesman sample:

These samples are generally produced in small quantities before going for bulk production and sent to retail outlets to check the response of customers or consumers and to book order.

6   Counter or reference sample:

Whenever the manufacturer sends sample to buyer they keep some sample for further reference. These help them to negotiate price and other factors with the manufacturer or concerned parties. These samples are called as counter or reference samples.

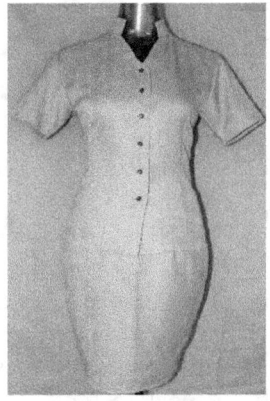

7   Approval & Approved Sample:

When an enquiry takes place the merchandiser will manufacture some samples of the order and sent to the approval from the buyer and when these samples are sent to them, they are known as Approval samples. When the approval samples are get approved it known as approved sample. Generally fit samples are sent for approval and are kept as approved.

PATTERN MAKING

Production Pattern

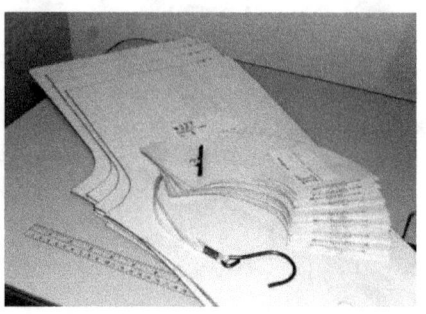

The pattern design is now taken for creating the production patterns. The production pattern is one which will be used for bulk production of garments. The pattern maker makes the patterns on standard pattern making paper. These papers are made-up of various grades.

Garment patterns can be constructed by two means: manual method, CAD/CAM method. Today many companies have developed CAD/CAM because of the ease of designing patterns, fluency and precision involved which cannot be guaranteed with the manual method and the economy in duplication and correction. Investing once into the CAD/CAM unit is worth in itself.

A garment sewing pattern or garment fabric & patterns draft is developed by calculating the data from the following means,

1. Direct Sample.

2. Specification Sheet/ Measurement Chart.

3. Actual body size measurements.

4. Ease Allowances.

5. Sewing Allowance.

These allowances are different for different type of fabrics and patterns.

GRADING

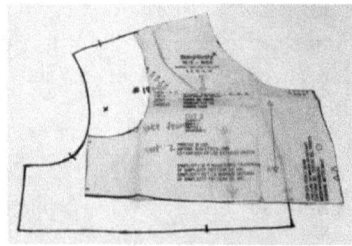

The purpose of grading is to create patterns in different sizes. Grading a pattern is really scaling a pattern up or down in order to adjust it for multiple sizes. Pattern grading by manual method is a cumbersome task because the grader has to alter the pattern on each and every point from armhole, to neckline, sleeve cap and wrist etc. by using

CAD it is much easier and faster.

MARKER MAKING:

The measuring department determines the fabric yardage needed for each style and size of garment. Computer software helps the technicians create the optimum fabric layout to suggest so that fabric can be utilized maximum. Markers, made in accordance to the patterns are attached to the fabric with the help of adhesive stripping or staples. Markers are laid in such a way so that minimum possible fabric gets wasted during cutting operation. After marking the manufacturer will get the idea of how much fabric he has to order in advance for the construction of garments.

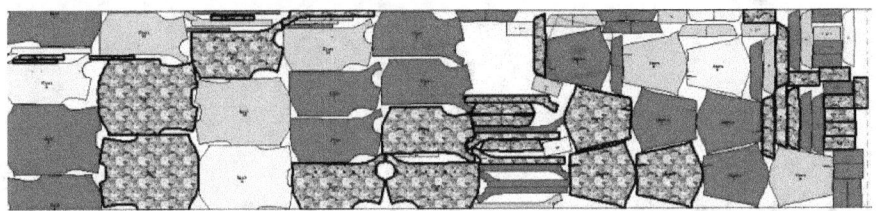

Computer marking is done on specialized software's. In computerized marking there is no need of large paper sheets for calculating the yardage, in fact, mathematical calculations are made instead to know how much fabric is required.

The Term to remember is *"Marker Efficiency"* is the total efficiency to cut maximum amount of fabric, can be calculated as " 100 x the total area of cut patterns / Total area of Marker" or "100 x total weight of the cut components / Weight of the lay"

SPREADING / LAYING

Spreading is the layering of fabric ready for cutting, the lay length will be calculated according to the marker and the lay height (number of lays) will be according to the cut order plan of the specific order.

Splicing:

Splicing is a process of cutting fabric across its width and overlapping layers in between the two ends of a lay. Splicing of lay is required some times to avoid faults found in fabric into the garment components. After splicing cut end is pulled back to overlap plies as far back as the next splicing mark. Overlapping length depends on splicing mark to cover complete garment components.

Splicing process is also used when one fabric roll ends in the middle of the marker and end bit length is enough to cover at least one complete garment components. Spreading of next roll starts from the splice mark.

Splice Marks:

Splice marks are marked on the edge of cutting table before spreading using reference of the marker. Splice marks are reference points from where overlapping of fabric is done after splicing of fabric. Spicing marks are shown in the following diagram.

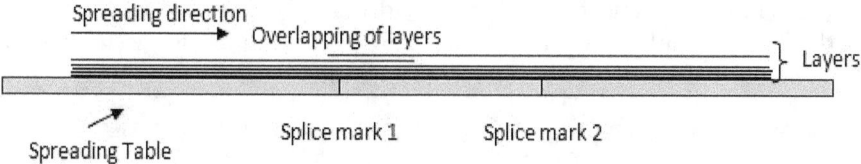

CUTTING

The fabric is then cut with the help of cloth cutting machines suitable for the type of the cloth. These can be a straight knife, band knife, Round knife, die clickers similar to die or punch press; or computerized cutting machines that use either blades or laser beams to cut the fabric in desired shapes

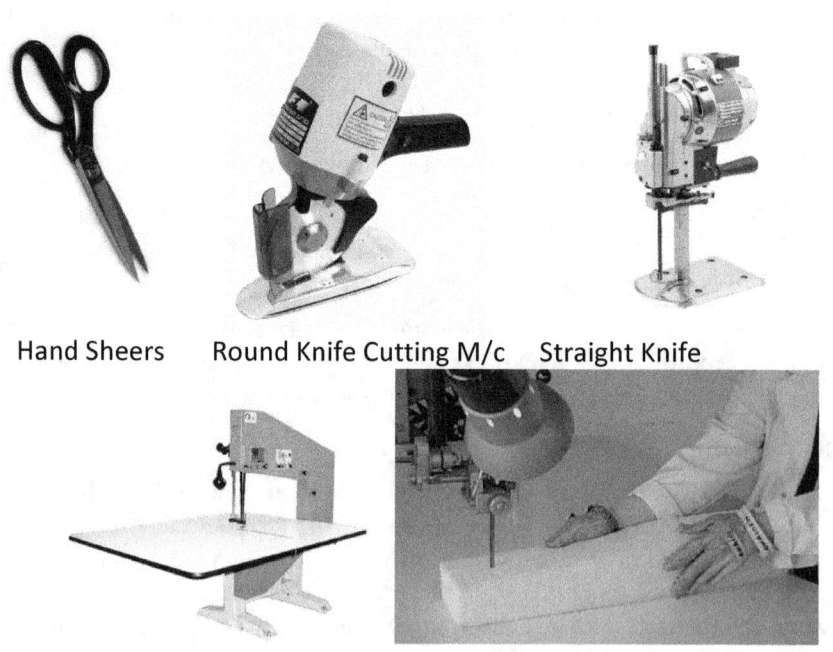

Hand Sheers   Round Knife Cutting M/c   Straight Knife

Band Knife cutting M/c

The main objective of cutting department is to get a precision cut so as to produce the right garment component in a way that it ensures the minimum fabric consumption because about 80% of the cost of a garment is spend on fabric, the cutting machine is selected according to the parts, for a high precision cut Band knife machine will be used. And general cutting straight knife machine used.

SORTING/BUNDLING:

The sorter sorts the patterns according to size and design and makes bundles of them. This step requires much precision because making bundles of mismatched patterns can create severe problems. On each bundle there are specifications of the style size and the marker too is attached with it. Each part is numbered for later matching.

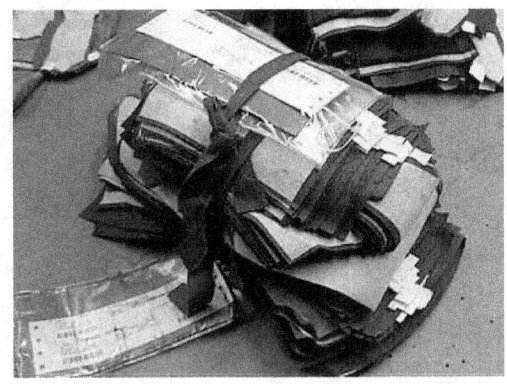

FUSING

Fusing is the method of joining interlining to the fabric to give strength and shape support after sewing, there are two type of fusing woven and non-woven fusing material is used for fusing, for minor production stages it uses a common iron box for fusing the interlining to the fabric, but industries use flatbed fusing or automated continuous feed fusing machines. The selection of machine is based on the size, shape and type of interlining and fabric used, The important factors verified and monitored in fusing is the Temperature of the heater, feed lattices etc. and the pressure inside the fusing area, the fusing defects are listed under the critical defect list of a garment inspection check list.

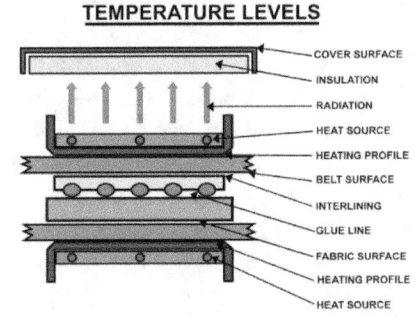

TEMPERATURE LEVELS

COVER SURFACE
INSULATION
RADIATION
HEAT SOURCE
HEATING PROFILE
BELT SURFACE
INTERLINING
GLUE LINE
FABRIC SURFACE
HEATING PROFILE
HEAT SOURCE

SEWING/ASSEMBLING

The sorted bundles of fabrics are now ready to be stitched. In this workplace, there are many operators who perform a single operation (generally for product which have more than 5 operations). One operator may make only straight seams, while another may make sleeve insets. Yet another two operators can sew the waist seams, and make  buttonholes. Various industrial sewing machines too have different types of stitches that they can make. These machines also have different configuration of the frame. Some machines work sequentially and feed their finished step directly into the next machine, while the gang machines have multiple machines performing the same operation supervised by a single operator. All these factors decide what parts of a garment can be sewn at that station.

INSPECTION

Open seams, wrong stitching techniques, non- matching threads, and missing stitches, improper creasing of the garment, erroneous thread tension and raw edges are some of the sewing defects which can affect the garment quality adversely. During processing the quality control section needs to check each prepared article against these defects. There are inline, end line, and final audits to control the defects and to separate critical defected garments from the lot.

PRESSING/ FINISHING

The next operations are those of finishing and/or decorating. Moulding may be done to change the finished surface of the garment by applying pressure, heat, moisture, or certain other combination. Pressing, pleating and creasing are the basic moulding processes. Creasing is mostly done before other finishing processes like that of stitching a cuff, decorating the  garment with something like a pocket, appliqués, embroidered emblems etc. There are lot of machineries used in finishing the garment. Pressing machine, steam presses, form press, etc.

FINAL INSPECTION

For the textile and apparel industry, product quality is calculated in terms of quality and standard of fibres, yarns, fabric construction, colour fastness, designs and the final finished garments. Quality control in terms of garment manufacturing, pre-sales and posts sales service, delivery, pricing, etc are essential for any garment manufacturer, trader or exporter. Certain quality related problems, often seen in garment manufacturing like sewing, colour, sizing, or garment defects should never be over looked

PACKING

The finished garments are finally sorted on the basis of design and size and packed to send for distribution to the retail outlets.

There are a lot of technology improvisation involved in the manufacturing of Garments, hence care will be take on all areas, for the better utilization of Man, Machine and Material

Types of Packing

- Stand up pack – Common Shirt packing method
- Flat Pack - Sportswear, Shirts, Trouser, Blouse etc.
- Hanger Packs- Blazers, Coats, Pants etc.
- Semi Stand up pack- Shirts
- Half fold pack - Pants

The cartons are size may wary from 12, 24 or 36 pieces in carton according to the retailer plan of delivery. And sometimes the cartons are packed with Size ration, colour ratio of even mixed packs are done.

PRODUCTION PROCESS FLOW CHART

Process chart is used to explain the complex production activities happening in the production floor or garment manufacturing process. It generally uses diagrams with links to identify the correct flow sequences. The below explain a basic process chart of a garment industry.

Flowcharts are prepared for specific garments and sometimes for specific styles to support the supervisor and other personnel's to identify the processes to be done in sequence for a particular product.

Apparel industry uses a hybrid mode of production structure, as the major output of the industry is based on 40% Machine and 60% human efforts with a combination of processes and sequences.

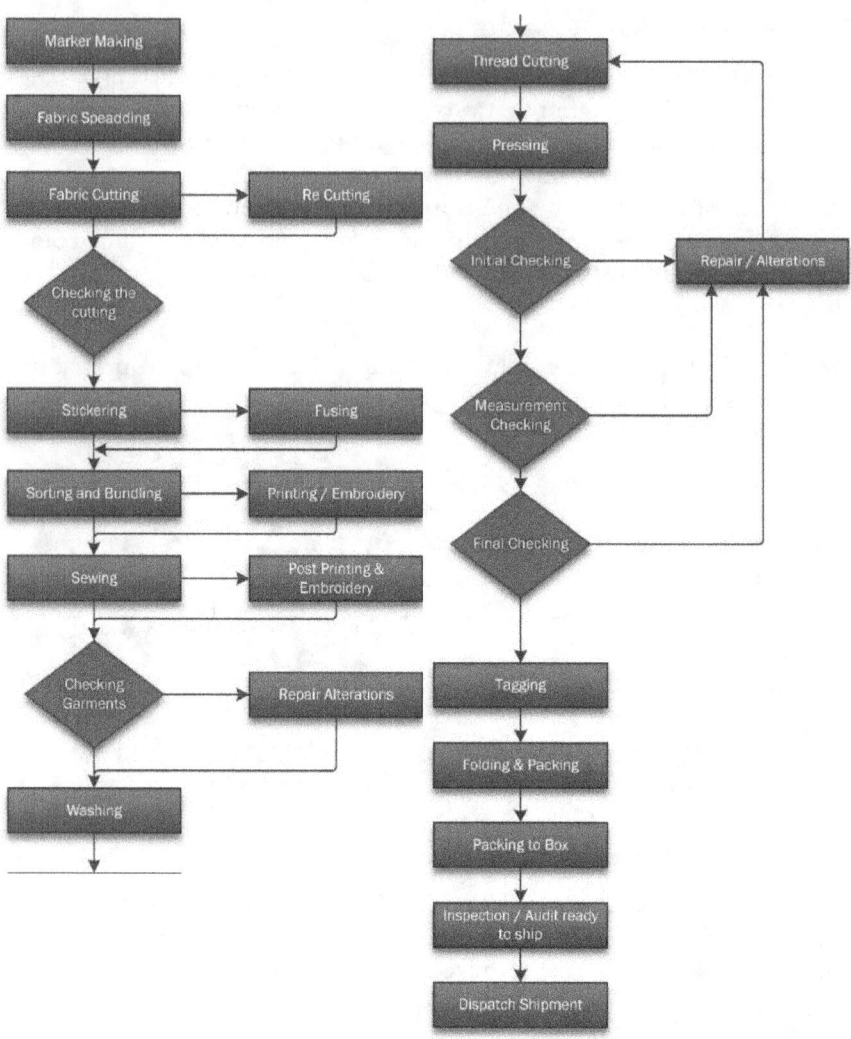

STORES

The Reason for keeping stock

Time :- The lead time of the production request the need of stock in hand

Uncertainty: - Inventories are maintained as buffers to meet uncertainties in demand, supply and movements of goods.

Economies of scale - Ideal condition of "one unit at a time at a place where a user needs it" may need to stock materials for the specific time of sale

Appreciation in Value - In some situations, some stock gains the required value when it is kept for some time to allow it reach the desired standard for consumption,

Inventory

Most manufacturing organizations usually divide their "goods for sale" inventory into:

- Raw materials - materials and components scheduled for use in making a product.
- Work in process, WIP - materials and components that have begun their transformation to finished goods.

- Finished goods - goods ready for sale to customers.
- Goods for resale - returned goods that are salable.
- Stocks in Transit.
- Consignment Stocks.

Role of a Store

The value of the item in the store department of an enterprise can represent a large proportion of the total value of its asset. Efficient store management will ensure that the correct item of the correct qualities will be available in the correct quantities when required, this avoiding losses of production, sales and profit

The basic role of the store in the apparel industry is related to,

- **Right time** :- purchase of Trims, accessories, fabric etc. in order to get the availability of the materials in time for production,
- **Right Quality:** - The purchase of the material has to be done without affecting the quality i.e. the quality of the materials should have the required quality parameters so that the production and faith of the company lay on it.
- **Lowest Price :-** the material are to be purchased in lowest cost in the market so that the company should same money
- **Right Quantity:-** There should be sufficient quantity of the material purchase so that the production should not stop for the materials and at same time there should be no excess stock so the excess stock of material is dead money

- **Proper inventory control: -** There should be proper inventory control of the materials in store, in production etc.so that the stores department should be aware of the flow of materials through the departments so as to control the cost of production and to reduce the dead money and wastage of materials.

MERCHANDISING

Merchandiser is the interface between Buyer & Exporter. He is the responsible from order analysis to shipment. So Merchandising is the very valuable department in the Apparel Industry. This Article explains the main responsibilities of merchandisers.

Merchandising is the department which mediates marketing and production departments. Some times, merchandising department will have to do costing and pricing also. In any case, the merchandiser is the person whose responsibility is to execute the orders perfectly as per the costing and pricing. So it is a very valuable department.

Following are the main responsibilities of merchandisers.

- Internal & external communication,
- Sampling,
- Labdips,
- Accessories & trims,
- Preparing internal order sheets,
- Preparing purchase orders,
- Advising and assisting production,
- Advising quality department about quality level,
- Mediating production and quality departments,
- Giving shipping instructions and following shipping,
- Helping documentation department,
- Taking responsibility for inspections and
- Following shipment.

As the other departments will follow the instructions given by the merchandising department, they have very high value. Other departments don't know the buyer's instructions; they know only the merchandising department's instructions. So it is the sole responsibility of merchandising department to instruct other departments the specifications and instructions of buyer's orders clearly.

16 PRODUCTION SYSTEMS IN RMG

Evaluation of production Systems

Based on the style, machine availability, operator availability, the operator skill, the production system can be evaluated. If we have few machines and operator skill is very good , we can set the machines based on model as described in section4 .If order quantity is large run and enough machines and operators are available we can use the system number -2 progressive bundling system. Based on the production requirement we can formulate the production Systems.

Equipment layout varies according to the production type of each factory. An apparel production system is an integration of material handling, production process, personnel and equipment's that direct workflow and generate finished products. Each system requires different types of:

- Management philosophy
- Material handling arrangement
- Floor layout
- Employee training
- Companies may combine the systems or use only one depending on their need.

Three types of production systems that are commonly used in the mass production,

1. Make Through System,
2. Modular Production System,
3. Assembly Line System.

MAKE THROUGH SYSTEM

It is the traditional method of manufacture in which an operator makes right through one garment at a time. In this system, one operator will do all the stages of the sewing operations of one garment and after completing it he will go for the next garment. The advantages of the make through system are,

- Quick throughput time
- Easy to supervise

The disadvantages of the make through systems are,

- Low productivity
- High labor cost
- Only very experienced operator can be used
- It is a system only suitable in couture and sample making.

MODULAR SYSTEM:-

"An organized group of individuals working together in a co-operative manner to accomplish a common purpose"

Working in modular system:

- The line layout is U -shaped with garments progressing around the line.
- Each operator is cross trained on a different portion of line (i.e. continuous operation) depending on skills and operation complexity. Ideally all the operators are cross trained on all the operations.
- Thus operators work to predominantly predetermined adjacent tasks.
- Each operator is assigned at least one operation.
- Operatives work on standing workstations.
- The first and last operations are uniquely assigned to the first and last operator respectively
- Work In Progress (WIP) is kept to a minimum.

ASSEMBLY LINE SYSTEM:-

Each operator is assigned to one operation only,

- Bundles of garment components are moved sequentially from operation to operation
- Bundles consist of garment parts needed to complete a specific operation or garment component.
- Some companies work with varied bundle sizes others with standard bundle sizes

- Bundles are assembled in cutting room where cut parts are matched.
- Bundle tickets consist of a master list of operations and corresponding coupons for each operation.
- Each bundle receives a ticket that identifies style#, size, shade and list of operations (is some cases)
- Bundles are assembled is cutting room where cut parts are matched
- Bundle receives a ticket that identifies style#, size, shade and list of operations.

There are four variations of the assembly line system being followed in the industries namely,

    a)   Unit production system (Basic System)

    b)   Progressive Bundle systems and

    c)   Bundle System by parts

    d)   Bundle System by Machine models.

UNIT PRODUCTION SYSTEM- UP (SYNCHRONIZED SYSTEM)

This system is suitable for mass production of a few styles. Each operation is synchronized; this system is called synchronized system. Every time the operator finishes one piece of garment and feed to the next operator. So the previous operation is per formed efficiently, it will increase efficiency of the operator so it massively increase the production. This system is not suitable for handling different styles of garments.

The features of this system are...

1. The unit of production is in single garment not in bundles.
2. The garment components are automatically transported from work station to work station according to a predetermined sequence.
3. The work stations are so constructed that the components are presented as close as possible to the operator's left hand in order to reduce the amount of movement required to grasp the component.

The operational principle is

1. All the components for one garment are loaded into a carrier at a work station.
2. The carrier itself is divided into sections, each section having a quick release clamp which prevents the components from falling out during movement through the system.
3. The loaded carriers are then fed on to the main powered line, which continuously circulates between the rows of machines.

4. The carriers get automatically opened on work stations if the work on a carrier is addressed to that particular station.
5. When an operator has completed work on one carrier, a push button at the side of the sewing machine is pressed and this activates a mechanism, which transport the carrier back to the main line.

Advantages

- Bundle handling is eliminated.
- Time for pickup and disposal is reduced.
- Output is automatically recorded.
- Automatically balance the work between stations.
- Up to 40 styles can be produced simultaneously on one system.

Disadvantages

- Require high investment.
- Proper planning is required.

PROGRESSIVE BUNDLE SYSTEM.

This system is based on the synchronized flow of work through each stage of producing a garment. Time synchronization is the most important factor of this system. For e.g. If one operation has a value of 1.5 minutes then all other operations in the line must have the same, or a very close value.

Advantages

- Labors of all level can be used.
- The quality of each component is checked during production, so quality is high.
- The components are moved as bundles, so this will avoid the problem of mixing the garment parts, shade variation, size variation.
- Specialization of the operators will increase the productivity.
- An effective production control system and quality control system can be easily implemented.
- Time study and Method study techniques.
- Bundle tracking is possible, so identifying and solving of the problem is so easy.

Bundle System By Garment Parts

It is difficult to strike a balance between the operations when you handle one item. However, if several kinds of items are flowing simultaneously, striking an average balance between the operations will be possible. Lay out the factory by parts of garments, such as front body, back body , accessories and assembly lines, or by machine models (or operations) , so that we do not have to change the layout according to the items you are dealing with. Since several kinds of items flow simultaneously, it is advisable that, at most each bundle is limited to 10 pieces of cutting.

Bundle System By Machine Models.

This kind of bundle system can be made by arranging the assembly machine models as per their application on the product manufacturing

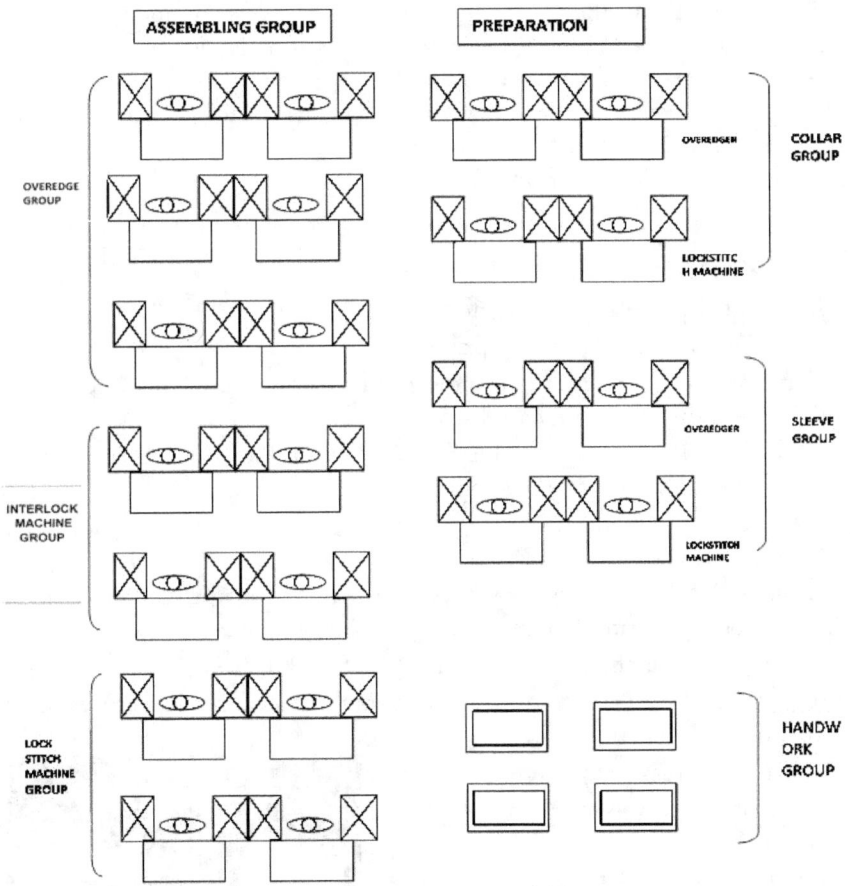

Belt Conveyer System

The operator is in charge of the transportation of this system. However, a belt conveyer performs a transporting operation in this system. Sewing machines and equipment's are placed along both sides of the conveyor. The person who operate the conveyor pick up and feed the cutting to be sewn in plastic containers for the operator in charge of each operation. It is effective for heavy weight cuttings like coats and denim. It is an expensive production system.

QUICK RESPONSE MANUFACTURING (QRM)

The main objective of QRM is to reduce internal and external lead times. (Lead time is the total time taken to dispatch a product after order confirmation), Shorter lead times to improve quality, reduce cost, and to eliminate non-value-added waste within the organisation while simultaneously increasing the organization's competitiveness and market share by serving customers better and faster. For this reason, companies making products in low or varying volumes have used QRM as an alternative or to complement other strategies such as Lean Manufacturing, Total quality management, Six Sigma or Kaizen.

QRM extends basic principles of time-based competition while including these new aspects:

- Singular focus on lead time reduction
- Focus on manufacturing enterprises
- Clarification of the misunderstanding and misconceptions managers have about how to apply time-based strategies
- Companywide approach reaching beyond shop floor to other areas such as office operations and the supply chain
- Use of cellular organization structure throughout the business with more holistic and flexible cells
- Inclusion of basic principles of systems dynamics to provide insight on how to best reorganize an enterprise to achieve quick response
- New material planning and control approach (POLCA)
- Specific QRM principles on how to rethink manufacturing process and equipment decisions
- Novel performance measure
- Focus on implementation and sustainability
- Manufacturing Critical-path Time (MCT) metric to measure lead times

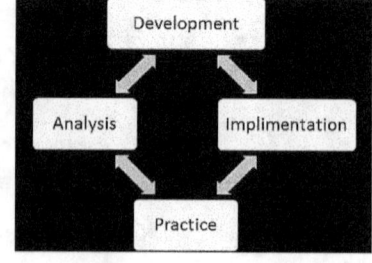

The QRM Strategies and Tools are,

1. Lead Time as the Management Strategy
2. Manufacturing Critical-path Time (MCT)
3. Organizational structure
1. Functional to cellular,
2. Top-Down control to Team ownership
3. Specialized Workers to a Cross-trained Workforce
4. Efficiency/Utilization Goals to Lead Time Reduction:
4. QRM Cell
5. System Dynamics
6. Create Spare Capacity
7. Optimize batch sizes,
8. Enterprise wide application
9. Office Operations
10. Material Planning
11. Production Control
12. Supply Chain
13. New product Introduction

QRM's strong focus on lead time reduction requires a comprehensive definition of lead time. To accomplish this, QRM introduces Manufacturing Critical-path Time (MCT). It is based on the standard critical path method; defined as the typical amount of calendar time from when a customer creates an order, until the first piece of that order is delivered to the customer.

A metric designed to calculate waste and highlight opportunities for improvement, MCT gives an estimate of the time it takes to fulfill an order, quantifying the longest critical-path duration of order-fulfillment activities

QRM requires four fundamental structural changes to transform a company organized around cost-based management strategies to a time-based focus:

Functional to Cellular: QRM cells are more flexible and holistic in their implementation compared to other cell concepts, and can be applied outside the shop floor

Top-down Control to Team Ownership: QRM cells manage themselves and have ownership of the entire process within the cell

Specialized Workers to a Cross-trained Workforce: Workers need to be trained to perform multiple tasks

Efficiency/Utilization Goals to Lead Time Reduction: To support this new structure, companies must replace cost-based goals of efficiency and utilization with the overarching goal of lead time reduction

17 OPERATION BREAK DOWN

How to Make an Operation Bulletin (OB) for a Garment?

An operation bulletin is one of the primary IE tools. An OB helps to set a production line with correct number of machines and manpower. Explained OB making process step by step. Prior to using these steps for making an OB it is also required to know how to determine operation SMV, calculation of machine requirement and how to make operation breakdown of a garment.

Step #1: Prepare An OB Format.

A basic operation bulletin contains following information. a data sheet will be prepared with the required details.

1. Daily working hours
2. Target output per day or per hour
3. Total SMV (Sewing SMV and Non-sewing SMV)
4. OB prepared by (Name of the Engineer)
5. Job code
6. Operation description
7. Machine description
8. SMV @ 100% Efficiency
9. SMV @ target efficiency%
10. Calculated production per hour
11. Name of the Folder and attachment if any used
12. Calculated no. of machines
13. Actual no. of machines
14. Estimated production per unit hours
15. Any remarks
16. Machine summary list

Step #2: Collect Correct Sample

Once the OB format ready, then the analysis of the approved sample will be done. Check for the sample so that it is approved and ready to cut.

Step #3: Make Operation Breakdown For The Sample

Look into garment construction in details. To have better understanding first break garment into parts (like collar, front, back etc.). Then list down operations in the note book according to the section made. Once listed all operations cross-check with garment again and visualize that if all operations are done as per the list and you will get exactly complete garment as per the sample garment. Now enter operations in the OB format as per sequence to be performed in line.

Step #4: Define Machine For Each Operation

Based on seam type used in a style it may need to use different types of sewing machines for different operations and manual work stations. Select one machine and enter into the sheet against each operation. Also enter name and description of attachments or folder or guides if needed for an operations.

Step #5: Enter SMVs For Each Operation

This step is the most critical in term of how we get SMVs, to find SMVs by conducting time study or existing database. Mention source of SMV (time study or MTM2 database). Convert SMVs in based on the target line efficiency%. It is optional.

SMV at Target Efficiency = SMV @ 100% efficiency / Target efficiency%

Step #6: Calculate Calculated Production Per Hour

Calculate production per hour at target efficiency%.

Calculated Production/Hour @ target efficiency = 60/Operation SMV @ target Efficiency

Step #7: Calculate Number Of Machines

To make garment as per the target it need install sufficient number of sewing machines. We will get fraction number of machines (with decimal) in this calculation. In the next column add number of machines manually round figure for machine numbers. Combine two operations in a single machine where possible, i.e. required machine no. is less or equal to half.

Calculated Machine number = (SMV @ target efficiency * Hourly production target/60)

Or

> Calculated Machine number = (SMV @ target efficiency * Daily production target/Total minutes in a shift day)

We can also use pitch time for the calculation of calculated machine no.

> Calculated Machine number =operation SMV / Pitch.

Step #8: Calculate Estimated Production Per Hour

It is calculated according to the machine assigned to each operation. It may be different for few operations than calculated production per hour (step #6) as we set machine numbers to round up value. Formula used -

> Estimated Production/Hour = (No. of machine assigned * Hourly target qty.)/Calculated no. of machines

Step #9: Calculate Machine Summary

At the bottom of the OB add one table for machine summary. This table will help you to quickly find how many actual machines are required for each machine types.

A basic Operation Break down is used to record the sequence of operations, machine and SMV only, and the Details OB will be prepared with the Balanced line structure giving the details of operator allocation, machine allocation etc.

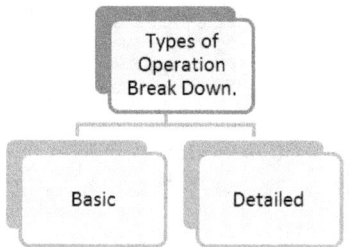

OPERATION BREAK DOWN OF TROUSER

The Operation Break Down of a trouser with Two Front Pockets, and two back pockets are as given below. This operation break down may vary according to machine to machine changes or style or design changes or workstations or layouts of production system changes. The operations needed to make a trouser are been listed section wise

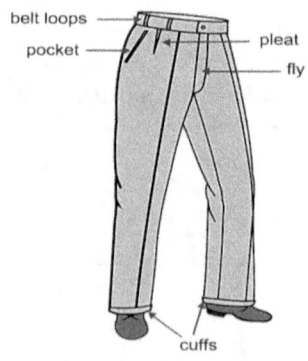

Operation Break Down of Trouser				
Section	No	Operation Description	Mc Type	SMV
Preparatory	1	Serge Front Panel with knee lining	Auto Serge	0.22
	2	Serge back Panel	Auto Serge	0.38
	3	Serge Right Fly	3T O/L	0.08
	4	Serge Back Rise	3T O/L	0.32
	5	Serge Front Rise	3T O/L	0.27
	6	Make Back Dart 2x2	Auto Dart	0.22
	7	Trim W/B	SNEC	0.25
	8	Attach Gripper	Gripper	0.45
	9	Make Fly Box	SNEC	0.20
	10	Fly Binding	SNLS	0.14
	11	Attach Front Pocket facing	Auto Facing	0.38
	12	Attach Back pocket facing	Auto facing	0.27
	13	Cut Waist Band	Indirect	0.12
	14	Waist Band checking		
Front	15	Tack Pocket Bag	SNLS	0.55
	16	Close Pocket bag with knitted tape	5T O/L	0.47
	17	Loading front and small parts	Indirect	0.40
	18	Attach left fly & TS with inside taking lining	SNLS	0.42
	19	Cut and attach pocket bag @ front with lining	SNLS	0.65
	20	Press Pocket & Fly	Ironer	0.46
	21	Top stitch @ Pocket Mouth	SNLS	0.54
	22	Tack pkt side & Waist	SNLS	0.48
	23	Attach fly box & Zipper with E/S @ Zipper	SNLS	0.62
	24	Front Checking		
Back	25	Fuse back dart	Ironer	0.46
	26	Make Back Bone	APW	0.53
	27	Back Loading	Indirect	0.35
	28	Press Back pocket bone	Ironer	0.52
	29	Attach Main label @ back pocket x1	SNLS	0.44
	30	Tack Tack back pocket corner with close facing	SNLS	0.77

	31	Make Eye Hole	BH	0.33
	32	Tack back pocket to pocket mouth	SNLS	0.55
	33	Close pocket bag with knitted tape	5T O/L	0.56
	34	Back Checking	CHK	
Assembly	35	Pairing	Indirect	0.45
	36	Join side seam and inseam with knee lining	SNCS	1.35
	37	Check side seam	SHK	
	38	Safety stitch	SNLS	0.39
	39	Press side and inseam	Ironer	0.59
	40	Assembly loading & Belt loading	Indirect	0.42
	41	Belt marking	Indirect	0.40
	42	Make round extension	SNLS	0.52
	43	Crotch Joint	SNLS	0.46
	44	Attach and close zipper	SNLS	0.42
	45	Loop Marking	Indirect	0.48
	46	Loop Attach	SNEC	0.76
	47	Attach W/B	SNUF	1.05
	48	Make Extension	SNLS	0.53
	49	Trim & Turn	Indirect	0.49
	50	Press belt & Extension	Ironer	0.42
	51	Hook & Eye att.	Hook & Eye	0.42
	52	Check W/B Extension	CHK	
	53	Tack fly in side	SNLS	0.20
	54	Make J Stitch	SNLS	0.52
	55	Sew Back rise	TNDM NDL	0.56
	56	Press Back rise	Ironer	0.42
	57	Check Back rise	CHK	
	58	Close Waist band (down stitch)	SNLS	0.76
	59	Attach W/B Label	SNLS	0.30
	60	Loop inner bar tack x 8	BT	0.48
	61	Loop upper bar tack x 7	BT	0.42
	62	Bar tack @ Side pocket x 5	BT	0.38
	63	Bar tack @ back pocket x 4	BT	0.30
	64	Loop cutting and Sticker removing.	Indirect	0.52
	65	Tack @ crotch x 5	Tacking	0.30
	66	Serge Bottom	3T O/L	0.40

	67	Bottom Hemming	BS	0.44
	68	Thread Trimming	Indirect	2.10
	69	Press Waist Band	Ironer	0.22
			TOTAL SMV	**29.87**

Abbreviations of Machine Name			
SNLS	1 Needle Lock Stitch	DNLS	2 Needle Lock Stitch
SNCS	1 Needle Chain Stitch	DNCS	2 Needle Chain Stitch
SNEC	1 Needle Edge Cutter	3T O/L	3 Thread Over Lock
BH	Button Hole	5T O/L	5 Thread Over Lock
BT	Bar Tacking Machine	BS	Blind Stitch
APW	Auto Pocket Welting	TNDM NDL	Tandem Needle Machine
4T O/L	4 Thread Over Lock	BA	Button Attach
CHK	Checking		

* The Procedure, Time, code used may change according to company, stile, design, method etc. Source : http://refergt.blogspot.in/

OPERATION BREAK DOWN OF FULL SLEEVE SHIRT – FORMAL MEN'S

The Operation Break Down of the formal men's Shirt with short sleeve, the components of the formal shirt are Front & Back body, Sleeves, Yokes, Collar (stand) and collar band, Cuff etc.

OPERATION BULLETIN FOR HALF SLEEVE SHIRT						
Target Output	**891**	Total workplaces	49		Total SAM's : 18.450	
Target Efficiency	70%	Total machines	37		Pcs./ machine	
Minutes per day	480	Absenteeism	10%		**SEWING SAM**	
			SAM	Machine	Attch	man	allot ted

COLLAR PREPARATION		SAM	Machine	Attch	man	allotted
1	Mark for run stitch collar	0.300	Helper Table		0.8	1.0
2	Run stitch Collar	0.650	SNEC		1.7	2.0
3	Trim & turn collar	0.350	Helper Table		0.9	1.0
4	Iron collar	0.350	Iron Table		0.9	1.0
5	Top-stitch collar	0.400	SNLS/ UBT	CR 1/4"	1.1	1.0
6	Hem collar band	0.400	Iron Table	Temp late	1.1	1.0
7	Attach collar band to collar	0.800	SNEC	Temp late	2.1	2.0
8	Turn / iron collar band corner	0.550	Iron table	Temp late	1.5	1.0
9	Trim & notch collar	0.450	Helper Table		1.2	1.0
		4.250			**11.3**	**11.0**

BACK YOKE		SAM	Machine	Attch	man	allotted
1	Attach back yoke	0.600	SNLS		1.6	2
2	Edge stitch back yoke	0.400	SNLS		1.1	1.0
		1.000			**2.7**	**3.0**

FRONT PREPARATION		SAM	Machine	Attch	man	allotted
1	Sew button hole placket MF 204	0.850	DNLS	11/2"	2.3	2.0
2	Iron button placket	0.300	Iron Table		0.8	1.0
3	Hem button placket	0.400	SNLS	1/32"	1.1	1.0

4	Iron pocket	0.650	Iron Table	Temp late	1.7	2.0
5	Hem pocket	0.300	SNLS		0.8	1.0
6	Attach pocket to left front	0.700	SNLS/ UBT	CR 1/16"	1.9	2.0
		3.200			**8.5**	**9.0**

SLEEVE PREPARATION

1	Iron sleeve hem	0.450	Iron Table		1.2	1.0
2	Hem sleeve	0.600	SNLS	Temp late	1.6	2.0
		1.050			**2.8**	**3.0**

ASSEMBLY

1	Match fronts & backs	0.200	Helper Table		0.5	1.0
2	Join shoulders	0.650	SNLS	T-Guide	1.7	2.0
3	Edge stich join shoulder	0.400	SNLS	CR 1/16"	1.1	1.0
4	Attach collar	0.650	SNLS		1.7	2.0
5	Prepare loop & tack hanger loop	0.400	SNLS		1.1	1.0
6	Close collar	0.900	SNLS	CR 1/16"	2.4	2.0
7	Attach sleeve	0.900	SNLS	corner Guide	2.4	2.0
8	Top-stitch arm hole	0.750	SNLS	CR 1/4"	2.0	2.0
9	Make side vent	0.800	SNLS		2.1	2.0
10	Close sides	0.900	FOA		2.4	2.0
11	Tack @ sleeve hem	0.400	SNLS		1.1	1.0
12	Hem bottom F-504	0.800	SNLS	a =1/4"	2.1	2.0
13	Line Check	1.200	Table		3.2	3.0
	32 OPERATIONS	**8.950**			**23.7**	**23.0**
	Total SM's	**18.450**			**48.94**	**49**
	Total sewing SAMs	**13.250**				
	M/c time/Total time	**72%**				

M/C TYPE	NO'S	
SNLS	26	
SNLS/UBT	3	
SNEC	4	* The Procedure, Time, code
DNLS	2	used may change according to
FOA	2	company, stile, design, method
Iron table	7	etc.
Helper table	4	
Checking table	3	
	51	

Calculation supports used for the development of Operation breakdown to an Operation Bulleting are,

$$SM\ @\ Tgt\ Effieciency = \frac{SMV\ @100\%}{Target\ Efficiency}$$

$$Production\ per\ Hr\ @\ Tgt = \frac{60}{Operation\ SMV\ @\ target\ Eff}$$

$$Calculated\ Machines = \frac{SMV\ @\ Target\ Eff * Hourly\ Prodn\ Tgt}{Total\ Minutes}$$

$$Calculated\ Machines = \frac{Operation\ SMV}{Pitch}$$

$$Pitch\ Time = \frac{Total\ SMV}{Number\ of\ Operations}$$

$$Production\ per\ Hr = \frac{Machines\ Assigned * Hourly\ target}{Number\ of\ M/c\ Calculated}$$

18 BASICS OF INDUSTRIAL ENGINEERING

Industrial engineering is a branch of engineering dealing with the optimization of complex processes or systems. It is concerned with the development, improvement, implementation and evaluation of integrated systems of people, money, knowledge, information, equipment, energy, materials, analysis and synthesis, as well as the mathematical, physical and social sciences together with the principles and methods of engineering design to specify, predict, and evaluate the results to be obtained from such systems or processes. Its underlying concepts overlap considerably with certain business-oriented disciplines such as operations management, but the engineering side tends to emphasize extensive mathematical proficiency and usage of quantitative methods.

STOP WATCH

A stopwatch is nothing but a handheld device that is designed to time the duration of an event. The basic function of this gadget is to measure how many minutes or seconds are taken by an athlete or swimmer to complete a particular round or lap. It is considered as an imperative device for trainers and athletes while they train and also when they are participating in the actual event. The stopwatch starts ticking with a push of a button when the starting gun fires and once the runners cross the finish line it stops.

Stopwatches are widely being used in lots of sporting events like swimming, running, track and field events, motor and car racing and much more. Even though the primary function of this gadget is to count time, but you'll notice that it is being used for wide ranging functions. It is most commonly being used as a training and practice gadget by athletes, team coaches as well as the entire athletic team. All you have to do is manually start it at the beginning of any event like racing, swimming, hockey or football match and stop it with the press of a button, the moment that particular event, game or race get finished.

Stop watches are available in two types, mechanical or digital.

Mechanical Stopwatches

The mechanical models have an analog face and resemble a pocket watch. These models are generally preferred over the digital ones because it provides a contemporary look, do not require batteries to operate and has the ability to anticipate time. These models are available for general purpose timing as well as sophisticated industrial timing. It is generally available in a silver-case, thus providing it a traditional look.

Digital Stopwatches

The digital ones are considered to be more accurate, come with more advanced features and looks more stylish and sporty. They are available in basic as well as advances models. The basic ones are inexpensive and used for general timing. It is provided with basic functions like start, stop and reset. Whereas, the advanced models are basically used for measuring sophisticated timing needs. Apart from all the functions like start, stop and reset present in the basic models, these advanced models are also provided with split, lap and multi-memory functions as well. Such types of models are generally preferred by runners, swimmers, bikers, car racers and track and field athletes for training and practice.

RESPONSIBILITIES OF IE

Though the time study and motion study are the most common function of Industrial engineer, the some other responsibilities are

1) Planning layouts
2) Monitoring Production flow system
3) Deicide the machines and attachments for all style
4) Pay system
5) Monitoring and improve the operator performance
6) Operator training
7) Production control system
8) Quality control
9) Other production improvement activities

NEED OF APPAREL ENGINEERING

One of the basic functions of Industrial engineer is to get facts. These facts may be in the form of a time study or a cost report. But either case, management is given information to act upon. The important necessities are

- Standardization of methods, equipment, and conditions.
- Production scheduling to work accurately helps to understand how long it takes to complete the work.
- Fair payment to employee

To ensure all the three above mentioned the apparel engineering is needed. These engineering efforts benefit the company like work simplification, increased productivity, increased profit, increased Earning.

BASICS OF INDUSTRIAL ENGINEERING

SMV (STANDARD MINUTES VALUE)

SMV is elaborated generally as Standard Minutes Value, it is represented in disseminates (1m/1000). The SMV value is the time calculated by the tool using time study, most commonly European systems of industrial engineering studies concentrate using the SMV. Usually SAM (Standard Allowed Minutes) and SMV are used miss placing the idea of both. SMV is generally calculated after a series of studies conducted, industry wide and operator wide for generating SAM of an operation, and after the series of calculations, a common SMV is generated from the series of SAM's so that it can be used industry wide and, operator wide for the operation. Nowadays PMTS are used to calculate the SMV of the operation (not for SAM)

$$SAM = (Cycle\ time\ X\ rating) + Allowances$$

SAM value of the operation may vary according to operator / industry / location for a single operation.

CYCLE TIME :- Cycle time is the brief time study conducted to set the target and to check if the operator is capable of achieving standard time.

PMTS (PRE-DETERMINED TIME AND MOTION SYSTEM)

PMTS is a pre-determined motion –time system (PMTS). It was designed specifically for the sewn products industry, its primary function is to rationalize manufacturing methods manufacturing methods and to produce an accurate evaluation of the time required to perform a specific task or function.

PMTS is a method study technique which identifies specific handling and sewing elements, each one of which has a pre-determined time, by adding each of these elements together and adding the required allowances one is able to establish a standard time for the operation. It produces standard times that are equally fair throughout the production environment. The standard times established in this way are equally fair and form the basis on which the following can be achieved.

- Establish the best method to do the operation
- Measure the performance of all the operators; this should include helpers and all the finishing operations
- Capacity planning and factory loading
- Line balancing
- Production targets
- Incentive payment systems
- Operator training (trough standardized methods)

Unlike time study, where industrial engineers uses stop watch and subjective rating concept to calculate the standard time, in PMTS the whole cycle operation is broken into elements and then to components of action, and then assign time values for each action and finally sums up the component action time to total standard time.

PMTS uses TMU (Time Measuring Unit) instead of seconds.

One TMU is = 0.00001 hrs (1/100000 Hrs) or 0.36 seconds.

ALLOWANCES

Allowances are the extra time added to each basic time to derive standard time from it. There are two kinds of allowances in use:

- The company sets their own allowance with respect to the national standards, and
- Some company follows the national standards only.

Reason for adding allowances to the basic time

- When a worker works for a long duration, there is no consistency in her pace. Also she requires some attention to personal needs, time is required for fixing needle in case of needle breakage, rethreading the needle in case of thread breakage, time lapsed due to machine breakdown, etc.

- The standard time is arrived at by adding up some allowances to the basic time. This will be a correct measure to set daily targets which are more practical or reliable.

While deciding the quantum of allowance to be added to the normal time, following types of allowances are considered.

Sl.	Condition	Rate	Details & Response
1	Personal and Fatigue	Sitting-11% Standing-13%	Toilets, drinking water, scratch, nose blowing, etc. for their personal fatigue
2	Machine Allowance	5% to 8%	S/N Chain stitch 5% Button sew Chain stitch 5% S/N Lockstitch 5% B/H Lockstitch 5% Multi needle Chain St 6% Over lock 6% Bar tack 6% Safety stitch 8% T/N Lockstitch 8%
3	Contingency Allowance	3%	Supervisory recording, quality information etc
4	Special Allowance	Vary according to physical condition of the industry	Periodic activity – bundling, bobbin change etc. Machine interference allowance- more m/c s Short run – periodic changes in fabric, threads Policy allowance – to line up standard – may vary from line to line

PRODUCTIVITY, EFFICIENCY AND PERFORMANCE

Productivity is the way to express the rate of production happened in specific line; productivity is generally expressed as the ration between the input and output of a line. The output refers to the goods or services produced and the input refers to all resources used in production of the output. It include one or all these;:

Land and buildings, Materials, Machines, People etc.

Productivity may be defined as" the ratio between output of wealth and input of resources of production". Output means the quantity produced and inputs are the various resources employed.

$$Productivity = \frac{output}{Input}$$

In the case of a garment manufacturing factory, "output" can be taken as the number of products manufactured, whilst "input" is the people, machinery and factory resources required to create those products within a given time frame.

The key to cost effective improvements in output –in "productivity" –is to ensure that the relationship between input and output is properly balanced.

For example, there is little to be gained from an increase in output if it comes only as a result of a major increase in input. Indeed, in an ideal situation, "input" should be controlled and minimized whilst "output" is maximized.

WAYS OF MEASURING PRODUCTIVITY

Productivity can be expressed in many ways but mostly productivity is measured as lab our productivity, machine productivity or value productivity.

These three terms can be defined as-

- Lab our Productivity: - Output per labour (direct +indirect) in a given time frame (in pieces).
- Machine Productivity: - Output per machine in a given time frame (in pieces).
- Value Productivity: - Total value of output in a given time frame.

MEASURE OF LABOUR PRODUCTIVITY

Within a factory, industrial engineers or factory managers and line supervisors measure the number of garments produced by a line of sewing machine operators in a specific time frame. Generally factory works 10 to 12 hours a day. Total production (output pieces) of a line and total labor involved in producing those pieces is required to calculate labor productivity.

See following example,

Assume that

Total production in day =1200 pieces
Total labor (operator +helpers) = 37
Working time = 600 minutes (10 hours)

So, Labor productivity per 10 hours is =Total pieces produced/ total labor input

$$= (1200/37) \text{ Pieces}$$
$$= 32.4 \text{ pieces.}$$

PRODUCTION VS PRODUCTIVITY

Production is the creation of goods, may be by the transformation of the raw material or by assembling many small parts to produce quality goods of sufficient quantity, whereas productivity is expressed in terms of percentage value related to the production and input with respective to operators in line.

Productivity refers to the efficiency of the production system. It is an indicator of how well the factors of production (land, capital, labor and energy) are utilized

$$Productivity = \frac{Production}{Resources\ Employed}$$

Productivity is said to be increased, when

- The production increases without increase in inputs
- The production remains same with decrease in inputs
- The output increases more as compared to input

TARGET SETTING

Target Setting is a line of sequential operations done through calculations. The first thing done is to balance the line taking the data from the daily production sheet and time study data sheet to prepare a perfect line in comparison with the operator matrix for operator allocation. Further, to make the line perfectly balanced without any bottle necks, there should be seldom difference in production levels between the operations. Once a perfectly balanced line is formed, if the hourly production rate drops the supervisor can easily detect the imbalance.

The target will be the quality of the line at perfect balance or its normal performance (75% to 80% according to line operations and product)

For example;

$$\text{SMV} \qquad\qquad\qquad = \quad 20 \text{ m}$$
$$\text{Avg. Efficiency achieved} = \quad 80\ \%$$

Number of Operators	=	30	
Absenteeism	=	5	

$$\text{Production time} = \frac{20}{80}\text{x } 100 = 25 \text{ min}$$

$$\text{Production Target} = \frac{30 \times 60}{25} = 72 \text{ garments}$$

If the absenteeism is 5 then actual

$$\text{Production Target} = \frac{35 \times 60}{25} = 60 \text{ Garments per hour}$$

There are also more other ways to balance the line in practice.

EFFICIENCY

Efficiency is another way of expressing productivity. Efficiency figures tell us how we perform against a target which has been set by industrial engineers and production planners through scientific means. As the target is expressed as a time per garment or a required level of production, the efficiency is quite easy to calculate.

Targets are normally set at a performance level of 100 %, and therefore if an operator reaches his/her target production, then his/her efficiency would be 100 %. Same as if the operator produces 80 % of his target then his efficiency is 80 %. In very rare conditions of balancing some operators may have capacity to produce more pieces, but also they can reach only up to 100% is according to the back feed arrangement.

$$Efficiency = \frac{\text{Time Allowed}}{\text{Time Taken}} \text{ x } 100$$

Where,

$$\text{Time allowed} = \text{Quantity produced x time per unit}$$

$$Efficiency = \frac{\text{Achieved Production}}{\text{Target Production}} \text{ x } 100$$

Productivity and efficiency improvements are keys to job security, better wages and lower prices.

TIME STUDY

Time study is a work measurement technique for recording the time and rates of working for the elements within specific conditions, and for analyzing the data so as to determine the time required to do a job at a defined quality level and performance

The objective of a time study is to develop and check production standards.

Common steps in making time study are

- Collecting details about the job
- Collecting details about the machine and tools used
- Observe the operation and study well before breaking the job into basic times.
- Take at least 15 cycles rating from time to time
- Convert to basic times
- Add the basic times for each element
- Give allowances required for the specific operation
- Calculate standard time and compare.

Time Study Equipment's

Basic time study equipment's consist of the following:

- **Stop watch** which includes cell phones, ordinary watches and decimal stop watch
- **Study board** which is simply a flat board, usually of plywood or simple plastic sheet, needed for placing the time study form.
- **Time study forms** which are used to record substantial amounts of data for an operation.

PERFORMANCE RATING

Performance Rating is the most controversial aspect of the time study. Only an experience hand can accurately rate the operation. There are many scales for rating the operator: 100/133, 60/80, 75/100, 0/100 etc. are the most used systems.

It is the work-study engineer who decides whether the operation is up to the idea of standard or not. There are errors like loose rating, tight rating, Flat rating, Steep rating; inconsistent rating etc. can affect the accuracy of the time study.

Cycle Time   =   Observed time X rating

Basic Time   =   Cycle time

Standard time =   Basic time + allowances

E.g.   Basic time = 0.73 m and P&F allowance = 13 % processing
Standard Time = 0.73 X 1.13 = 0.825 Mins

60/80	BS	100/133	REMARKS
40	50	67	Very slow pace, fumbling movements operator appears half asleep with no interest in the job
60	75	100	Steady, deliberate, unhurried pace as of a worker not an incentive scheme but under proper supervision. Looks slow but time is not being intentionally wasted whilst under observation.
80	100	133	Brisk business-like performance as of an average trained worker on incentive work. Necessary standard of quality and accuracy achieved with confidence.
100	125	167	Very fast, operator exhibits a high degree of assurance, dexterity and co-ordination of movement well above that of average trained worker.
120	150	200	Exceptionally fast, requires intense effort and concentration and is unlikely to be kept up for long periods; an outstanding performance only achieved by a few worker

METHOD STUDY

Method study is the systematic study about how a work is done. It includes systematic recording, examination and improvement of doing work in order to develop a better method. The study can be conducted in various means, generally close observation is the base of study, and according to technology developments high speed cameras are being used for doing the method study. Method study is the careful writing down of how a job is done, checking the way it is done, and trying to find a better or simpler way of doing the job.

The result of method study is to develop a new simplified method of operation sequence for doing the work. For this, each elements and movements of the operator (finger to legs) are recorded sequentially and observed for the unwanted movements during the operation. These unwanted movements are removed in order to develop a new and simplified method, and further the new method is implemented to the operator and checked for efficiency.

Objectives of Method Analysis

The main objectives of method analysis are:

- To train the individual worker in its practice as per standardized method
- To standardize the method, obtained after conducting the motion study
- To reduce fatigue and boredom of work by avoiding unnecessary movements
- To improve the design of work place layout
- To have more effective utilization of materials, machines and workforce
- To find the best way of doing a job
- To eliminate wastage of time and labour.

Basic Procedure for Method Analysis

Method study steps are as follows:

- Select the job to be studied by.
- Record every detail about the job
- Examine all the details
- Consider alternatives for improvement and develop the most suitable.
- Define all jobs other than those performed on standard machine tools or specialized machine where the process and machines are virtually controlled by the machine.
- Install new method by making sure it is understood.
- Maintain the new method by continually checking that it is still being performed correctly.

PREPARATION OF PROCESS CHART

The flow process chart in industrial engineering is a graphical and symbolic representation of the processing activities performed on the work piece. In 1947, ASME adopted the following symbol set derived from Gilbreth's original work as the ASME Standard for Process Charts.

Symbols used in Preparation of Process Chart

- Operation: to change the physical or chemical characteristics of the material.
- Inspection: to check the quality or the quantity of the material.

- Move: transporting the material from one place to another.
- Delay: when material cannot go to the next activity.
- Storage: when the material is kept in a safe location.

SYMBOL	ACTIVITY	RESULT
○	OPERATION	Produces, Accomplishes, furthers the process
⇨	TRANSPORT	Travels, Movements
▽	STORAGE	Holds, Keeps or retains
D	DELAY	Interferes or delays
□	INSPECTION	Verifies quantity and or quality

When to use it

It is used when observing a physical process, to record actions as they happen and thus get an accurate description of the process.

It is used when analyzing the steps in a process, to help identify and eliminate waste.

It is used when the process is mostly sequential, containing few decisions.

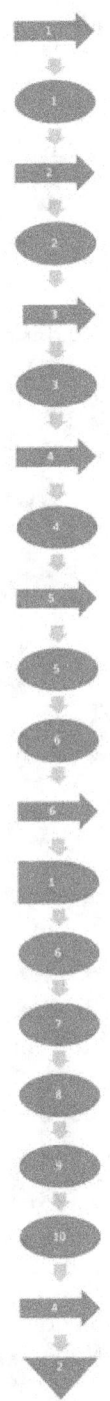

Making a cup of coffee (sample operation)

1. Walk to work top

2. Unplug kettle

3. Walk to sink

4. Fill kettle with water

5. Walk to work top

6. Plug in kettle / power on

7. Walk to cupboard

8. Get coffee, cup, spoon etc.

9. Walk to table

10. Place coffee, cup and spoon

11. Put coffee in cup

12. Walk to work top

13. Wait for kettle to boil

14. Unplug kettle

15. Walk to table

16. Pour water in cup

17. Walk to work top

18. Plug in kettle / power off

19. Walk to table

20. Take up coffee

21. Walk to cup board

22. Put away coffee

23. Walk to table

24. Take up cup & Spoon

25. Walk to door

* Sample Flow chart

Primary questions asked when preparing for the examination of selected work

Purpose : for which the activity is done

What is done? Why is it done? What else might be done?

What should be done?

Place   : at which the activity is being carried out

Where is it done? Why is it done there?

Where else might it is done? Where should it be done>

Sequence   : in which the activity is being performed

When is it done? Why is it done? When might it be done?

When should it be done?

Person   : by whom activity is being performed

Who does it? Why does that person do it?

Who else might do it? Who should do it?

Means   : by which activity is being accomplished

How is it done? Why is it done that way?

How else might it be done? How should it be done?

INSTALLATION

The installation of a new method is not as simple or as easy as it appear to be, Detailed preparation must be made before the actual installation takes place, as follows

- One Person only should have responsibility during the installation,
- The installation stages must be selected to be convenient for both personnel and process
- Prepare a timetable in stages of changes, should be available for reference
- All layouts should be checked for necessary machines and equipment's availability
- Prepare any new clerical records if required
- Select and train operators as required
- Provide the necessary training away from the production line
- Notify everyone concerned of the plans and timetable for the installation

Installing new method

- The changeover of the machines , workplace should be done outside working hours
- The first few days of operating the new method are critical, extra supervision will be necessary
- A small reserve of labour is useful
- Anny minor modifications to the new method which should be completed quickly
- A close watch should be kept on the effect of the new method
- Tact, encouragement and training are required through the period of installation

Assessment

After the installation the operation and the productivity have to be measured for the improvement, and through analysis have to be made.

The inspection loop fill continue for the continues production improvement

HOW TO IMPROVE THE METHOD?

Once a new method is being developed the improvements may be in machine placement, machine attachments, operation sequence, or even modifications in workplace lay out. The improvement of a method is done for creating more efficient operator for efficient operations.

Pitch time.

Pitch time is the ratio between the total SAM of the garment with the total number of operations for the particular garment

$$Pitch\ Time = \frac{\text{Total SAM}}{\text{Number of Operations}}$$

Pitch diagram is prepared for each plan sheet with graphical representation of pitch time with individual SAM of the garment. It is generally used to analyze the machine requirement and Line balancing. Etc.

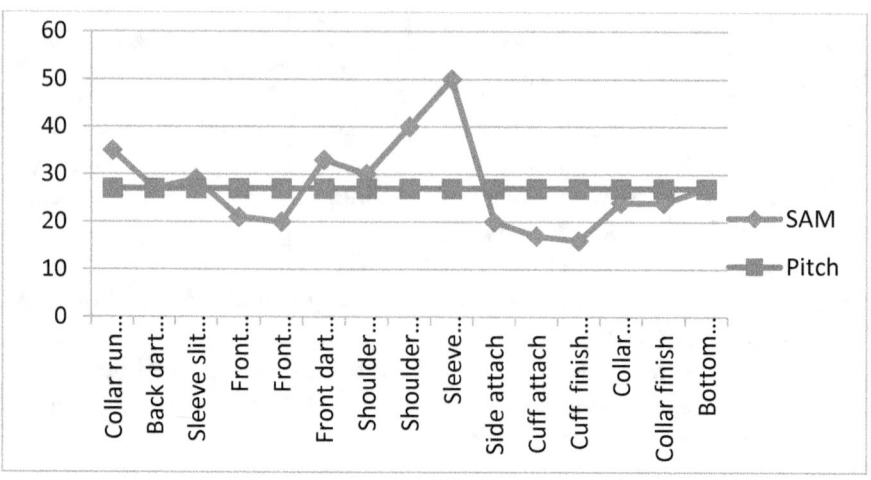

Short Cycle Time Study - format					
Date	1/1/2013	Analyst		Factory	Dreams
Operator	398	CL.NO	1	Study	30-Jan
Machine	SNLS	W AID	A33 Folder	Style	#3214 S
Garment	Ladies Tops	Cloth	Cotton 3242	Size	S 32

Readg	Cycle Time (dec Min)			Operation	
1	33				
2	36				
3	38				
4	32				
5	35				
TOT	174				
AVG	34.8				
100%	35				

Machine Allowance	5%	1.75	Tot	44
Contingency	3%	1.00	STD Time (m)	0.440
P&F	13%	4.50	TGT	1090
Special Allowance (bundle Handling)	5%	1.75	TGT @ 75% Normal EFF	800

General Sewing Data tools and symbols,

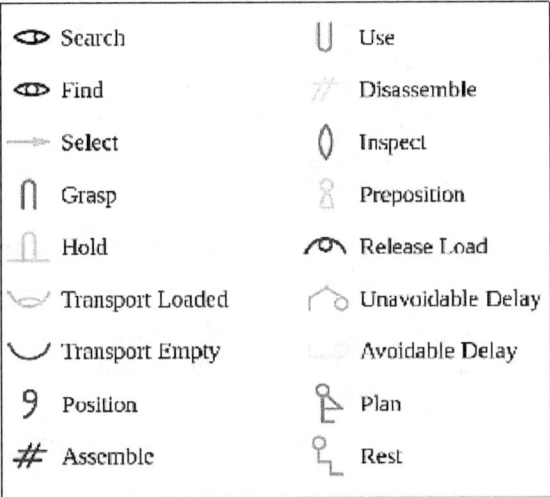

Symbol	Name	Symbol	Name
⬭	Search	∪	Use
⬤	Find	//	Disassemble
—→	Select	〇	Inspect
∩	Grasp	🎗	Preposition
∏	Hold	⌒	Release Load
⌣	Transport Loaded	⌒	Unavoidable Delay
∪	Transport Empty		Avoidable Delay
9	Position	🗲	Plan
#	Assemble	🗲	Rest

Time Study Sheet

OPERATION	ATTACH POCKET
OPERATOR	A
TYPE OF MACHINE	SINGLE NEEDLE LOCK STITCH
DATE	20-May-05
ANALYST NAME	X

SL.NO	OBS SC	RATING FACTOR	FREQUENCY
1	0.8	0.8	1
2	0.75	0.85	1
3	0.76	0.85	1
4	0.78	0.8	1
5	0.77	0.75	1
6	0.74	0.8	1
7	0.79	0.85	1
8	0.73	0.8	1
9	0.75	0.8	1
10	0.76	0.8	1
TOTAL	7.63		
AVERAGE	0.763	0.81	1

BASIC TIME (SC TIME X RF)	0.618
MA	12.50%
PF	20%
BH	0.03%

SAM=[(BT x (1+MA) x (1+PF))] +[BH x (1+PF)]	0.87

METHOD ENGINEERING

This topic involves method engineering at the individual work place. It is important to note that methods engineering is greatly influenced by the basic sewing room design. For this purpose it is necessary to plan methods and sewing room design simultaneously. Machinery selection also related to method engineering. The method engineering tools are discussed below.

1. Process charting

Here the different types of charts are used to analyses the operator work, work flow etc.

- Multiple activity chart - For assembly line
- Man – machine chart – For operator study related to machine
- Micro motion study chart - Micro motion study
- Left hand and Right hand chart - For typical sewing operation

2. Principles of motion economy.

While we analyzing the basic motions formally, it is possible to apply the laws of motion economy. These rules have been researched extensively by Professor Ralph M. Bames of the University of California. These rules are most important in sewing room. The rules are,

- Two hands should begin and complete their motion at the same time
- Two hands should not be ideal at the same time other than rest time
- Motions of the arms should be made in opposite, symmetrical and simultaneously.
- There should be fixed and definite place for all tools and materials.
- Tools, materials and controls should locate close and direct to the operator.
- Gravity feed bins and containers should use to deliver the material.
- Drop deliveries should use whenever possible
- Two are more tools should combined where ever possible

3. General classification of hand motions

The hand motion generally categorized follows

- Finger motion
- Motion involving finger and wrist
- Motion involving finger, wrist and fore arm
- Motion involving finger, wrist, forearm and upper arm
- Motion involving finger, wrist, forearm, upper arm and shoulder.

4. Precision

This method is to reduce precision I the required finger motions by use of such device as edge guides and label dispensaries as well as sewing tolerance of the stitch line.

5. Work Flow

Many parts of garment assembly are sequential; therefore, each operation is dependent on the previous operation. This has significant implications in planning work flow and assembly. Work flow is the movement of materials and garment parts through the conversion processes. It can be impacted by any part of a production process and the constraints that develop. A slow operator, a machine that malfunctions, or flawed fabric may all be constraints to work flow.

6. Balancing

Balancing is the process of planning a smooth work flow with a steady supply of work for each operation. Balancing involves planning and scheduling input based on the demand for finished parts and products. Demand originates from both internal and external need for parts and finished goods. External demand is established by customers outside the firm and internal demand is created by succeeding operations as parts and components are needed to assemble products. Pull through production is customer driven which means that the next operation is an internal customer. Products or parts are produced as needed but not in anticipation of future use.

7. through Put Time (TPT)

In seeking to maintain a steady work flow, it is essential to determine the operation that is consistently the slowest. If all work on a particular style must go through the specific slow operation that operation will dictate the rate of work flow and the volume of finished goods that can be completed in a specific time period. This operation is often referred to as a bottleneck, a constraint to throughput, because it limits the volume of work that can be completed in a work day.

Throughput time (TPT) is the time taken by particular volume of work to complete.

8. WIP (Work In Progress)

Work in process (WIP) is the number of garments under production at a given time. Once a bottleneck is determined, engineers study the operation to determine whether it can feasibly be improved. It may mean operating during breaks and lunch, adjusting routings, using other methods, scheduling the operation a second shift, buying an additional machine, or changing to new technology for the operation. Other factors that affect work flow are plant layout, materials handling, the production system, and operator skill and training.

9. Plant Layout

Plant layout is the spatial arrangement and configuration of departments, work stations, and equipment used in the conversion process. Layout of an apparel production plant directs the flow of material and work in process from start to completion and integrates materials handling and equipment. A good layout has the flexibility to be changed to meet requirements of the product line, delivery schedules, and anticipated volume.

10. Line Layout

A line layout operates on the principle that each unit is produced exactly the same and that operations are performed in a specified sequence. Work flows from work station to work station until the garment is completed. Line layout is most efficient with long runs (high volume of identical products) when the sequence of operations and equipment does not have to be changed frequently. Depending on the volume required, a plant may have several lines making the same style or several lines each making different styles.

Line layout does not necessarily mean each machine is different. There may be several operators performing the same operation. The goal is steady work flow through succeeding operations. If a style requires only one operator to hem the pockets and three operators to set pockets in order to keep work in process moving, then engineers will build that into the layout.

THE BENEFITS OF INDUSTRIAL ENGINEERING

1. **Work Simplification** : - One of the main benefits of almost any engineering effort is that it makes work simpler to perform. This holds true for operators, supervisors, and top management. When an engineer analyses any area of work, he does so with the thought in mind. Do not be misled about into thinking, however, that work simplification means people always will be doing less work. They may, in fact, do more work but within the same amount of time as before. Because work has been simplified, people's ability to produce is increased.

2. **Increased Productivity** :- The ability to produce more within the same amount of time is a company's insurance for survival. This ability means that the company can now accept more work. It means that costs can be lowered by avoiding overtime. It means that fixed costs can be spread out over more units of production. It means that profits Improve.

3. Increased Profits :- When a company's profits increase, everyone involved is in a better position. Owners and stockholders prosper. Management and supervision are rewarded for their performance. Money is available to do more for the operators. A company is able to expand which creates more Jobs.

4. Increased Earnings :- Most engineering projects not only increase company profits, but also result in higher earnings for employees. Most companies are willing, and in fact eager, to share with its employees the financial gains that are available through engineering.

APPLICATIONS OF INDUSTRIAL ENGINEERING

The roles and responsibilities of the industrial engineering department are not just limited to timing operators and making operation bulletins as it is only a part of the job. The I.E function can contribute significantly to improvement in working and productivity of almost all the departments of apparel manufacturing. Let us discuss few of the activities of various sections of apparel manufacturing which can be associated with industrial engineering:

1. Merchandising

In merchandising section the Industrial engineer can work closely in following:

a. Product Analysis-

- Determine the optimum method of construction to achieve required finished product efficiently.
- Establish the operation sequence (Operation bulletin).
- Specify the equipment type and work aids to be used

Operation Bulletin is an important tool used for product analysis. Operation bulletin is a documented form of sequence of operations in a product. It contains all the information about the machine required and the total no. of operations, total no. of operator required. Operation bulletin contains the standard times for each operation.

Operation bulletin also contains some other parameters as follows:

- Output (pieces per day)
- Target efficiency
- Minutes per day
- Total standard time
- Total no of work places

In simple way we can say that operation bulletin is a record of

- Equipment type
- Machine attachments
- Workplace engineering aids
- Standard time for each operation

It can be extended to include

- Hourly/ period targets for each operation
- Manpower Requirements
- Equipment Requirements

It should cover all operations that can be directly related to single unit of a product e.g.

- Spread and cut
- Sew including manual operations
- Finish and pack

The operation bulletin is a fundamental planning tool used for many functions such as

- Capacity planning
- Methods engineering
- Line planning
- Performance measurement
- Manpower planning
- Investment appraisal
- Incentive payment
- Factory loading

The operation Bulletin should be developed at the earlier stage of product development.

- Hourly/ period targets for each operation
- Manpower Requirements
- Equipment Requirements

It should cover all operations that can be directly related to single unit of a product e.g.

- Spread and cut
- Sew including manual operations
- Finish and pack

The operation bulletin is a fundamental planning tool used for many functions such as

- Capacity planning
- Methods engineering
- Line planning
- Performance measurement
- Manpower planning
- Investment appraisal
- Incentive payment
- Factory loading

The operation Bulletin should be developed at the earlier stage of product development.

a. Costing

- The first stage is to calculate the SMV of the garment
- To calculate the production cost for that particular garment by multiplying the total SMV of the garment with the average cost incurred by the factory to produce one SMV.

2. Production Planning

Production planning is an essential prerequisite to production control. It involves management decisions on the resources that the firm will require for its manufacturing operations and selection of these resources to produce the desired goods at the appropriate time and at the least cost.

Production planning is defined as, "the technique of foreseeing or picturing ahead, every step in a long series of separate operations, each step to be taken in the right place, of the right degree and at the right time, and each operation to be done at maximum efficiency."

Production planning provide a line for effective, balanced flow of product, incorporating line and individual (operation) productivity standards. The end product of production planning efforts is the formulation of production plans. The plans are formulated in light of specified future period. The plans are to be implemented in the light of the estimated cost and agreed policies

- Plant capacity can be calculated by I.E dept. so that planning can book order as per the available capacity.
- I.E can assist in better planning by helping in better style allocation to different units or lines.
- I.E can formulate an efficiency/performance build-up for a particular style based upon the work content or past performance. This can inform the planning dept. that a particular line will take how many days to

produce a specific quantity of a style. This will help the planning dept. to plan the availability of resources and material in advance.

3. Production

Industrial engineering is a key part of a production process. One of the basic functions of engineering is to get facts. These facts may be in form of a time study, the engineer has made or cost report the engineer has designed. So we can say that the basic need for engineering is the need for management information.

4. Work-In-Progress (WIP) Control-

WIP is made up of all garments and their parts that are not completely finished. For example a bundle of shirts that has everything attached but has no bottom hem. There are two cost areas that can be reduced if WIP is controlled:

- *Investment in inventory-* Inventory is money invested in raw materials. When we don't move the goods through the plant quickly we are affecting cash flow directly.

- *Ability to reduce the production cycle-* By having low inventory between operations, garments usually have less waiting time and go through the production cycle in less time. Large inventory levels between operations keeps goods waiting longer to be processed. This increases the overall throughput time.

Managing WIP:

- *Production planning-* This requires planning from marketing and sales to determine what will sell and what needs to be produced and when. This provides the basis to determine how many operators and machines will be needed. I.E can calculate the required resources to any style and block the capacity for this style at a specific efficiency build up.

- *Trims control-* Trims are buttons, zippers, labels, thread, elastics, and so on. A cut should enter the production line only when someone has verified that all the trims needed are available. An updated inventory of trims should be kept.

    i. A missing label could halt a 12,000 unit cut. Holding the 12,000 units in inventory is not acceptable and could lead to other problems.

- *Production Build-up-* Careful consideration should be given to loading the production lines. If you feed into the line more product that can be processed you will overload the line with work that will just sit stagnant. I.E can provide

  i. Figures in terms of production to be expected from any line which can help in feeding control and thus managing the WIP.

- *Balancing-* Even if you load the line based on its capacity, you might find the inventory accumulating due to an unbalanced production. Absenteeism and turnover can greatly affect the line's balance. A change in style and irregular

  i. Feeding are two other factors that can put a line off-balance. To keep a line balanced you need information on the inventory levels. While allocating operator to the operation, the skill requirement for that operation should be kept in mind. To help regain balance in an unbalanced situation industrial engineer can use Utility operators, operator transfers and overtime as the last option.

- *Cut Flow Control-* In order to keep control over WIP and to keep the cycle times low you need to have cuts go as close as FIFO as possible. For this reason strict control must be placed on the tracking of cuts as they flow through the production floor.

The industrial engineering is very useful in:

- *Standardization-* You can appreciate the need for standard convocations in managing your department. Think of confusion that would result if each operator on a job performed his or her work differently from anyone else. Suppose quality specifications changed every day so that what passed yesterday rejected today.

- *Production Scheduling-* In order to run your department efficiently, you need a firm schedule of production. Suppose there was no way of knowing how more work your section could handle, engineering data helps to make this decision.

- *Fair Payment of Employees-* In order to pay employees fairly, we need to know the value of the work they produce, since part of engineering function is to measure work.

- *Prevention of Chaos-* Any attempt to run a department without standardized conditions, without a production schedule, and without fair payment to the employees is doomed to chaos and failure.

Main production functions of engineering are:

i. Develop detailed production methods, from detailed manual moments to major decisions on technology.
ii. Documents all the methods using manuals, computer based system as appropriate.
iii. Justify all changes based on analyses of the work content in the operation, taking account of skill requirements
iv. Define the appropriate WIP level and develop WIP measuring and control techniques.

5. Maintenance

Proper maintenance leads to better capacity utilization of same asset, avoiding thus the investment in addition facilities. So far industries have a tendency to neglect maintenance function, thinking it be a not so important job, however necessary. It has been taken just for granted. Plant maintenance is important and inevitable service function of an efficient production system. It helps in maintaining and increasing the operational efficiency of plant facilities and thus contributes of the revenue by reducing the operating cost and increasing the quality of quality of the production

6. Quality

Quality is an asset, which may be offered to the potential customer of a product. There are two aspects of quality, which contribute to the ultimate quality of the product. Quality of design is the first aspect, which depends on the type of materials used, specs specified by the buyer, method of production, knowledge of the design and skill level of the person. The degree to which this quality is achieved in production that is the quality of conformance is the second aspect.

Industrial Engineering can help converting quality specifications into technical parameters to ensure that quality requirements are met with during the manufacturing process. I.E helps in selecting the equipment's and method of the job so as the final product conforms to the specifications.

7. Human Resource

- *Manpower Planning-* I.E can calculate the manpower required to perform a specific job at a certain performance level. Once the work content of any job is analyzed by I.E dept., the next step is to find out the resources required to complete that job. This principle can be applied successfully especially on the production floor where work content of each job is measured using time study techniques. The manpower can also be calculated as per the capacity of the plant using standard ratios like Man to Machine ratio. The number of people for a factory having x number of machines can be fixed through this ratio

- *Skill Matrix-* Skill matrix refers to the database of available worker skill in the factory. The workers' skill is analyzed on different jobs and based upon his/her performance on a particular job a grade is given. This grade defines the level of performance that operator can achieve on that specific job. This matrix is used in 2 ways:

    - While allocating workers to a job as per the skill requirement of that job.

    - To analyze the skill availability and distribution throughout the factory.

availability to achieve at the training requirement. This shortfall in availability of any skill can be overcome by conducting a specific training program or through recruitment also.

- *Skill Matrix* helps in allocating right person for the right job which helps in achieving desired performance level.

- Performance Measurement- For measuring the performance of any individual first step is to define the targets and second step is to develop performance measuring tools. An industrial engineer can help in setting up of measurable goals and targets, which could be time standards for an operator and key performance indicators for middle & senior management. Next step is to set up systems and define a methodology to capture the performance on regular basis and analyze the results

- *Training-* Industrial engineering should be responsible of working on a scientific recruitment methodology for workers so as to check the basic skills are already present in the selected personnel. The training methodology for these trainees should target towards efficient and rapid learning with proper control tools in place. This training could be as per the results of the skill matrix to train people on skills which are not available at present but are required on regular basis or in near future.

8. Production Follow up

"Follow up" means that someone "checks and Stays with" something until the desired results have been achieved. Many worthwhile plans and projects have failed because someone did not follow up. So for the purposes of this training, follow up means to stay on top of something until the desired results are achieved."

Elements	OR	OT	OR	OT	OR	OT	OR	OT	OR	OT	Cycle		
												Date	Study No
												Operator	Clock No
												Machine	RPM
												Attach	
1													
2													
3													
4													
5													
6													
7													
8												SKETCH	
9													
10													
11													
12													
13													
14													
15													
Total Time													
Total Rating													
Avg. Time													
Frequency													
Basic Time													

TIME STUDY SHEET * format

Allowances		Machine			
		Cont			
		P& F		Std. Time	
		Bundling		Target	

1. Basic Time   = Observed time X rating
2. Standard Time   = (Observed time) x (Rating Factor) x (1+ PFD Allowances)

9. Allowances Added

1.Personnel & Fatigue   =   11 % (for sitting operations)
                         =   13 % (for Standing Operations)
2. Machine Allowance
1.SN Chain Stitch   =   5 %
2.Chain Stitch B/S =   5 %
3.SN Lock Stitch   =   5%
4.Lock Stitch B/S   =   5%
5.Multi Chain Stitch =   6%

6. Over lock   =   6%

7. Bar tack   =   6%

8. Safety Stitch   =   8%

9. TN Lock Stitch   =   8%

3. Contingency Allowance   =   3%

4. Special Allowances   =   as per local or government norms and requirements

HOW TO CALCULATE SAM OF A GARMENT?

SAM or Standard Allowed Minute is used to measure task or work content of a garment. This term is widely used by industrial engineers and production people in the garment manufacturing industry. For the estimation of cost of making a garment SAM value plays a very important role. In past scientists and apparel technicians did research on how much time to be allowed to do a job when one follows standard method during doing the job. According to the research study minute value has been defined for each movement needed to accomplish a job.

Method #1: Calculation of SAM Using Synthetic Data

In this method 'Predetermined Time Standard' (PTS) code are used to establish 'Standard Time' of a garment or other sewing products.

Step 1: Select one operation for which you want to calculate SAM.

Step 2: Study the motions of that operation. Stand by side of an operator (experienced one) and see the operator how he is doing it. Note all movement used by the operator in doing one complete cycle of work. See carefully again and recheck your note if all movement/motion are captured and correct. (for example motions are like - pick up parts one hand or two hand, align part on table or machine foot, realign plies, etc.)

Step 3: List down all motion sequentially Refer the synthetic data for TMU (Time measuring unit) values. Or Sewing Performance Data table (SPD). Now you got TMU value for one operation (for example say it is 400 TMU). Convert total TMU into minutes (1 TMU=0.0006 minute). This is called as Basic Time in minutes. In this example it is 0.24 minutes.

Step 4: Standard allowed minutes (SAM) = (Basic minute + Bundle allowances + machine and personal allowances). Add bundle allowances (10%) and machine and personal allowances (20%) to basic time.

Now you got Standard Minute value (SMV) or SAM.

SAM= (0.24+0.024+0.048) = 0.31 minutes.

Method #2: Calculation of SAM through Time Study

Step 1: Select one operation for which you want to calculate SAM.

Step 2: Take stop watch. Stand by side of the operator. Capture cycle time for that operation. (Cycle time is the total time taken to do all works needed to complete one operation, i.e. time from pick up of first piece to next pick up of the next piece). Do time study for consecutive five cycles. Discard if found abnormal time in any cycle. Calculate average of the 5 cycles. Time you got from time study is called cycle time. To convert this cycle time into basic time you have to multiply cycle time with operator performance rating.

[Basic Time = Cycle Time X performance Rating]

Step 3: Performance rating Now have to rate the operator at what performance level he was doing the job seeing his movement and work speed. Suppose that operator performance rating is 80%. & suppose cycle time is 0.60 minutes.

Basic time = (0.60 X 80%) = 0.48 minutes

Step 4: Standard allowed minutes (SAM) = (Basic minute + Bundle allowances + machine and personal allowances).

Add bundle allowances (10%) and machine and personal allowances (20%) to basic time.

Now you got Standard Minute value (SMV) or SAM. SAM= (0.48+0.048+0.096) = 0.624 minutes.

LOST TIME AND ITS REDUCTION

Lost time is the time an operator loses which is outside of his/her control. This time will affect the efficiency of an operator unless it is taken into consideration.

Categories of lost time are:

- Waiting for work
- Machine trouble
- Doing the other person's repairs
- Doing samples
- Power failures
- Meetings etc.

Since the above points cannot be controlled by the operator, the time spent is subtracted from the attended minutes of the operator when calculating the daily efficiency.

For example:

If no lost time occurred operator efficiency is calculated as,

$$\frac{Produced\ Time}{Attended\ Time} \times 100 = efficiency$$

$$\frac{350\ min}{540\ min} \times 100 = 64.8\ \%$$

If, however the operator had waited for work for $= 30$ min

$$\text{Done sample for} \quad = 40\ \text{min}$$

$$\text{Machine trouble for} = 30\ \text{min}$$

$$\text{Total} \qquad = 100\ \text{min}$$

The calculation would now be worked as

$$\frac{350}{540-100} \times 100 = 79.5\ \%\ efficiency$$

LOST TIME REPORT ** FORMAT

Name				Clock No.			Week Ending		
A) Machine B/Down			B) No Supply			C)No Cut Work		D) INSTR/ Supervisor	
E) Repairs			F) Samples			G) Cutting Room fault		H) Trimming Supply	
I) Others									

	ON	OFF	Code/ Total	ON	OFF	Code/ Total	ON	OFF	Code/ Total	ON	OFF	Code/ Total
Monday												
Tuesday												
Wednesday												
Thursday												
Friday												
Saturday												

Source: http://refergt.blogspot.in/

The lost time is calculated to find out the exact efficiency obtained to the operator.

WORK PLACE LAYOUT

A Layout essentially refers to the arranging & Grouping of machines which are meant to produce goods. According to the methodology used for the production of the particular product for the maximum output, the method of arrangement f the machineries, work areas are differed, and the method of such arrangement is called as a Layout.

The following factors should be taken into consideration while planning a layout:

- Minimization of manufacturing cost,
- Feeding the materials and parts at highest possible speed and in one direction without any backtracking or overlapping flow of products,
- Minimization of work transfer among the processes from acceptance of raw materials till delivery of finished product with properly defined spaces for each process, and
- Provision of future expansion plans.

The layout planning should be done based on factory site selection and arrangement of building and machines.

GENERAL STEPS FOR MAKING A PLANT LAYOUT

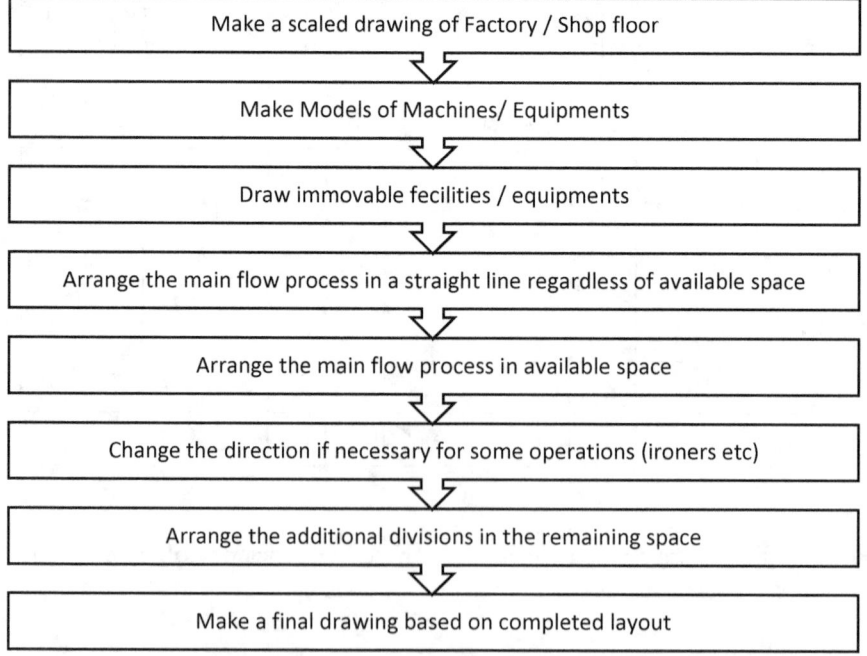

Make a scaled drawing of Factory / Shop floor

Make Models of Machines/ Equipments

Draw immovable fecilities / equipments

Arrange the main flow process in a straight line regardless of available space

Arrange the main flow process in available space

Change the direction if necessary for some operations (ironers etc)

Arrange the additional divisions in the remaining space

Make a final drawing based on completed layout

TYPES OF LAYOUTS

- Process Layout is the floor plan of a plant, which is installed by industrial engineers to improve the efficiency by arranging equipment according to their functions.

- Product Layout; the workstations and equipment are located along the line of flow of the work units. Usually, work units are moved along a flow line which is powered by a conveyor.

- Static Layout is used mainly in manufacturing. When huge items are to be manufactured and the item cannot be moved from work station to work station the items remains stationary and the different processes of manufacturing are brought to it.

- Cellular Layout,; machines are grouped together according to the families of parts produced. The major advantage is that material flow is significantly improved, which reduces the distance travelled by materials, inventory and cumulative lead times.

- Hybrid Layout is the mixture of all the layouts, the most commonly used layout for Apparel production is hybrid layout. For example in cutting room we use Static Layout, in some conditions we have preparatory sewing and production line there we uses Process and product layouts, according to the availability and requirement

19 LINE BALANCING

A line is defined as a group of operators under the control of one production supervisor, doing a particular garment production.

Line balancing is the equal distribution of the work among the workers of a particular line, in the basis of time taken for each operation.

Line balancing is a vital key in the efficient running of a line. The object of the process is to "Balance the work load" of each operator to make sure that the flow of the work is smooth and no bottlenecks are created. Line balancing is intended to reduce the waiting time to a minimum. The method of line balancing can vary from factory to factory, type of garment,

SETTING UP THE LINE

Before the actual production of a garment it is necessary to prepare the operation break down of the garment and to calculate how many operators will be necessary to achieve the given production rate per hour. Management must have this information before the commencement of the order, so that the line can be balanced and layed out in such a way as to maximize productivity.

The methods which can be used to set up the line are,

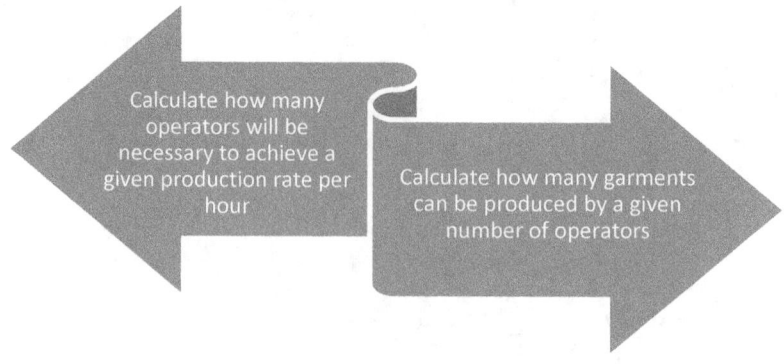

Calculate how many operators will be necessary to achieve a given production rate per hour

Calculate how many garments can be produced by a given number of operators

Using either technique, the information required are,

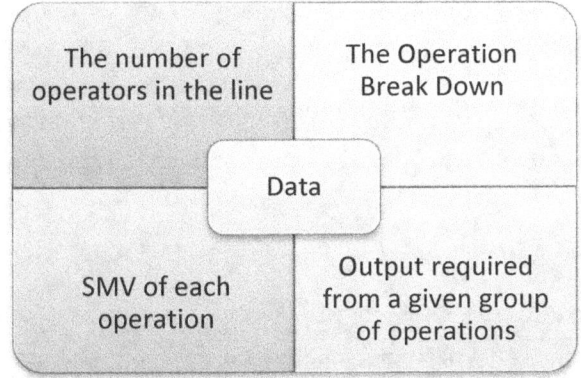

Other physical requirements are,

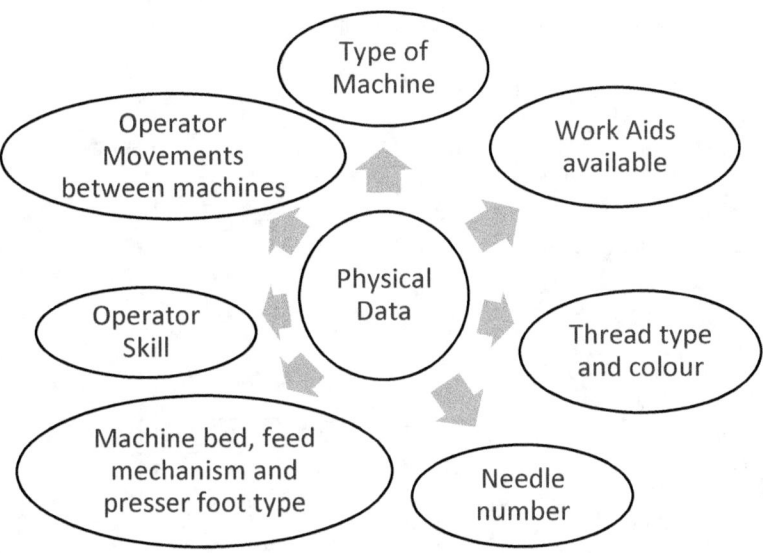

METHOD OF LINE BALANCING,

1. Add up the operation times
2. Establish percentage of operations time
3. Calculate theoretical balance & round
4. Production Required per hour (Operators x 60/SMV)
5. List type of Equipment's required
6. Calculate Theoretical Output Operators x 60 / SMV
7. Calculate Balance Efficiency (Lowest output/ Theoretical output)
8. Calculate Line forecast (Efficiency x Theoretical Out Put)
9. Manually distribute operators

Base formulas in use

Theoretical output = Number of Operators x (SAM / Total SMV) /100

Output = Number of Operators x 60 /SMV

Balance Efficiency = Lowest Output x 100 / Theoretical Output

Line Forecast @60%= Theoretical output x Eff. x (100 –absenteeism)

Line Balancing example,

Number of Operators = 12

Sl	Operation	SMV	M/c	%	Operator	Actual Op	Output	Rem
	Balancing of Shirt Collar							
1	Pinning to profile	0.234	Manual	6.46	0.84	1	256	
2	Run Stitch Collar	0.219	SNLS	6.05	0.79	1	274	
3	Trim Collar	0.285	Manual	7.87	1.02	1	211	
4	Clip and Turn Collar	0.223	CT	6.16	0.80	1	269	
5	Crease Collar	0.381	Press	10.52	1.37	1.5	236	1 op 5 & 10 does
6	Top Stitch Collar	0.42	SNLS	11.60	1.51	1.5	214	1 op 6 & 9 does
7	Run stitch Collar Band	0.291	SNLS	8.04	1.04	1	206	
8	Crease Collar Band	0.317	Press	8.75	1.14	1	189	
9	Insert Collar in Neck Band	0.799	SNLS	22.07	2.87	2.5	188	0.5 with 6
10	Turn and Crease Collar	0.452	Press	12.48	1.62	1.5	199	0.5 with 5
	TOTALS	**3.621**		**100**	**13**	**13**	**188 pc**	

Theoretical output = 13 x 60 / 3.621   = 215 pcs / Hr

Balance Efficiency = 188 / 215   = 87.5 %

Line Forecast @ 75 = 215 x 75 x (100-5% abs)/100   = 153

I.e. Line Target   = 153 @ average performance of 75%

OPERATOR PLANNING & ALLOCATION

The Major part of the production operation if the allocation of right operators to the right operation. For the easy identification of operators they are basic classified as,

1. *Un Skilled Operators :* are those who are fresh to the industry or not knowing any skill about the sewing operation, even in some cases key knows how to operate the machine but don't know how to sew, these men can only be used for manual support or those which have very low SAM and require less skill

2. *Semi-Skilled Operators:* They know to sew and some basic operations like straight lines or some simple joints, they can sit in line with low SAM and normally works with 50 to 60 % efficiency.

3. *Skilled Operators :* These category can be suit in any operation and can achieve up to 90% efficiency

4. *Floaters:* Floaters are highly skilled operators even know all operations and skilled in more than one machine, even some times all of the machines. They are used as substitutes for absenteeism or even in some times Supervisors..

SKILL MATRIX & OPERATOR ALLOCATION

A skill matrix is a table that clearly shows the skills held by individuals and in a team and the skills gaps within a team. Codes used are

I	Can complete the task	L	Can Complete the task to required standard
U	Can complete the task in Required Standard and in time	☐	Could do all and train others also

In some cases we uses efficiency also for preparing skill matrix.

By comparing the operator efficiency in the previous orders processing of the same operation may also helpful to prepare their skill matrix for the specific operation in the style, for this the previous reference efficiency matrix have to be prepared regularly for each operator for different operations.

Sample Skill Matrix

Name	SNLS	DNLS	4T O/L	MN CS	Zigzag	Bar tack	Button Sew
Operator A	40			85			
OP-B	50		85				
OP-C					90		
OP-D						90	
OP-E			70				60
OP-F					55	80	
OP-G			80	50			

Operator allocation is always in comparison to the Line balancing sheet and the Skill Matrix

Operator Allocation

Operation	Machine	SMV	Percent	Theo. Operatr	Actual Operator	Output	Operator
Close First Side	4T O/L	0.50	21.43	1.50	1.50	180	OP-G & B
Elastic Waist	MNCS	0.33	14.06	0.98	1	183	OP-A
Lace to waist	Zigzag	0.72	30.86	2.16	2	167	OP-C & F
Close 2nd Side	4T O/L	0.45	19.29	1.35	1.5	200	OP- E & B
Bartack x2	Bartack	0.34	14.36	1.01	1	179	OP - D
Total		2.33	100	7.00	7	180	7

20 QUALITY CONTROL

Quality means customer needs is to be satisfied. Failure to maintain an adequate quality standard can therefore be unsuccessful. But maintaining an adequate standard of quality also costs effort.

From the first investigation to find out what the potential customer for a new product really wants, through the processes of design, specification, controlled manufacture and sale. Factors on which quality fitness of garment industry is based such as - performance, reliability, durability, visual and perceived quality of the garment.

Quality needs to be defined in terms of a particular framework of cost.

IMPORTANCE QUALITY CONTROL

Quality is of prime importance in any aspect of business. Customers demand and expect value for money. As producers of apparel there must be a constant endeavor to produce work of good quality.

"The systems required for programming and coordinating the efforts of the various groups in an organization to maintain the requisite quality". As such Quality Control is seen as the agent of Quality Assurance or Total Quality Control.

In the garment industry quality control is practiced right from the initial stage of sourcing raw materials to the stage of final finished garment. For textile and apparel industry product quality is calculated in terms of quality and standard of fibers, yarns, fabric construction, colour fastness, surface designs and the final finished garment products. However quality expectations for export are related to the type of customer segments and the retail outlets.

Quality control and standards are one of the most important aspects of the content of any job and therefore a major factor in training.

TOTAL QUALITY CONTROL

"To ensure that the requisite quality of product is achieved".

To ensure, at minimum practicable cost, that the requisite quality of product is being achieved at every stage of manufacture from raw materials to boxed stock

Objectives

• To maximize the production of goods within the specified tolerances correctly the first time.

• To achieve a satisfactory design of the fabric or garment in relation to the level of choice in design, styles, colour, suitability of components and fitness of product for the market.

Approach

• Itemize the variables that occur in fabric and garment production in order to provide a complete specification.

• Develop a specification in a number of parts or sections to ensure that all design and production staff has a clear idea as to what is needed.

• Establish acceptable working tolerances in relation to all values on the specification.

• Establish fault rate recording systems.

• Improve technical understanding of the product including,

• Fabric geometry and the interrelationship of yarn count, loop length, pick count, relaxation and fabric properties.

• Sewing problems.

• Causes and prevention of seam breakdown.

• The effects of various factors on the apparent shade of goods affecting shade matching.

VISUAL INSPECTION

The Visual inspection method is the most common used inspection system for the garment, for the easy categorizing defects are classified into three,

• *Critical Defects* are those defects which will effect either the appearance, quality, feel, or design or may sometimes effects both. (E.g. Tearing,

Button Missing, etc.) When doing the inspection the critical defects are treated as the rejection points (details according to AQL inspection systems) hence no critical defects are entertained in any stage of garment manufacturing.

- *Major defects* are the one which may affect look of quality or sometimes both, there is some limitation of this class of defects, and are according to the zones of the garment

- *Minor defects* are those defects which will not effect on look, feel, quality or properties but are defects,

Any minor or major defect can be a critical defect according to where it is present for example if a joint stitch is found in the color point then it is treated as critical defect even though it is minor one. For the proper identification of defects.

ZONES OF THE GARMENT

Most of the cases apparel buyers provide garment figures with marking zones in their quality manual. And provide a list of defects that fall under major or minor categories.

- *A Zone :-* These are the area of the garment with most appearance, generally collar, cuffs, pockets, front sleeve area etc. and parts which will be visible after packing are also included, nay minor defects coming in this area are treated as major defects, but any defects visible (minor or major) after packing can be treated as critical defects. Normally no defects are acceptable in this zone.

- *B Zone:* - all other parts of the garment front and back are B zone, minor defects may be acceptable in the B zone.

- *C Zone:-* this is the area of inner side of the garment, most of the defects are treated as minor except open seams, loose threads, cut seams, or sharp seams etc.

QUALITY STANDARDS

The Apparel Industry has set lot of quality standards to be followed from Design development Stage till the packing and dispatching activity involved in the sequential operations. The major quality check points in each session of production are as follows

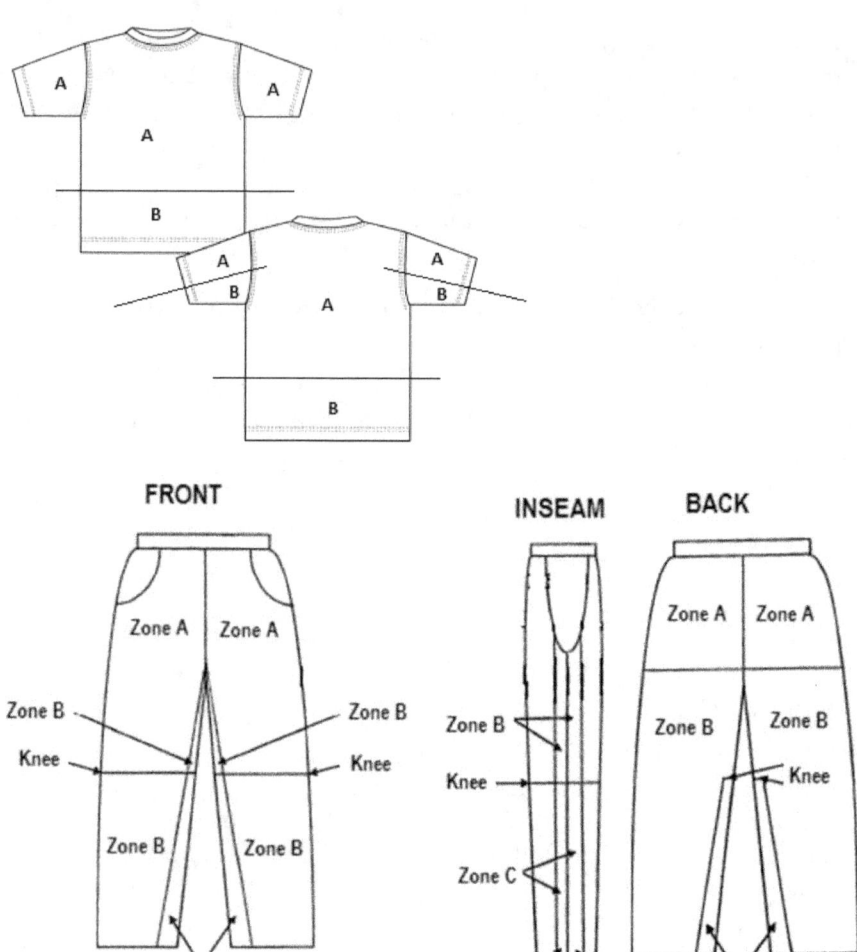

TRIM CARDS

Trim cards are the document prepared along with the tech pack, it has all the technical details of the trims and accessories used for manufacturing the garment. Trim cards are used to convey the design aspects and construction requirement to the production.

Quality inspections is always done in verifications with the Trim card of the particular design so as to avoid any change in design, shape, colour or placement changes in the product with reference to the original sample. Any minor changes may be treated as critical defects as it will alter the product design.

TOLERANCES

Tolerance is the approved possible difference from the actual product specification, they are set in accordance with the process, fabric, construction & finishing methods used for the manufacturing of the product and are mostly set to avoid risk of production variances, in most of the case the tolerance are given in a range plus and minus to the actual requirement, for example if the seat measurement of the trouser is 32 inches, then there may be a ±1 inch tolerance given, that means the seat measurement of the finished trouser can be measured from 31 inches to 33 inches. For the critical A zone checking points there will be no tolerance given, there may be variation of the standards according to buyer or designs.

SUPERVISORS RESPONSIBILITY FOR QUALITY

The supervisor is the person who is coordinating with the sewing machine operators and other floor level staffs to achieve Production without losing the quality.

The supervisor have to take preventive methods to reduce the defects generating from the sewing or production department.

To prepare and train the operators to follow the proper method of sewing or operation procedures, continuous monitoring of the operators so as to ensure the proper quality is been produces as per the requirement.

Quality In Various Departments

There are various points of checks conducted by an apparel industry to ensure the right quality product is been produces. Some of the check are onetime, some are periodical and most are routine checks, the data collected from each check point is analyzed using the TQM (Total Quality Management) methods and preventive actions are prepared and acted to reduce or eliminate the quality parameter issues, and to produce a proper quality product. The main check points in various departments are as follow,

2. Cutting Quality Check List:
   - Pattern to Cutting Garments Measurement Check.
   - Fabric diameter Measurement Check.
   - Cutting Lay Check.
   - Fabric Roll to Roll Shade Check.
   - Fabric G.S.M Check.
   - Bundle Mistake Check.

- Size Mistake Check.
- Fabric Color Mistake Check.
- Yarn contaminated Check.
- Any Fabric Problem Check.

3. Sewing Line quality Check List:
   - Buyer Approved Sample & Measurement Sheet Check.
   - Sample Wise Input Check.
   - Buyer Approved Trims Card Check.
   - Buyer Approved Sample Wise Style Check.
   - All Machine Thread Tension Check.
   - Style Wise Print & Embroidery Placement Check.
   - All Process Measurement Check.
   - All Machine Oil Spot Check.
   - All Process S.P.I Check as Per Buyer Requirement.
   - Input Time Shading, Bundle Mistake & Size Mistake Check.
   - Buyer Approved Wise Contrast Color Check.
   - As per Buyer Requirement Wise Styling Check.
   - All Machine Stitch Tension Balance Properly.

4. Sewing Table Quality Check List:
   - Style Wise Garments Check.
   - All Process Measurement Check.
   - Front Part, Back Part, Sleeve & Thread Shading Check.
   - S.P.I Check for All Process.
   - Print/Embroidery Placement Check.
   - Main Label, Care Label, Size Label &Care Symbol Check.
   - Size Mistake Check.
   - All Process Alter Check.
   - Any Fabric Fault /Rejection Check.

5. Finishing Quality Check List:
   - As Per Buyer Requirement Wise Iron Check..
   - Buyer Approved Sample Wise Style Check.
   - Front Part, Back part, Sleeve, Rib Thread & Contrast Color check.
   - Print/Embroidery Quality & Placement Check.
   - All process S.P.I check.
   - Oil Spot/Dirty Spot Check.

- Main Label Care label & Care Symbol Check.
- Any Fabric Fault & Fabric Reject Check.
- All process Measurement Check.
- Blister Poly & After Poly Getup Check.
- Hang tag & Price Sticker Check.
- Assortment Every Carton Pcs Quantity Check.
- Buyer Requirement Wise Carton Size, Poly Size, & garments Size Check.

6. Out Side Print & Embroidery Quality Check List:
   - Buyer Approved Sample or Artwork Wise Bulk Sample Print & Embroidery Design Check.
   - Size Wise Approved Pattern Placement Check.
   - As per Sample Wise Print Design, Color & Quality Check.
   - Bundle & Size Wise Print/Embroidery Check.
   - Fabric Top Side in Side Check.
   - Print / Embroidery Pattern Placement Check.
   - As Per Sample Wise Print/Embroidery Design, Thread Color Quality Check.
   - Print/Embroidery Color Wise Wash Test Check.

7. Store Quality Check List:
   - Buyer Approved Trims Card Check.
   - Buyer Approved Sample Wise Main, Size & Care Label Check.
   - Buyer Approved Sample Wise Care Symbol Check.
   - Thread Color Shading & Quality Check.
   - Buyer Wise Hang tag & Price Sticker Check.

COST OF QUALITY

It's a term that's widely used – and widely misunderstood. The "cost of quality" isn't the price of creating a quality product or service. It's the cost of NOT creating a quality product or service. Every time work is redone, the cost of quality increases. Obvious examples include:

- The reworking of a manufactured item.
- The retesting of an assembly.
- The rebuilding of a tool.
- The correction of a bank statement.

- The reworking of a service, such as the reprocessing of a loan operation or the replacement of a food order in a restaurant.

In short, any cost that would not have been expended if quality were perfect contributes to the cost of quality.

FABRIC INSPECTION

Fabric quality is based on the quality of each component used to produce and finish the fabric. Quality is cumulative of all properties of the components of fabric

Defect is defined as non-conformance of some characteristic from its required level or performance

Systems of Fabric inspection

Fabric is inspected to identify type, number, size, and location of defects. The cumulative of these defects is used to determine the grade of the fabric and its acceptability for the next process. A grade is a numerical value assigned to a fabric based on number, size and severity of defects. The most used fabric grading systems are ASTM 4 Point system and 10 point system of grading.

ASTM 4 POINT SYSTEM

This system is mostly used to grade all type of fabrics such as woven, knit, grey or finished fabrics are inspected in this system. The fabric is inspected using a fabric inspection machine where fabric is continuously fed and observed, once a defect is observed, it will be measured for length and according to the length and status of impact on fabric defect points are added. The inspection is a 100% inspection, the defect point allocation is as

Defect length	Demerit Points
Less than 3 inches	1
Over 3 inches but not over 6 inches	2
Over 6 inches but not over 9 inches	3
Over 9 inches	4
Fabric holes	4

- No running yard will be penalized more than 4 points for warp and weft defects,
- No more than 4 points is assigned to a single defect.
- For fabric width exceeding 64" – 66" maximum penalty points can be increased above 4 per linear yard on proportion to width.
- The defects appearing within one inch of the selvedge will be ignored.
- The grading is done in linear yard basic with an acceptable tolerance of 20 points in 100 linear yard. Or a 28 points per square yard for each individual roll of fabric.
- The system no provisions for the probability of minor defects
- The defect is graded regardless the end product

Calculation formula used to find the grade of the fabric according to defect

$$\text{points per square yard} = \frac{\text{Points scored in bulk x 100 x 36}}{\text{Width of the roll in inches x total yards inspected}}$$

TEN POINT SYSTEM FOR FABRIC INSPECTION.

The 10 point system of fabric inspection was developed in early 1950's. The system assigns penalty points for each and every defect depending on the length of the defect. Penalty points are assigned separately for warp and weft defects. The penalty point distribution is as below.

Warp Defects		Weft Defects	
Defect length	**Penalty**	**Defect length**	**Penalty**
Up to 1 inch	1 point	Up to 1 inch	1 point
1" to 5 inches	3 point	1" to 5 inches	3 point
5" to 10 inches	5 point	5" to Half Width of fabric	5 point
10" to 36 inches	10 point	Full width	10 point

Under the Ten Point system a piece is graded as "First" if the total penalty points do not exceed the total yardage of the piece. The piece is graded as "second" if the total penalty points exceeds the total yardage. For example a 100 yard piece got penalized 70 points then the piece is First grade, if exceeds 100 then it has to be "second"

- No one yard should be penalized more than 10 points

- Any warp or weft defect occurring repeatedly throughout the entire piece makes it "second"

- A combination of warp and weft defects when occurring in one yard should not be penalized more than 10 points

Requirements for Fabric Inspection

For initiating a quality inspection the below requirements are to be considered.

1. Area for inspection
   a. The inspection area should be Open, Clean and dry
   b. Proper light have to be maintained for good vision

2. Equipment's

   a. *Inspection frame* :- equipped with proper light and measuring facilities

   b. *Inspection speed:-* the frame should be capable of running up to 30 yards per minute (27 meters per minute) and should have both forward and reverse controls

   c. *Viewing distance;-* the inspection should be performed from an observation distance of 2 to 4 feet's (60 to 20 cm) so as to get full vision of the fabric width

   d. *Lighting.* - overhead customer requirement lighting should be maintained. The surface illumination level should be a minimum of 1075 lux (lux is the unit of measuring light)

QUALITY CONTROL INSPECTION & AUDITING.

"in-process quality control" is actually quality control steps that take place thought the process of fabric production or garment production. This is also often referenced as "inline" inspections or inline audits.

The primary purpose of the in-process auditing is to identify problems as early as possible. A problem may be caused by the operator, the machine, or other factors. The inline audits will help you find specific problems in production. The only way to fix a problem is to find the problem. It is important to find errors as quickly as possible so that they can be corrected as fast as possible.

Some companies will do their own inline inspections and others will utilize inspection services.

FINAL STATISTICAL AUDIT:

Final Statistical Audits are very important in catching quality problems. This is the last check before the goods are sent to the customer. Skilled auditors are required to perform this job because many of the defects at this point require the attention of a skilful eye. If one of these auditors rejects a cut, then the whole cut it to be checked 100% for that defect.

Elements of the Final Statistical Audit

Verification- It must be verified that the garment at hand is what is desired by the customer.

Inspection for Workmanship Defects- A statistically determined number of units from the lot must be thoroughly inspected in order to evaluate the quality of the stock.

Inspection for Size Problems- A few garments from each size must be measured for size after being inspected.

General Requirements for Inspection:

- Work area must be well lighted and the measuring table should be large enough to hold the entire garment spread out flat and buttoned.

- Use a soft fibre glass ruler or a metal ruler that has been calibrated against a rigid steel ruler.

- Cuts should be stored in the auditing storage area to facilitate the access of the boxes for the auditor.

- Sample boxes must be randomly obtained. Cuts that are only partially boxed are not ready for the final statistical audit and should not be audited until all boxes are complete. Samples must be randomly obtained from finished sealed boxes.

- Final Statistical Audits are done following a 4.0 AQL.

- Auditors should establish a routine for inspecting garments in order to eliminate the possibility of overlooking an operation.

- The auditor must be aware of the specifications of the garment.

- Round measurements are made to the nearest 1/8th unless specifications require that it is taken to the 1/16th.

- All operations must be checked in the final audit. Also, tacks, shading, long threads, raw edges, skip stitches and other defects must be checked.

- Garments with major defects are to be marked by colour tape and set aside for repair.

- Detailed records should be recorded and major defects must be properly recorded with their code.

- Cuts that have not passed a final audit or that have only been partially audited should not be loaded on the truck.

- After inspection, the remainder of the garments in the box must be counted and checked for size. The label on the exterior of the box must reflect what is inside the box.

- Garments that have passed the inspection must be returned to the box in the same manner that they were in when they were taken out. All repairs should be set aside and marked.

- Detailed records of any defects must be recorded

Trouser Inspection Procedure:

- Lay garment face up and visually check the front for shading, fabric defects, and soil.

- Measure the waist with a metal or fiberglass ruler. Check that the measurement of the waist is the same as the size on the label.

- Check that pockets are functional and have no shaded pieces, missing tacks, and are overall correct.

- Check the placement of the button and that it lines up with the hole. Button and unbutton the garment to ensure that there are no problems with function.

- Check the zipper making sure it is properly placed, the right length and that it is functional (must zip and unzip smoothly).

- Check that the crotch has the correct tacks and no "dog ears". A slight pull should be administered to the crotch area to ensure that all the seams are secure.

- Measure the inseam and verify that it is the same as the size label. Also, measure the inseam to ensure that both legs are the same length.

- Flip garment over and visually inspect the back for shading, fabric defects, and soil.

- Check that the back pockets are properly aligned, have tacks, and are not too open (exposing the inside of the pocket).

- Compare the sober in the back pocket to the paper ticket and the woven size label to be sure that the garment is correctly labelled.

- Check belt loops for correct size, attachment, and alignment.

- Ensure that the label is properly placed and aligned correctly.

- Turn the pants inside out and inspect all seams and operations.

- Then turn the garment outside in and re-button, zip and fold the garment.

Shirt Inspection Procedure:

- Visually inspect the front of the garment for any defect.

- Check that the two sides of the shirt are the same length and evenly meet at the bottom.

- Check that all buttons line up with their button holes and are properly placed. (Also, be sure that the number of buttons is correct and that all of them are securely attached to the garment.)

- Buttons should be checked for function (button and unbutton to ensure that no button holes are too small).

- When checking short sleeve garments, both arm holes must be checked for size.

- Pockets must be checked for shading, tacks, and placement. Crooked or uneven pockets are unacceptable. Pockets of a patterned fabric must line up according to the print. (A pocket set even slightly off can be very apparent when using a patterned fabric.)

- Garments must be turned inside out and all seams must be checked.

- 3 garments of every size must be measured. (Bust, sweep, collar, yoke, cuff, arm hole, natural shoulder, and pockets must all be measured and compared to the specifications of the garment.

Lot Failure:

If a lot fails, then a 100% inspection must occur. First 20% must be inspected and those results should be combined with the failure results if the lot still fails then continue to check 100%.

ACCEPTED QUALITY LEVEL (AQL)

AQL is one of the most frequently used terms when it comes to quality in the apparel export industry.

The inspection is the tool that is used for assessing the conformance of the merchandise to the agreed specifications or the requirements. Though inspection is important and it gives us an idea about the acceptance level of a product, it may not be possible to carry out 100% inspection of all the units in a particular shipment or a lot. This is mainly due to following reasons:

- It is costly.

- 100% inspection is seldom 100% accurate and dependable.

- It may be impractical and not desirable as it leads to excessive handling of goods which results in goods losing their freshness.

What is AQL?

The AQL is the maximum per cent defective that for the purpose of sampling inspection can be considered satisfactory as a process average." In layman's language this means, when a buyer specifies a particular AQL for sampling inspection, it is an indication that as long as the percentage of defective garments in the shipments (lots) supplied by a manufacturer is lower than the AQL, most of the shipments will be accepted.

Process Average means the average percentage of defective products (percent defective) in the lots submitted for the first inspections.

Acceptable Quality Level (I= Inspection Qty, A= Accepted Points)								
Lot Size	1.5		2.5		4.0		6.5	
	I	A	I	A	I	A	I	A
Less than 151	8	0	5	0	13	1	8	1
151-280	8	0	20	1	13	1	13	2
280-500	32	1	20	1	20	2	20	3
501-1200	32	1	32	2	32	3	32	5
1201-3200	50	2	50	3	50	5	50	7
3201-10000	80	3	80	5	80	7	80	10
10001-35000	125	5	125	7	125	10	125	14
35001-150000	200	7	200	10	200	14	200	21
150001-500000	315	10	315	14	315	21	200	21
500001 & Over	500	14	500	21	315	21	200	21

** NAME OF THE COMPANY **

Final Audit Measurement Report

Date:_____   Customer:_____

Invoice:_____

Cut:_____   No. of Units:_____   Line:_____

Style:_____

Point of Measure. Eg. Waist				
Size	Spec	1	2	3

Point of Measure				
Size	Spec	1	2	3

Point of Measure				
Size	Spec	1	2	3

Point of Measure				
Size	Spec	1	2	3

Supervisor:_____

Date:_____

This format is generic used for direct measurement taking from the garment at the finishing stage or at any level after sewing, there may be modifications according to the requirement of the style, design or company

** NAME OF THE COMPANY **

Final Audit:_____

Re-Audit:_____

Date:_____   Customer:_____

Cut Number:_____   Inspector:_____

Style/ Model/ Color:_____   Cut Size:_____

Line Number:_____   Sample Quantity:_____

     Acceptable Amount:_____

Check Off List		X= Problem	v= Satisfactory
Specs	Care Label	Stains	Packing Problems
Hem	Woven Label	Fabric Flaws	Sizes/ Pack
Button	Elastic	Shading	Scale
Holes	Zipper	Mfg. Seconds	Packing Slips
Buttons	Strings	Other	Pair Count
Pressing	Raw Seams		Documents
Belt Loops	Skipped		Container Loading
Stitching	Stitch		

Description of Defects	No. of Defects	Total

Number of Total Major Defects:_____

Number of Pairs With a Major Defect:_____   Number of Seconds Found

Accept:_____   Reject:_____   Reject for 100% inspection:_____

Notes on Other Minor Defects and/or Other Comments:

There are many other formats used in Quality auditing, the formats will be developed according to brand, product, etc.

12 COMMON DEFECTS

Defects – Defects are all those non-conformances that are not acceptable by end customer. Like imbalanced shape of the garment, broken button or other trims, holes in fabrics, slip stitch, broken seam etc. In a defective garment there may be more than one defect.

Defective Pieces – Defective pieces are those pieces, which are separated for alteration during checking may be for any causes.

For the quantitative measure there is two measuring unit as Defects per hundred units and percentage defective.

Defects per hundred units (DHU) – DHU is the number of total defects in 100 checked garments. The formula for calculating DHU is

DHU = Total no. of defects found X 100 / Total pieces checked

Percent Defective (%) – total number of defective pieces in 100 checked garments.

Percentage defective = Total no. of defective pieces X 100 / Total pieces checked

Example: - In a day one table checker checked 200 pieces. He found total 15 defective pieces and in those 15 pieces total 60 defects were found. So, quality measure of that lot in terms of DHU is 30 (60*100/200) and Percentage Defective is 7.5%.

Pattern defects in garment:

- Some parts of pattern are missing, probably because the marker did not include the correct number of parts. Mixed parts, probably because the marker is not correctly labeled, resulting in a marriage of wrong sized parts.

- Patterns not facing in correct direction on napped fabrics. Not all patterns facing in same direction (either way) on a one-way fabric. Patterns not aligned with respect to the fabric grain. Poor line definition (e.g. too thick chalk; indistinctly printed line, perforated lay not powdered) leading to inaccurate cutting.

- Skimpy marking, caused by either the marker did not use the outside edge of the pattern; or the pattern was moved or swung after partial marking to squeeze the pattern into a smaller space for economizing the fabric.

- Marking back from miniature markers also can cause trouble unless the miniature marker making is in the hands of experienced operators. Alternatively the full size pattern may be having worn out edges.

- Wrong check boxing, i.e. checks are not showing a full or partial box across the seam. Notches and drill marks omitted, indistinct or misplaced.

Spreading defects in garment:

- Not enough plies to cover quantity of garments required. Plies misaligned, resulting in garment parts getting cut with bits missing in some plies at the edge of the spread.

- Narrow fabric, causes garment parts at the edge of the lay getting cut with bits missing. Incorrect tension of plies, i.e. fabric spread too tight or too loose. This will result in parts not fitting in sewing, and finished garments not meeting size tolerances.

- Not all plies facing in correct direction (whether 'one way' as with nap, or 'one way either way' as with some check designs). This happens when fabric is not spread face down, face up, or face to face as required.

- Spread distorted by the attraction or repulsion of plies caused by excessive static electricity. Plies are not spread accurately one above another for cutting. This results in mismatching checks.

Cutting defects in garment:

- Failure to follow the marker lines resulting in distorted garment parts. Top and bottom plies can be a different size if the straight knife is allowed to lean, or if a round knife is used on too high a spread.

- Notches, which are misplaced, too deep, too shallow, angled, omitted, or wrong type to suit fabric.

- Drill marks, which are misplaced, wrong drill to suit fabric, omitted, not perpendicular through the spread. Frayed edges, scorched or fused edges, caused by a faulty knife, not sharp enough, or rotating at too high a speed.

- Garment part damaged by careless use of knife, perhaps overrunning cutting previous piece. Marker incorrectly positioned on top of spread. Garment parts have bits missing at edge of lay. If too tight or too loose then garment parts are distorted. Slits opened inaccurately or omitted.

Garment Twist

- A rotation, usually lateral, between different panels of a garment resulting from the release of latent stresses during laundering of the woven or knitted fabric forming the garment.

- Twist may also be referred to as Torque or Spirallity

VARIOUS TYPES OF DEFECTS IN KNITTED FABRICS

It is very natural that in the course of knitting fabrics, imperfections occur. The imperfections may be the result of faulty yarn, knitting machine malfunction or improper finishing. The defects in knitting construction are considered in terms of appearance and nature.

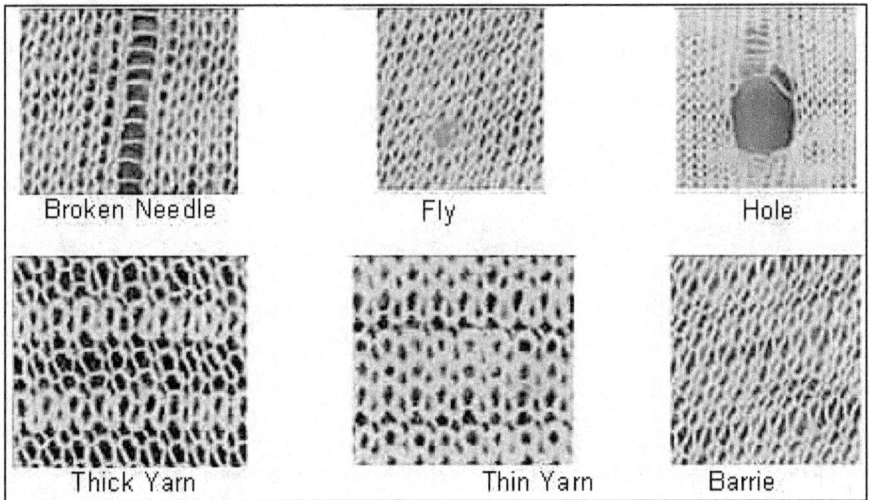

| Broken Needle | Fly | Hole |
| Thick Yarn | Thin Yarn | Barrie |

Bands and Streaks

There are different kinds of bands and streaks that may occur in knitting. Some of the popular defects are as follows:

Barrie Effect: A Barrie effect has the appearance of a stripe with shaded edges. It is horizontal in weft knits and vertical in warp knits. The Barrie effect is caused by various factors like:

- Lack of uniformity in yarn size, color or luster.
- Mush tension on the yarns during knitting one section of the fabric.
- Uneven shrinkage or other finishing defects.

Bowing: A line or a design may curve across the fabric. This bowing is the distortion caused by faulty take-up mechanism on the knitting machine.

Streak or Stop Mark: A straight horizontal streak or stop mark in the knitted fabric is due to the difference in tension in the yarns caused by the machine being stopped and then restarted.

Skewing: Skewing effect is seen as a line or design running at a slight angle across the cloth.

Needle Lines: Needle lines or vertical lines are due to a wale that is either tighter or looser than the adjacent ones. This is caused by needle movement due to a tight fit in its slot or a defective sinker.

STITCH DEFECTS

There are various kinds of stitch defects like:

- Boardy: The knitted fabric becomes Boardy (a stiff or harsh hand) when the stitches have been knit very tightly.

- Cockled or puckered: If the knitted fabric is cockled or puckered, it is due to uneven stitches or uneven yarn size.

- Dropped Stitch: This is an un-knitted stitch caused either by the yarn carrier not having been set properly or the stitch having been knitted too loosely.

- Run or ladder: A run or ladder indicates a row of dropped stitches in the wale.

- Hole: A large hole or a press off is the result of a broken yarn at a specific needle feed so that knitting cannot occur.

- Tucking: This is the result of an unintentional tucking in the knitted fabric. This is also called the bird's eye defect.

- Float: This is caused by a miss stitch which is the result of failure of one or more needles to have been raised to catch the yarn.

Broken Stitches - Needle Cutting:

Where the thread is being broken where one seam crosses another seam (ex: bar tacks on top of waistband stitching, seat seam on top of riser seam) resulting in stitch failure.

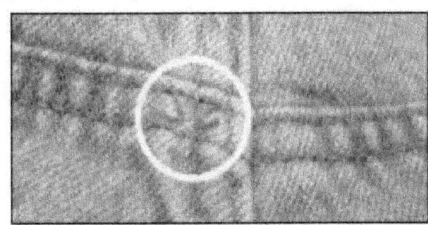

Minimizing broken stitches due to Needle Cutting

- Use a higher performance Perma Core or D-Core thread.

- Use a larger diameter thread on operations where the thread is being cut.

- Make sure the proper stitch balance is being used. On a chain stitch seam on denim, you normally would like to maintain a 60%/40% relationship of Needle thread to looper thread in the Seam.

- Use needles with the correct needle point.

- Change the needles at regular intervals on operations where the Needle Cuts are occurring frequently.

Broken Stitches:

Where thread on the stitch line is broken during stone-washing, sand blasting, hand sanding, etc. Broken stitches must be repaired by re stitching over the top of the stitch-line.

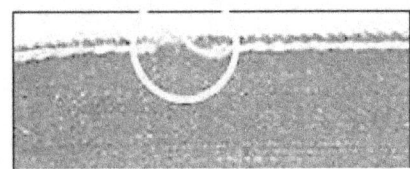

Minimizing broken Stitches due to abrasion

- Use a higher performance Perma Core or D-Core thread;

- Use a larger diameter thread on operations where excessive abrasion is occurring

- Make sure stitches are balance properly,

- Use a Magic air entangled thread in the Looper due to its lower seam profile making it less susceptible to abrasion

- Monitor the Finishing Cycle for compliance to specs.

Broken Stitches by Chemical Degradation

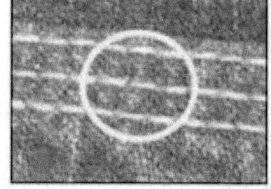

Where thread is being compromised by the chemicals used during laundering resulting in loss or change of color and seam failure

Minimizing broken stitches due to Chemical Degradation:

- Use a higher performance Perma Core NWT that has greater resistance to chemical degradation.

- It is recommended to go to larger thread sizes when the Denim Garments will be subject to Harsh Chemical washes.

- To achieve the best laundering results make sure that the water temperatures and PH Levels are correct and that the proper amounts and sequence of chemical dispersion are within guidelines.

- Make sure the garments are being rinsed properly to neutralize the chemicals in the fabric.

- Monitor the drying process, cycle times, and temperatures to make sure they are correct so that the best possible garment quality can be achieved

Unraveling Seams:

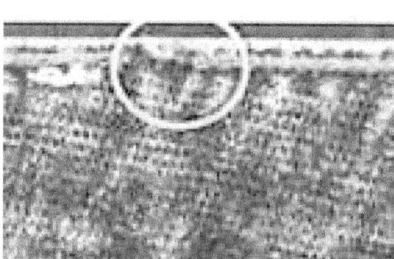

Generally occurs on 401 chain stitch seams where either the stitch has been broken or a skipped stitch has occurred. This will cause seam failure unless the seam is Re stitched.

Minimizing unraveled Stitches:

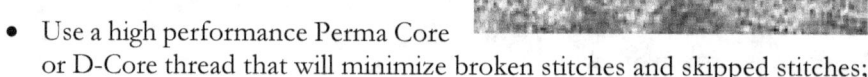

- Use a high performance Perma Core or D-Core thread that will minimize broken stitches and skipped stitches;

- Insure proper machine maintenance and sewing machine adjustments;

- Observe sewing operators for correct material handling techniques.

Re Stitched Seams

Where there is a "splice" on the stitch line. If this occurs on Topstitching, then the seam does not appear to be 1st quality merchandise. Caused by:

- Thread breaks or thread run-out during sewing; or

- Cut or broken stitches during a subsequent treatment of the finished product (I.e., stone washing).

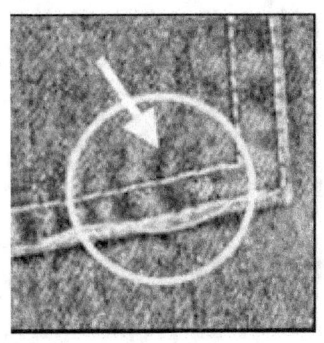

Minimizing Re stitched Seams:

- Use a better quality sewing thread. This may include going to a higher performance thread designed to minimize sewing interruptions.

- Insure proper machine maintenance and sewing machine adjustments;

- Make sure sewing machines are properly maintained and adjusted for the fabric and sewing operation

- Observe sewing operators for correct material handling techniques.

Sagging or Rolling Pockets:

Where the pocket does not lay flat and rolls over after laundering.

Minimizing Sagging or rolling front & back Pockets:

- Make sure the sewing operators are not holding back excessively when setting the front pocket.

- Make sure the hem is formed properly and that excessive fabric is not being put into the folder that will cause the hem to roll over.

- Check to make sure pocket is cut properly and that pocket curve is not too deep.

- Use a reinforcement tape on the inside of the pocket that may help prevent the front panel from stretching along the bias where the front pocket is set.

- The type and weight of denim, along with the fabric construction, may contribute to this problem.

Skipped Stitches:

Where the stitch forming device misses the needle loop or the needle misses the Looper loop. Skips are usually found where one seam crosses another seam and most of the time occurs right before or right after the heavy thickness.

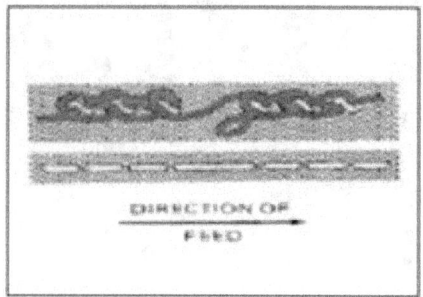 

Minimizing Skipped Stitches:

- Use core spun thread.

- Use minimum thread tension to get a balanced stitch.

- Use the ideal foot, feed and plate that help to minimize flagging.

- Training sewing operators NOT to stop on the thickness

- Make sure the machine is feeding properly without stalling.

- Make sure the machine is not back feeding.

Ragged / Inconsistent Edge

Where the edge of the seam is either extremely "ragged" or "rolls" inside the stitch.

Solutions to Ragged / Inconsistent Edge:

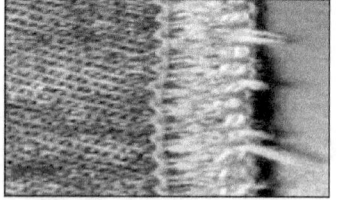

- Make sure the sewing machine knives are sharpened and changed often;

- The knives should be adjusted properly in relationship to the "stitch tongue" on the needle plate to obtain the proper seam width or width bite.

Wavy Seams on Stretch Denim:

Where the seam does not lay flay and is wavy due to the fabric stretching as it was sewn or during subsequent laundering and handling operations.

Solutions for wavy seams on stretch Garments

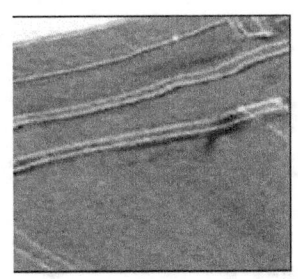

- Use minimum presser foot pressure

- Instruct sewing operators to use proper handling techniques and not stretch the fabric as they are making the seam.

- Where, available, use differential feed to compensate for the stretch of the fabric.

Ropy Hem:

Where hem is not laying flat and is skewed in appearance.

Solutions for Ropy Hems

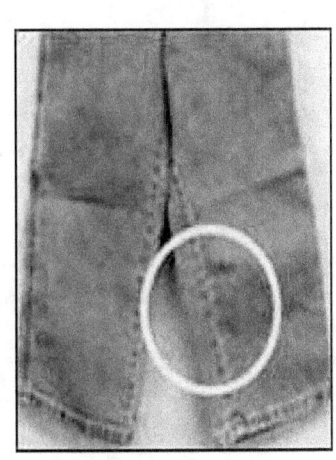

- Usually caused by poor operator handling.

- Instruct the sewing operator to make sure they get the hem started correctly in the folder before they start sewing. Also, make sure they don't hold back excessively as the seam is being sewn.

- Use minimum roller or presser foot pressure.

Twisted Legs:

Is where the side seam twists around to the front of the pant and distorts the appearance of the jeans.

Solutions for Twisted Legs:

- Usually caused by poor operator handling. Instruct the sewing operator to match the front and back properly so they come out the same length. Sometimes notches are used to insure proper alignment. They should NOT trim off the front or back with scissors to make them come out the same length

- Make sure the cut parts are of equal length coming to the assembly operation.

- Check fabric quality and cutting for proper skew

- Make sure the sewing machine is adjusted properly for uniform feeding of the top and bottom plies.

Disappearing Stitches in Stretch Denim:

Is where the thread looks much smaller on seams sewn in the warp direction than in the weft direction of the fabric.

Solutions to minimizing disappearing stitches on stretch Denim:

- Use a heavier thread size on topstitching.
- Go to a longer stitch length (from 8 to 6 SPI).
- Make sure the thread tensions are as loose as possible so the thread sits on top of the fabric rather than burying in the fabric on seams sewn in the warp.

Thread Discoloration After Laundry

It is the thread picks up the indigo dyes from the fabric giving the thread a 'dirty' appearance. A common discoloration would be the pick-up of a greenish or turquoise tint.

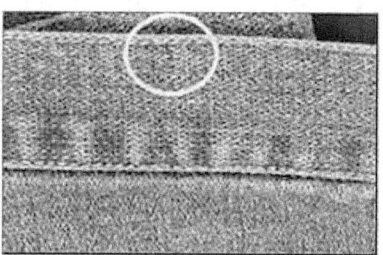

Solutions to Thread Discoloration

- Use thread with proper color fastness characteristics
- Correct PH level (too low) and Water Temperature (too low) during laundry
- Use the proper chemicals & laundry cycles.
- Use Denim col PCC in wash or similar additive
- Do not overload washers with too many garments at one time.

Poor Colorfastness after Laundry

Poor Colorfastness after Laundry is where the thread does not wash down consistently in the garment or changes to a different color altogether.

Solutions to poor Colorfastness after Laundry:

- Use thread with proper color fastness characteristics

- Use threads from the same thread supplier and do not mix threads in a garment.
- Always do preproduction testing on denim garments using new colors to assure that they will meet your requirements.

Improper Stitch Balance – 301 Lock Stitch

Where loops are seen either on the bottom side or topside of the seam. This is particularly evident with different colour needle and bobbin threads. Also, where the stitch is too loose.

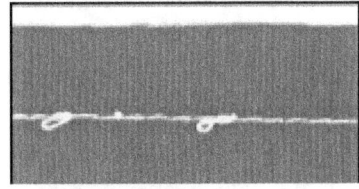

SOLUTIONS:

- Use a quality thread with consistent frictional characteristics;
- Properly balance the stitch so that the needle and bobbin threads meet in the middle of the seam. Always start by checking the bobbin thread tension to make sure it is set correctly, so that the minimum thread tension is required to get a balanced stitch

Improper Stitch Balance - 401 Chain Stitch

Where the loops on the bottom-side of the seam are inconsistent and do not appear uniform.

SOLUTIONS:

- Use a quality thread with consistent frictional characteristics;

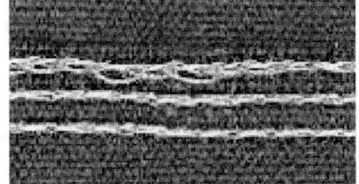

- Properly balance the stitch so that
when the Looper thread is unravelled, the needle loop lays over half way to the next needle loop on the underside of the seam.

Improper Stitch Balance - 504 Over Edge Stitch

Where the needle loop is not pulled up to the underside of the seam and the "purl" is not on the edge of the seam.

SOLUTIONS:

- Use a quality thread with consistent frictional characteristics;

- Properly balance the stitch so that when the Looper thread is unravelled, the needle loop lays over half way to the next needle loop on the underside of the seam.

Needle Cutting on Knits

Where needle holes appear along the stitch line that will eventually turn into a "run". Generally caused by the needle damaging the fabric as it is penetrating the seam.

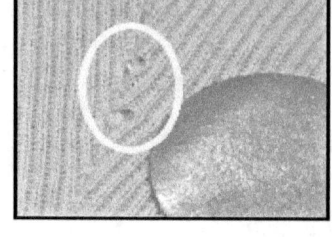

Minimizing needle cutting on knits:

Make sure the proper thread size and needle type and size are being used for the fabric Make sure the fabric has been properly stored to prevent drying out and has been finished properly;

Open Seam - Seam Failure - Fabric

Where the stitch line is still intact but the yarns in the fabric have ruptured.

Minimizing seam failures - fabric:

- Reinforce stress points with Bartack. Make sure the Bartack are the proper length and width for the application;
- Check to make sure the patterns have been designed for proper fit;
- Make sure the ideal seam construction is being used;

Open Seam - Seam Failure - Stitch

Where the threads in the seam have ruptured leaving a hole in the stitch line. Caused by

- Improper stitch for application;
- Inadequate thread strength for seam;
- Not enough stitches per inch.

Minimizing seam failures - stitch:

- Use a better quality sewing thread. This may include going to a higher performance thread designed to give greater seam performance.
- Use the proper size thread for the application;

- For knit fabrics, check for "Stitch Cracking". Stitch Cracking can be caused by any of the following: not enough stitches per inch; improper seam width or needle spacing for application; improper stitch balance; and improper thread selection.

Puckered Seams - Knits & Stretch Woven

Where the seam does not lay flat after stitching.

SOLUTIONS:

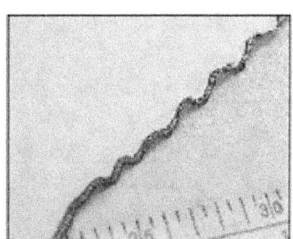

- If sewing machines are equipped with differential feed, set them properly for the fabric;
- Use minimum presser foot pressure during sewing; and
- Observe operator for correct handling techniques. Too much stretching of the fabric by the sewing operator will cause this problem

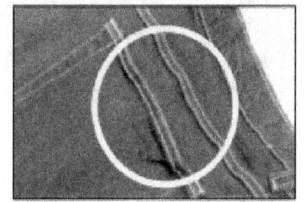

Excessive Seam Puckering – Woven

The seam does not lay flat and smooth along the stitch line. Caused by one of the following:

- Feed Puckering - where the plies of fabric in the seam are not being aligned properly during sewing;
- Tension Puckering - where the thread has been stretched and sewn into the seam. The thread then causes the seam to draw back and pucker;
- Yarn Displacement or structural jamming - caused by sewing seams with too large of thread that causes the yarns in the seam to be displaced, giving a puckered appearance.

Minimizing excessive seam puckering:

- Use the correct thread type and size for the fabric. In many cases, a smaller, higher tenacity thread is required to minimize seam puckering but maintain seam strength
- Sew with minimum sewing tension to get a balanced stitch;
- Make sure machines are set up properly for the fabric being sewn;

- Check for proper operator handling techniques.

Ragged/Inconsistent Edge - Over edge or Safety stitch Seams

Where the edge of the seam is either extremely "ragged" or "rolls" inside the stitch.

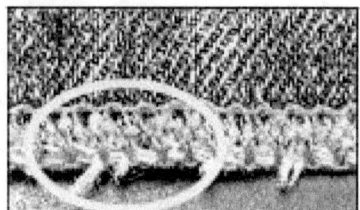

Solutions:

- Make sure the sewing machine knives are sharpened and changed often;
- The knives should be adjusted properly in relationship to the "stitch tongue" on the needle plate to obtain the proper seam width or width bite. In the photo, the trimming knives have been set wider than the "stitch tongue" on the needle plate causing the "ropy" appearance.

Re-stitched Seams / Broken Stitches

Where a "splice" occurs on the stitch line. If this occurs on Topstitching, then the seam does not appear to be 1st quality merchandise.

Caused by

- Thread breaks or thread run-out during sewing; or
- Cut or broken stitches during a subsequent treatment of the finished product (i.e., stone washing).

Minimizing Thread Breakage:

- Use a better quality sewing thread. This may include going to a higher performance thread designed to minimize sewing interruptions.
- Insure proper machine maintenance and sewing machine adjustments;
- Make sure sewing machines are properly maintained and adjusted for the fabric and sewing operation
- Observe sewing operators for correct material handling techniques.

Unravelling Buttons

Where a tail of thread is visible on the topside of the button and when pulled, the button falls off.

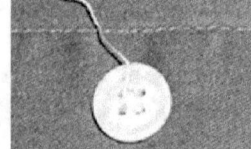

Solutions:

- Use a quality sewing thread to minimize skipped stitches;
- Specify attaching the buttons with a Lockstitch instead of a single thread Chain stitch Button sewing machine.

Excessive Seam Grin

Where the stitch balance is not properly adjusted (stitch too loose) and you can see the seam opening up. To check for Seam Grin, apply normal seam stress across the seam and then remove the stress. If the seam remains opened, then the seam has too much "grin through".

Solutions:

To correct, readjust the sewing machine thread tensions so that the proper stitch balance is achieved. Too much tension will cause other problems including seam failures ("Stitch Cracking"), excessive thread breakage, and skipped stitches.

Seam Failure - Seam Slippage

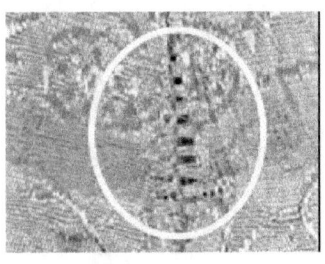

Where the yarns in the fabric pull out of the seam from the edge. This often occurs on fabrics constructed of continuous filament yarns that are very smooth and have a slick surface. Also caused by loosely constructed fabrics.

Minimizing Seam Failures - Seam Slippage:

- Consider changing the seam construction to a French seam construction;
- Increase the seam width or width of bite;
- Optimize the stitches per inch;
- Contact your fabric supplier

Skipped Stitches

Where the stitch length is inconsistent, possibly appearing as double the normal stitch length; or where you can see that the threads in the stitch are not properly connected together. Caused by the stitch forming device in the sewing machine missing the thread loop during stitch formation causing a defective stitch. On Looper type stitches, this will allow the stitch to unravel causing seam failure.

Minimizing Skipped Stitches:

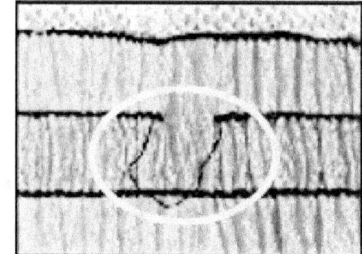

- Use a better quality sewing thread. This may include going to a higher performance thread designed to minimize sewing interruptions.
- Insure proper machine maintenance and sewing machine adjustments;
- Make sure sewing machines are properly maintained and adjusted for the fabric and sewing operation.

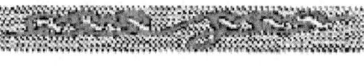

- Observe sewing operators for correct material handling techniques.

Apart from these defects there are many other defects occurs, this will be according to the style, fabric, thread used, attachments used to sew etc. the details of the stitch will be illustrated in the specific techpack of the garment to be checked.

22 COMPLIANCE

Compliance is all about the quality of products from the factory which must meet the audits and inspections and to give a proper environment for working. The demand for compliance is growing rapidly in today's business scenario as the buyers from the global markets are insisting on ethically manufactured products. As the export of garment products from India has increased, the demand for social compliance has also risen in the Indian garment Industry.

Social Compliance

Social compliance refers to how a business treats its employees, the environment and their perspective on social responsibility. It refers to a minimal code of conduct that directs how employees are treated with regards to wages, working hours and work conditions. To ensure that the company meets standards of various environmental laws, it may be necessary to conduct a compliance audit.

Compliance Audit

Audits and assessments provide vital management control for Process Safety Management, Process Security Management, and Risk Management Programs. Audits focus on the policies and procedures to verify compliance with regulatory requirements and industry standards. They help to ensure programs are properly designed and implemented. Further, audits also identify program deficiencies so that recommendations can be developed for corrective action.

Compliance audit in India includes an examination of rules, regulations, orders and instructions for their legality, adequacy, transparency and prudence. Auditors gather information through visual observation at the site, document reviews and interviews of staff. This data is then compared to the applicable permits and regulations to evaluate how well the operation is conforming to the applicable legal requirements.

Phases of Audit

There are three main phases of compliance audit in India:

1. Pre-Audit :- It includes planning and organizing the audit; establishing the audit objectives, scope and etiquette; and reviewing the design of the program by inspecting documentation

2. On-Site audit :- It includes conducting personnel interviews, reviewing records, and making observations to assess program implementation

3. Post-Audit :- It includes briefing the management on audit findings, and preparing a final report, Therefore, Indian apparel manufacturers need to follow Government guidelines, and social compliance standards not only within their sphere of operations, but also insist their vendors, distributors, and other collaborators involved in the supply chain to do the same.

A garment factory can fulfill its social responsibility in the following manner:

- By providing a competitive and challenging work environment to the employees
- By having ethical recruitment, remuneration, promotion and other policies
- By providing opportunities to the employees to voice their opinion and complaints and have an effective policy for the solution of these complaints
- Ensuring a safe working environment for the employees
- Ensuring not to adopt child or forced labour in the industry
- Having fair policies for the solution of employee disputes

Why Code Of Ethics Is Required

The code of ethics is all about the quality of the products from the factory and the working environment that should meet the requirements of audits and inspections. An individual running an export business needs to follow these ethics sincerely. These ethics are required for:

- Increasing national competitiveness in terms of social compliance
- Increasing competitiveness of small scale manufacturers

- Reducing burden on manufacturers
- Some of the compliance codes in Indian garment industry are listed below.

Working Hour & Wage Rate Compliance

Garment factory must ensure that employees should get at least minimum wages according to the domestic law and as per the time spent by them in the industry. Employer should pay equal wages to both men and women employees, for performing the same work or work of a similar nature. Worker employed for more than nine hours on any day or for more than 48 hours in any week, shall be entitled to wages at premium legal rates for such overtime work

Every worker should be given one holiday (for a period of 24 consecutive hours) in a week. Whenever a worker is required to work on a weekly holiday, he is to be allowed a compensatory holiday for each holiday so lost

Every worker is to be allowed at least half an hour rest interval after a maximum working of 5 hours at a stretch Workplace & work environment compliance

- Organizations should ensure proper ventilation, sufficient light and air to provide the employees with standard work environment

- Indian garment industries should provide the workers with comfortable sitting chair with back support and proper leg space

Non-discrimination compliance

Organizations should not discriminate employees on the basis of physical characteristics, beliefs and cultural characteristics. All the terms and conditions of employment should be based on an individual's ability to do the job. They should provide equal employment opportunities for all employees and associates irrespective of the employees' race, color, religion, age, sex, creed, national origin, marital status, etc.

CODE OF CONDUCT (COC)

Social Accountability standards have been developed by the international organizations such as Fair Labor Association (FLA), Worldwide Responsible Apparel production (WRAP), Council on Economic Priorities Accreditation Agency (CEPAA), The Ethical Trading Initiative (ETI) and Business for Social Responsibility (BSR).

Reputed brand buyers in large supply chain have taken the guideline from those organizations and formulated their own standard of COC and also the acceptance criteria.

The basic principles of COC have been derived from the principles of international human rights norms as delineated in International Labour Organization Conventions, the United Nations Convention on the Rights of the Child and the Universal Declaration of Human Rights.

It has nine core areas to be addressed upon. These are as follows:

1. Child labour
2. Forced labour
3. Health and safety
4. Compensation
5. Working hours
6. Discrimination
7. Discipline
8. Free association and collective bargaining
9. Management systems

While following the above criteria is compulsory for satisfying COC, local culture and regulation of Govt. cannot be overlooked. For instance, limit of working hours and compensation for extra work may not be the same for all geographical zones in the globe. Minimum basic wage also depends on the economic situation of a particular country in question. The introduction of rights of free association and collective bargaining is guided by the political environment, the maturity level of workforce and above all the basic training of the management of the organization.

By keeping in mind the complex scenario, several case studies in Bangladesh have been made with respect to the information obtained through actual social compliance audits performed by leading auditors of internationally well-known consumer products service companies.

Social compliance audits conducted as per the COC of different brand buyers of USA and Europe were basically based on the following steps:

1. Opening meeting with the factory management (informed the scope of audit)
2. Factory Tour (observed working condition)
3. Document Review (payroll, time card, personal file, age documentation etc.)
4. Employees Interview
5. Closing meeting with factory management (discussed audit findings and recommended necessary improvements).

IMPORTANCE OF SIGNS AND SYMBOLS IN INDUSTRY

The signs and symbols are used to give proper direction to the workers or personals whenever any risk to health and safety have not been avoided by other means. In addition, also need to train the staff in the meaning of safety signs and symbols. The reason being signs and symbols are used than writing is, Most of the skilled workers in industry may be illiterate or migrated from other countries, states, or may be not be knowing a common language. When on an emergency situation like fire or such accidents happening, they have to be lead to the safe zone, and also symbols are easy to understand and create

SIGN	MEANING	DETAILS
	Prohibition "Stop!"	**Colour: -** A red circular band with diagonal cross bar on the white background, the symbol within the circle to be black
		Purpose: - To indicate that a certain behaviour is prohibited.
	Hazard " Danger"	**Colour:-** a Yellow triangle with black border and black symbol
		Purpose:- To warn any type of Hazard
	Mandatory "Obey"	**Colour:-** a blue circle with a white symbol
		Purpose:- Indicates that a specific course of action must be taken
	Fire Equipment " Fire"	**Colour:-** A red oblong or square with a white symbol
		Purpose:- to describe the location of firefighting equipment
	Safe Condition "Safety"	**Colour:-** a green oblong or a square with a white symbol or text
		Purpose:- to provide information about safe conditions, emergency safe areas, first aid location etc.
	Restriction " Care"	**Colour:-** A red circle with black writing or symbol
		Purpose:- to provide strict information to follow the guidelines and cautious to avoid accidents.

Where to place the Signs,

The signs should be placed,

- Near a person's eye sight,
- In a clear space where they are unlikely to be covered
- In a position that gives adequate warning of the hazard
- Signs may be grouped where they have a common purpose and do not confuse the reader
- Fire exit navigation signs are generally marked on the floor with black words or symbols in yellow and on a path way mark arrow leads to the safe zone or fire exit

Commonly used symbols in Apparel Industry and its details.

There are a lot of other machines are in use and the symbols are made according to the standards by buyer restrictions There are a lot of symbols and markings are used as part of the compliance requirement in an apparel industry so that the workers of the industry are properly guided to and the information's are passed and acted accordingly . all the boards, signage's, standees, posters, etc. are placed according to the colour codding and standards.

Compliance Requirements for Apparel Factory:	
	**Danger Signs been put up** - All areas / machines which can be dangerous to any extent to human being needs to be marked properly with right colour & sign. Fire Extinguishers & First Aid Boxes should be identified with proper sign.
	**Unsafe Staircase in factory** Unsafe stairs should not be in use for workers, especially the fire exit should not lead to such openings.
	**Unclean & insufficient Water arrangement –** Drinking water arrangement has to be clean & hygienic. Toilets provided to workers should be clean and sufficient in numbers.
	**Marked Aisles** The walking area in production floor needs to be marked with yellow lines & red arrow towards exit.

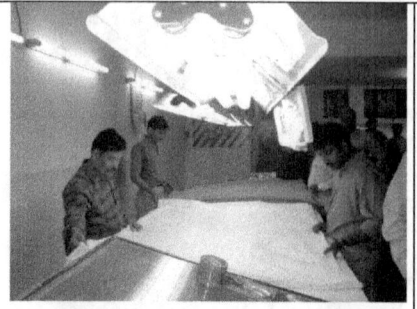	**Fabric Inspection Area** Proper lighting should be provided at all work places. Sewing operators should have sufficient lights at the sewing side of the sewing machine.
	**Production Area** Clean production floors with sufficient walking area between 2 lines and also distance between two machines giving enough space for operator movement.
	**Face Mask** Protective Equipment's like mask, gloves, rubber boots, and apron are necessary to be provided to workers.
	**No Open electric Wires near garments** All electric fittings should be properly closed. Care should be taken not to keep garment or any combustible material near electric connections.

Some Common Indian Garment Industry Compliance Code Guidelines Are:

- Exporters must not be involved in unfair labour practices including but not limited to interferences in matters concerning freedom of association

- There shall be no differences in workers remuneration for work of equal value on the basis of gender, race, religion, age, disability, sexual orientation, nationality, political opinion, or social or ethnic origin

- Exporters shall not threaten female workers with dismissal or any other employment decision that negatively affects their employment status in order to prevent them from getting married or becoming pregnant

- Exporters shall ensure that proper ventilation systems are installed within their premises to prevent airborne exposures which may affect the health of workers

- Members shall not use any form of physical or psychological violence, threats, harassment, or abuse against workers seeking to form organizations or participating in union activities, including strikes

- Workers shall be entitled to at least 24 consecutive hours of rest in every seven-day period. If workers must work on a rest day, an alternative consecutive 24 hours rest day must be provided

- Exporters shall provide workers with paid annual leaves as required under local laws, regulations and procedures. Exporters shall not impose any undue restrictions on workers' use of annual leave or taking any type of sick or maternity leave

- Exporters shall pay workers at least the legal minimum wage or the prevailing industry wage, whichever is higher. In today's scenario, it is the most essential code of compliance for Indian Industry

- Exporters shall compensate workers for all hours worked. Workers on a piece rate payment scheme or any other incentive scheme should be paid accordingly

- Exporters shall not unreasonably restrain the freedom of movement of workers, including movement in canteen during breaks, using toilets, accessing water, or to access necessary medical attention, as a means to maintain work discipline

- Garment exporters must ensure that the minimum age requirement to non-hazardous employment shall not be less than 14 years. This is the most important concern in India nowadays. Further, each worker has the right to enter into and to terminate their employment freely

Indian apparel makers need to follow all the compliance guidelines to comply with global standards.

23 SEWING MACHINE

SINGLE NEEDLE LOCK STITCH MACHINE

Lock Stitch

The lockstitch uses two threads, an upper needle thread and a lower bobbin thread, together in the hole in the fabric which they pass through. The upper thread runs from a spool kept on a spindle on top of or next to the machine, through a tension mechanism, through the take-up arm, and finally through the hole in the needle. Meanwhile the lower thread is wound onto a bobbin, which is inserted into a case in the lower section of the machine below the material.

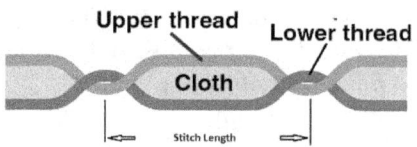

To make one stitch, the machine lowers the threaded needle through the cloth into the bobbin area, where a rotating hook (or other hooking mechanism) catches the upper thread at the point just after it goes through the needle. The hook mechanism carries the upper thread entirely around the bobbin case, so that it has made one wrap of the bobbin thread. Then the take-up arm pulls the excess upper thread (from the bobbin area) back to the top, forming the lockstitch. Then the feed dogs pull the material along one stitch length, and the cycle repeats

THREADING THE MACHINE

Needle – DB x 1 or DA x 1 or DP x 5

Max Stitch Length – 4mm to 5 mm

Presser foot lift – 10mm to 13 mm

Sewing speed – 4000 to 5000 rpm

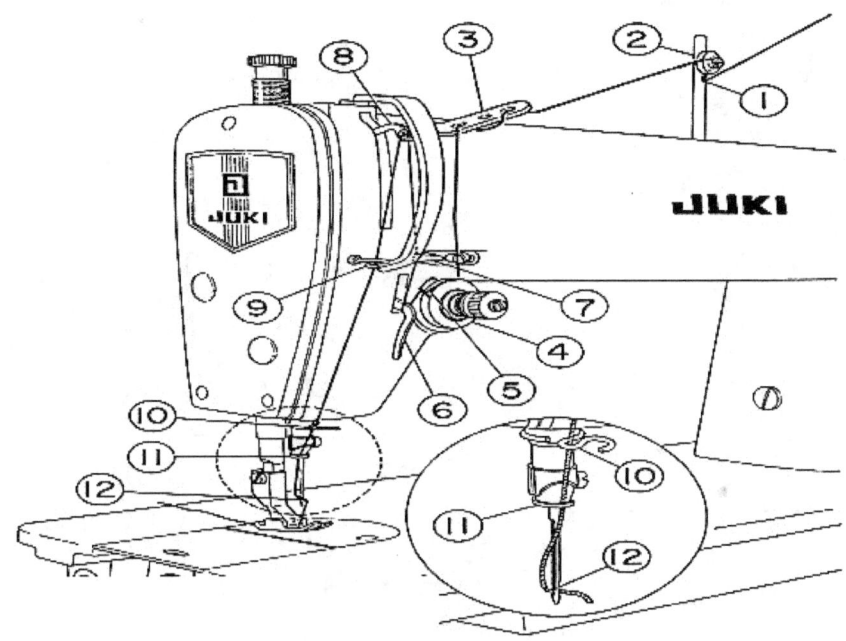

The needle thread need to be placed in the thread post and then drawn through the points 1 to 12 respectively so that the threads must not cross anywhere and should run in water flow manner.

Parts of a Single Needle Lock Stitch Machine

1. Power Switch
2. Operation Panel (based on advanced machines, conventional m/c don't have a panel)
4. Synchronizer – Drive Pulley getting drive from motor
5. Thread Stand
6. Power Motor / Drive control
7. Head of the Machine
8. Motor
9. Pedal
10. One touch reverse feed
11. Wiper assembly – pressure foot lifter

12. Machine stand
13. Presser foot
14. Needle Plate & Feed Dog
15. Back tack liver
16. Knee lifter

There are more other parts in the machine as Hock Set, Needle Bar, thread Tension assembly etc.

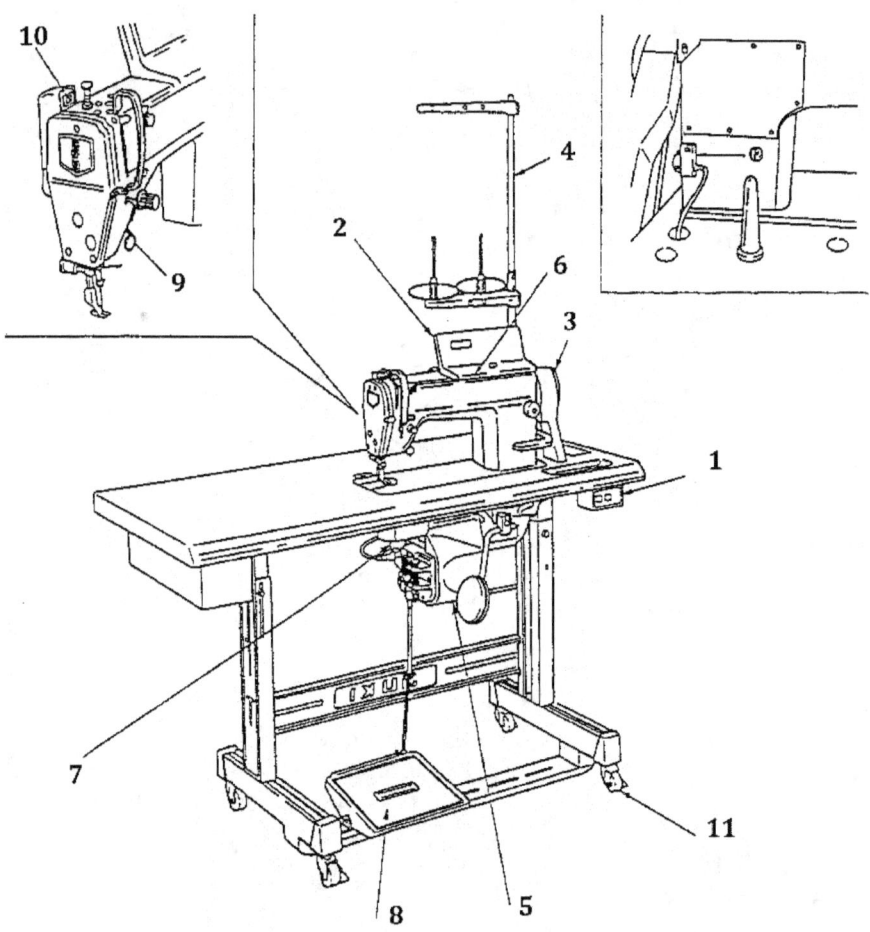

The Stitch Formation in a Lock Stitch machine.

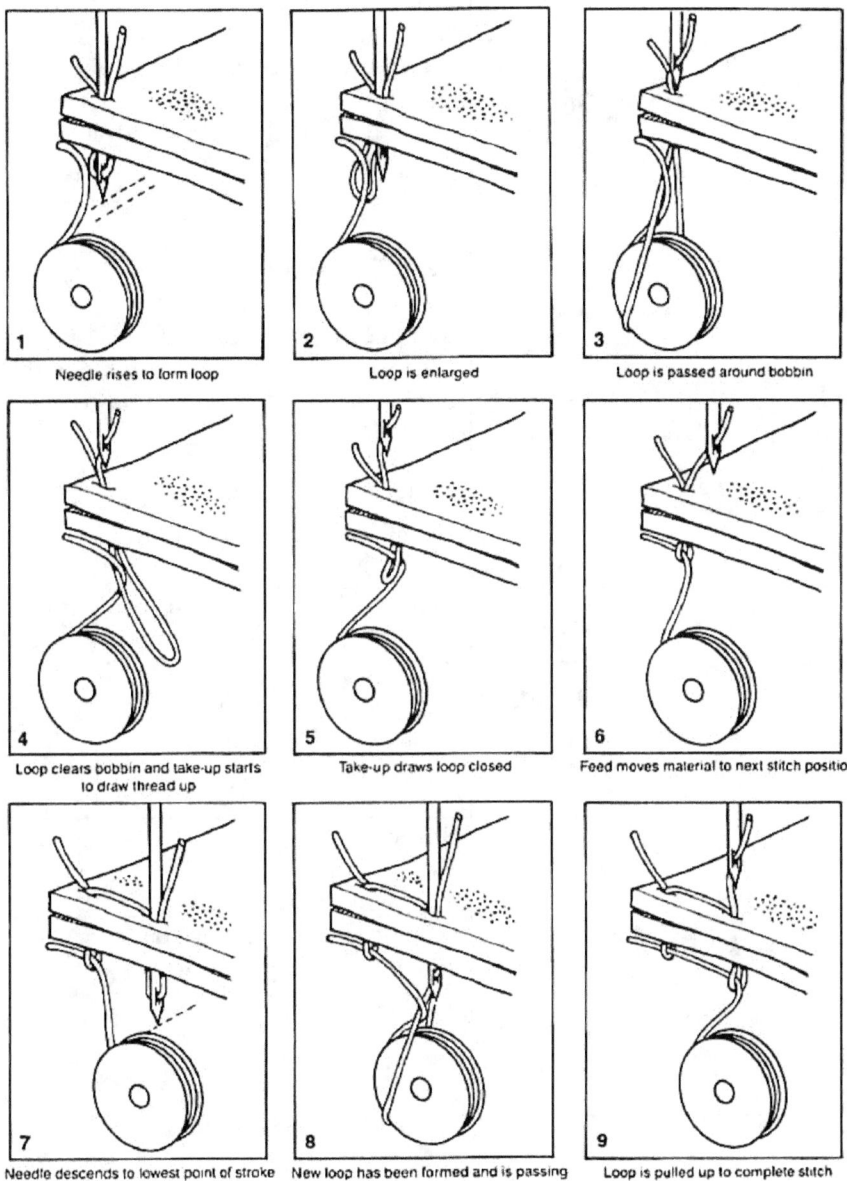

1. Needle rises to form loop
2. Loop is enlarged
3. Loop is passed around bobbin
4. Loop clears bobbin and take-up starts to draw thread up
5. Take-up draws loop closed
6. Feed moves material to next stitch position
7. Needle descends to lowest point of stroke
8. New loop has been formed and is passing around bobbin
9. Loop is pulled up to complete stitch

Major parts of a SNLS Machine – Identification

	Hook Set The rotating part carries the Bobbin and allows the needle thread to pass through and making the interlacing possible.
	Feed Dog & Presser Foot The Feed dog makes the fabric advancing after the stitch formation the distance being id moves is the stitch length Presser foot holds the fabric together and allows to keep the fabric together.
	Needle Thread Tension Assembly To control the tension in needle thread to for the right stitch
	Stitch Dial To control Stitch length, the marking in the dial is the distance between stitches in millimetre

OVER LOCK MACHINE

An overlock stitch sews over the edge of one or two pieces of cloth for edging, hemming or seaming. Usually an overlock sewing machine will cut the edges of the cloth as they are fed through some are made without cutters. An overlock sewing machine differs from a lockstitch sewing machine in that it uses loopers fed by multiple thread cones rather than a bobbin. Loopers serve to create thread loops that pass from the needle thread to the edges of the fabric so that the edges of the fabric are contained within the seam.

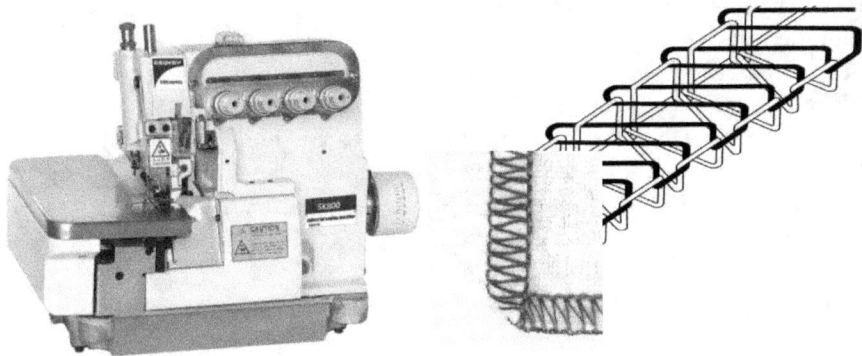

Over locking is also referred to as "over edging", "merrowing" or "serging". Though "serging" technically refers to over locking with cutters, in practice the four terms are used interchangeably.

Types Of Overlock Stitches

Overlock stitches are classified in a number of ways. The most basic classification is by the number of threads used in the stitch. Industrial overlock machines are generally made in 1, 2, 3, 4, or 5 thread formations. Each of these formations has unique uses and benefits:

- 1-thread: End-to-end seaming or 'butt-seaming' of piece goods for textile finishing.
- 2-thread: Edging and seaming, especially on knits and woven, finishing seam edges, stitching flat lock seams, stitching elastic and lace to lingerie, and hemming. This is the most common type of overlock stitch.
- 3-thread: Sewing pin tucks, creating narrow rolled hems, finishing fabric edges, decorative edging, and seaming knit or woven fabrics.
- 4-thread: Decorative edging and finishing, seaming high-stress areas, mock safety stitches which create extra strength while retaining flexibility.

- 5-thread: In apparel manufacturing, safety stitches utilizing 2 needles create a very strong seam. For every 1 cm of seam length you would require 20 cm of thread to sew it.

Technical Details

No of threads used - 3 to 6 threads based on machine
Feed system   - Differential Feed
Needles used   - 1 to 3 based on model
Number of looper   - 2 to 3 based on model
Stitch length   - 0.8 mm to 4 mm
Needle gauge   - 2.0, 2.4, 3.2 mm to 2.0, 3.2, 4.0, 4.8 mm
Over edge width   - 1.6 mm to 6.4 mm based on model
Gathering stitch   - 1:2 to 1: 4 max on standard adjustments
Stretching stitch - 1:0.7 to 1: 0.6 Max on standard adjustments
Type of Needle   - DC x 27 or DC x 1
Presser foot lift - 7.0 mm
Sewing speed   - 6000 rpm to 8000 rpm

fabric can be gathered

rear feed dog   front feed dog

Threading The Machine

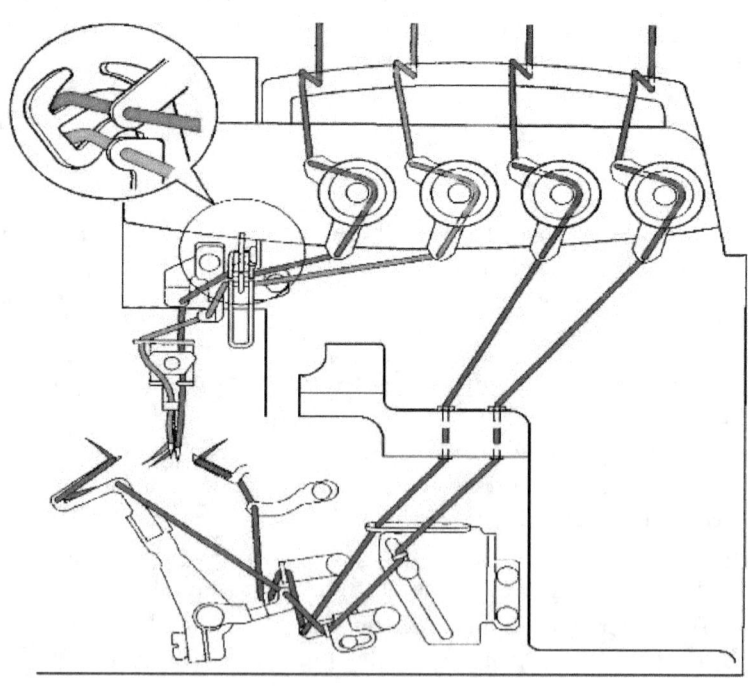

The Formation Of An Overlock Stitch

- When the needle enters the fabric, a loop is formed in the thread at the back of the needle.
- As the needle continues its downward motion into the fabric, the lower looper begins its movement from left to right. The tip of the lower looper passes behind the needle and through the loop of thread that has formed behind the needle.
- The lower looper continues along its path moving toward the right of the serger. As it moves, the lower thread is carried through the needle thread.
- While the lower looper is moving from left to right, the upper looper advances from right to left. The tip of the upper looper passes behind the lower looper and picks up the lower looper thread and needle thread.
- The lower looper now begins its move back into the far left position. As the upper looper continues to the left, it holds the lower looper thread and needle thread in place.
- The needle again begins its downward path passing behind the upper looper and securing the upper looper thread. This completes the overlock stitch formation and begins the stitch cycle all over again.

Machine Parts

	**Looper** Upper & Lower looper will carry the looper threads to form the chain stitch & covering stitch in the Over locking process
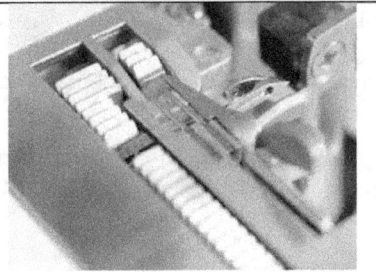	**Feed Dog** Two feed dogs as Overlock machine has the Differential feed mechanism

	**Thread Tension Assembly** The perfect stitch can only be produced with a right tension provided on each of the threads used for sewing. All the looper and needle threads are passed through the tension assembly.
	**Feed control mechanism** Two feed dogs as Overlock machine has the Differential feed mechanism. Adjusting the feed between two feed dogs will create stretch or gather stitching
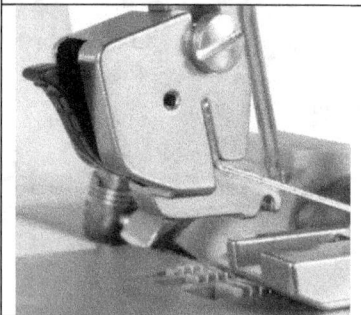	**Thread cutter & Guide** Overlock machine needs continuous operation and need to cut threads on an easy and perfect way so that the SAM should be less, hence an attached thread cutter with the presser foot will give the action of cutter.

SEWING MACHINE PRACTICAL TRAINING.

The operators and supervisors should have good handle over sewing machines, supervisors especially should have handle over most of the machineries used in the production line so as to identify the task and to understand and allocate proper operators to the specific machine and operation.

In apparel industry there are many methods used to give handle and speed to the operators , the below list of procedure is basic, to develop a flotter mode operator.

N	Exercise	Machine	Aim
1	Paper – Straight Line	SNLS	Pedal Control with maximum speed
2	Paper – precise Start Stop	SNLS-UBT	Pedal Control and Precise start stop practice in UBT
3	Paper – Straight Stitch	SNLS	Straight line stitching at Maximum Speed
4	Paper – U Stitches	SNLS-UBT	Change Direction with Needle Down
5	Paper –Sewing Curve (parabolic)	SNLS	Sewing Curve lines with one hand
6	Paper – ZIG ZAG Stitching	SNLS-UBT	Stitching Zigzag lines in maximum speed
7	Paper – Sewing Circles	SNLS-UBT	Stitching Circles in Maximum speed
8	Paper- Straight Line	Over Lock	Sewing straight Line in an Over lock Machine
9	Paper – Stop & align	Over lock	Exact stops and changing alignment in O/L
10	Paper – Sewing Curves	Over Lock	Practicing Curve Stitching in O/L
11	Fabric- Loop Stitching	SNLS	Practicing High Speed stitching in single bust
12	Fabric- Turn & parallel Stitch	SNLS-UBT	Stitch Parallel lines and Exact Turn
13	Fabric- Back Tack	SNLS/UBT	Practice Back Tack in same position Parallel Stitches
14	Fabric- Edge Stitching	SNLS/UBT	Practice high speed edge stitching without guides.
15	Fabric- Hem	SNLS	Hem and Edge stitch
16	Fabric-French Seams	SNLS UBT	Preparation of a French seam
17	Fabric- Shirt Placket	SNLS	Preparation of a Shirt front Placket – 2 piece
18	Fabric-Flat Fell Seam	SNLS	Seam Practice
19	Fabric- Sleeve Placket – Diamond	SNLS	Preparation of a Shirt Sleeve placket – diamond top

20	Fabric-Shirt Pocket stitching	SNLS – ES	Sew a Shirt pocket using Edge guide
21	Fabric- Shirt Collar	SNLS/ES	Sew a Two piece Shirt Collar
22	Fabric- attaching Zipper	SNLS/ES	To know how to attach a zipper on a trouser
23	Fabric – Bone Pocket and Top stitch	SNLS	To learn how to sew a bone pocket in trouser
24	O/L- Curve Stitches	O/L	Learn how to sew on Over lock machine in max speed
25	O/L- Circle Sewing	O/L	Learn how to sew on Over lock machine in max speed
26	Flat Lock – Knit Hem	FL	Learn to sew in Flat lock Machine
27	FOA – Sleeve Loop	FOA	Learn how to sew on a FOA machine in top speed
28	Bar Tack –	LK	Put bar tacks on the markings
29	Button Sew	LK	Put Buttons in all the dots
30	Button Hole	LBH	Make button holes in all markings
31	Stitch- Shirt - Woven		Learn how to sew a basic shirt
32	Stitch – Polo Shirt - Knit		Learn how to sew a polo Shirt

Operation can be selected according to the specific need of the industry and operator based on operation. The shapes of the Paper practice are as follows, it is done in paper to get maximum handle.

Paper Exercise – Straight Line - SNLS

SAM - 0.10 min

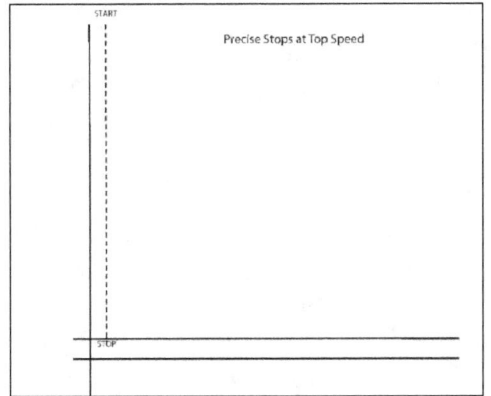

Paper Exercise – Precise Stop at Top Speed - SNLS

SAM 0.10 min

Objective - to learn the precise stopping of a clutch machine.

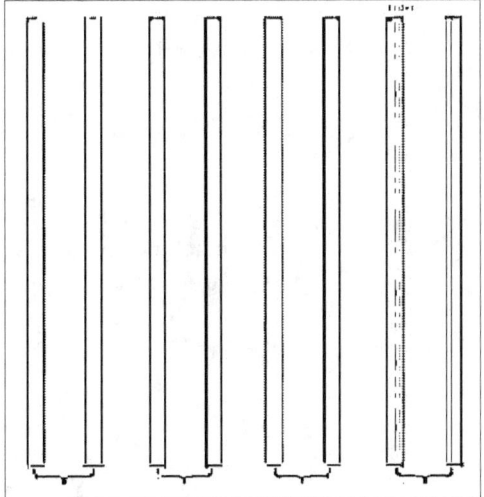

Paper Exercise – Straight Line Stitches

SAM - 0.17 min

Objective - to learn the SNLS machine operation in Full speed

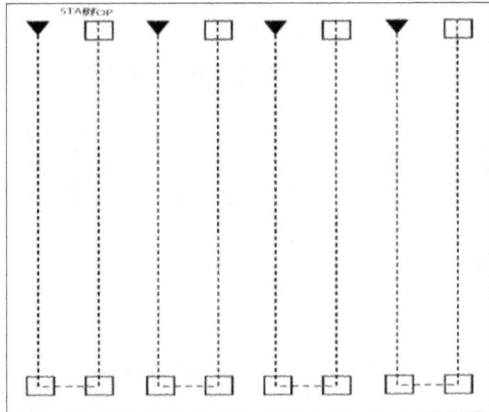

Paper Exercise – Turn and Stitch

SAM - 0.17 min

Objective - to learn the SNLS machine for precise Turn and Straight line stitch

Paper Exercise – Curve Stitches

SAM - 0.33 min

Objective - to learn the SNLS machine for precise curve stitches

Paper Exercise – Judging Turns

SAM - 0.330 min

Objective - to learn the SNLS machine for precise Turn and Straight line stitch

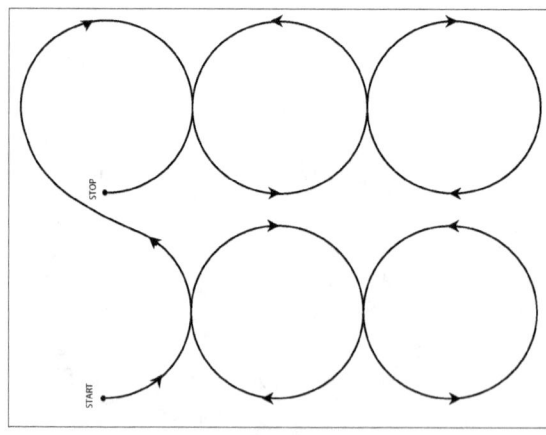

Paper Exercise – Sewing Circles

SAM - 0.570 min

Objective - to learn the SNLS machine for precise circles

Paper Exercise – Straight Line Stitch - Over Lock

SAM - 0.20 min

Objective - to learn the over lock machine Stitching

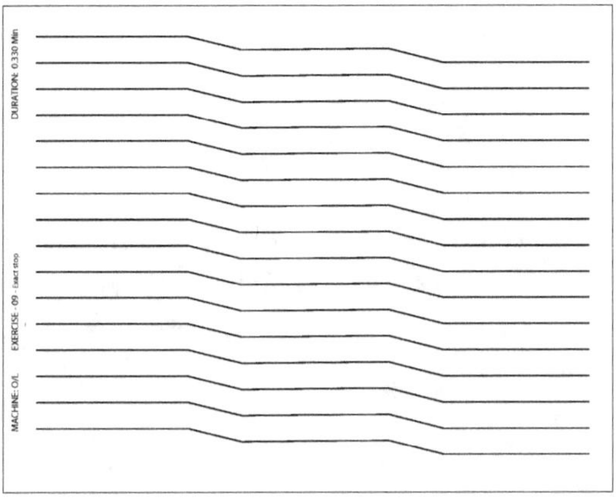

Paper Exercise – Precision stop and align - Over Lock

SAM - 0.330 min

Objective - to learn the over lock machine Stitching

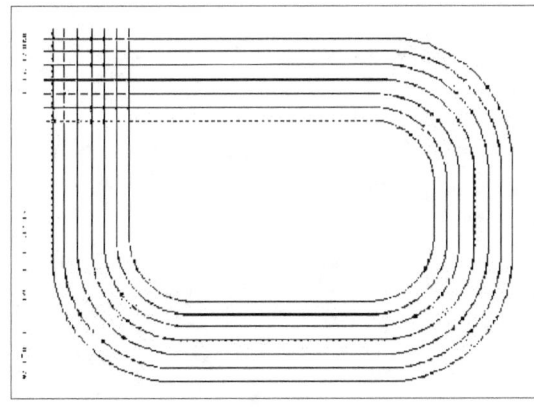

Paper Exercise – Sewing Curves - Over Lock

SAM - 0.250 min

Objective - to learn the over lock machine Stitching

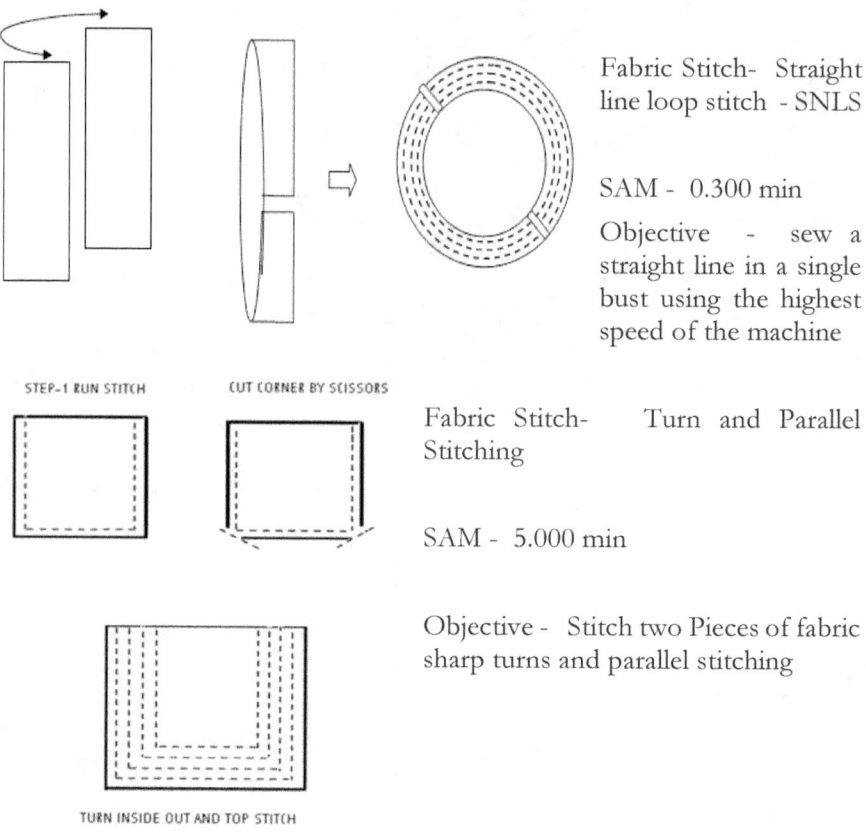

STEP-1 RUN STITCH   CUT CORNER BY SCISSORS

TURN INSIDE OUT AND TOP STITCH

Fabric Stitch- Straight line loop stitch - SNLS

SAM - 0.300 min

Objective - sew a straight line in a single bust using the highest speed of the machine

Fabric Stitch- Turn and Parallel Stitching

SAM - 5.000 min

Objective - Stitch two Pieces of fabric sharp turns and parallel stitching

The other exercises are can be followed as per the industry basics

24 IMPORTANCE OF DISCIPLINE

Discipline is very essential for a healthy industrial atmosphere and the achievement of organizational goals. Discipline in industry may be described as willing cooperation and observance of the rules and regulations of the organization. Discipline is essential to a democratic way of life. According to Brembless: "Discipline does not mean a strict and technical observation of rigid rules and regulations. It simply means working, co-operating and behaving in a normal & orderly way, as any responsible person would accept an employee to do"

Importance of Discipline in industry.

Discipline is the very essence of life. The goals or objectives of industrial discipline should be clearly stated.

- To ensure that employers & employee recognize each other's rights and obligations.
- To promote constructive cooperation between the parties concerned at all levels.
- To maintain discipline in industry.
- To secure settlement of disputes & grievances by negotiation, cancellations voluntary arbitration.
- To eliminate all forms of coercion violence in industrial relation.
- To avoid work stoppages.
- To facilitate the free growth of trade unions.
- Respect for the human personality.
- Management personnel should set high standards.

Code Of Discipline In Industry

To maintain harmonious relations and promote industrial peace, a Code of Discipline has been laid down which applies to both public and private sector enterprises. It specifies various obligations for the management and the workers with the objective of promoting cooperation between their representatives.

The basic objectives of Code of Discipline are to:

- Maintain peace and order in industry.
- Promote constructive criticism at all levels of management and employment.
- Avoid work stoppage in industry
- Secure the settlement of disputes and grievances by a mutually agreed procedure
- Avoiding litigations
- Facilitate a free growth of trade unions
- Eliminate all forms of coercion, intimidation and violations of rules and regulations governing industrial relations.

Importance of Attendance

Timely and regular attendance is an expectation of performance for all employees in an organization. To ensure adequate staffing, positive employee morale, and to meet expected productivity standards throughout the organization, employees will be held accountable for adhering to their workplace schedule. In the event an employee is unable to meet this expectation, he/she must obtain approval from their supervisor in advance of any requested schedule changes. This approval includes requests to use sick, vacation and/or personal time, as well as late arrivals to or early departures from work. Departments have discretion to evaluate extraordinary circumstances of a tardy, absence or failure to clock-in or clock-out and determine whether or not to count the incident as an occurrence. HR Consultants are available to advise supervisors regarding the evaluation of extenuating circumstances.

Importance of Team Work

A group of individuals who are working together to achieve a common goal is known as teamwork. "Teamwork is the ability to work together toward a common vision. The ability to direct individual accomplishments toward organizational objectives. It is the fuel that allows common people to attain uncommon results." Teamwork is a process of working together and achieving common goals. In order to understand teamwork better, we need to differentiate between teamwork and group.

The fashion industry rarely relies on a single individual to handle all aspects of a project. Although one person might have the initial vision, various teams bring that vision to life. These teams include everything from design teams to production teams to sales team. There is usually a team maintaining a web presence for the design company. The success of the fashion company is the overall output of the teams, or we can say the success of the teams of teams.

Advantages of Team Work.

- Increased work Efficiency
- Improved employee relation
- Increased accountability
- Increased learning opportunities

Importance of Volunteer Work

Volunteer work is defined by ILO as "Volunteering is an unpaid non-compulsory work; that is, time individuals give without pay to activities performed either through an organization or directly for others outside their own household"

The key points defined are,

- Volunteering involves work:- volunteering involves activities that produce goods and or services which contribute something of potential value to its receivers

- Volunteering is unpaid:- it is without pay or compensation, in cash or any means, except the volunteers may be reimbursed for their out-of-pocket expenses may incur in their assignment, and may receive stipends intended to cover their own living expenses

- It is non-compulsory:- persons engaging in these activities should be willingly, without being legally obliged or otherwise coerced to do so. Unpaid apprenticeships required for entry into a job and internships and student volunteer work required for graduation or continuation in a school or training program violates the non-compulsory feature of the definition and should not be considered as volunteer work.

25 WORK ETHICS

Work ethic is a value based on hard work and diligence. It is also a belief in the moral benefit of work and its ability to enhance character. A work ethic may include being reliable, having initiative, or pursuing new skills.

Value of Work Ethics

The top 10 values of work ethics that and employer expects from an employee

1. Strong Work Ethic
2. Dependability and Responsibility
3. Possessing a Positive Attitude
4. Adaptability
5. Honesty and Integrity
6. Self- Motivated
7. Motivated to Grow & Learn
8. Strong Self- Confidence
9. Professionalism
10. Loyalty

1. Strong Work Ethic

Employers value employees who understand and possess a willingness to work hard. In addition to working hard it is also important to work smart. It's also important to care about your job and complete all projects by saving time while maintaining a positive attitude. Doing more than is expected on the job is a good way to show management that you utilize good time management skills and don't waste valuable company time attending to personal issues not related to the job. Downsizing in today's job market is quite common so it's important to recognize the personal values and attributes employers want to improve your chances of job security should a layoff occur.

2. Dependability and Responsibility

Employer's value employees who come to work on time, are there when they are supposed to be, and are responsible for their actions and behavior. It's important to keep supervisors abreast of changes in your schedule or if you are going to be late for any reason. This also means keeping your supervisor informed on where you are on all projects you have been assigned

3. Possessing a Positive Attitude.

Employers seek employees who take the initiative and have the motivation to get the job done in a reasonable period of time. A positive attitude gets the work done and motivates others to do the same without dwelling on the challenges that inevitably come up in any job. It is the enthusiastic employee who creates an environment of good will and who provides a positive role model for others. A positive attitude is something that is most valued by supervisors and co-workers and that also makes the job more pleasant and fun to go to each day.

4. Adaptability

Adaptability means adapting to the personality and work habits of co-workers and supervisors. Each person possesses their own set or strengths and adapting personal behaviors to accommodate others is part of what it takes to work effectively as a team. By viewing change as an opportunity to complete work assignments in a more efficient manner, adapting to change can be a positive experience.

Employers seek employees who are adaptable and maintain flexibility in completing tasks in an ever changing workplace. Being open to change and improvements provides an opportunity to complete work assignments in a more efficient manner while offering additional benefits to the corporation, the customer, and even the employee.

5. Honesty and Integrity

Employers value employees who maintain a sense of honesty and integrity above all else. Good relationships are built on trust. When working for an employer they want to know that they can trust what you say and what you do. Successful businesses work to gain the trust of customers and maintain the attitude that "the customer is always right". It is the responsibility of each person to use their own individual sense of moral and ethical behavior when working with and serving others within the scope of their job.

6. Self – Motivated

Employers look for employees who require little supervision and direction to get the work done in a timely and professional manner. For self-motivated employees require very little direction from their supervisors. Once a self-motivated employee understands his/her responsibility on the job, they will do it without any prodding from others

7. Motivated to Grow & Learn

In an ever-changing workplace, employers seek employees who are interested in keeping up with new developments and knowledge in the field. It has been noted that one of the top reasons employees leave their employers is the lack of opportunity for career development within the organization. Learning new skills, techniques, methods, and/or theories through professional development helps keep the organization at the top of its field and makes the employee's job more interesting and exciting. Keeping up with current changes in the field is vital for success and increased job security

8. Strong Self – Confidence

Self-confidence has been recognized as the key ingredient between someone who is successful and someone who is not. A self – confident person is someone who inspires others. A self-confident person is not afraid to ask questions on topics where they feel they need more knowledge. The self-confident person does what he/she feels is right and is  willing to take risks. Self- confident people can also admit their mistakes. They recognize their strengths as well as their weaknesses and are willing to work on the latter. Self-confident people have faith in themselves and their abilities which is manifested in their positive attitude and outlook on life.

9. Professionalism

Employers value employees who exhibit professional behavior at all times. Professional behavior includes learning every aspect of a job and doing it to the best of one's ability. Professionals look, speak, and dress accordingly to maintain an image of someone who takes pride in their behavior and appearance. Professionals complete projects as soon as possible and avoid letting uncompleted projects pile up. Professionals complete high quality work and are detail oriented. Professional behavior includes all of the behavior above in addition to providing a positive role model for others.

Professionals are enthusiastic about their work and optimistic about the organization and its future. To become a professional you must feel like a professional and following these tips is a great start to getting to where you want to go.

10. Loyalty

Employers value employees they can trust and who exhibit their loyalty to the company. Companies offering employee growth and opportunity will ultimately gain a sense of loyalty from their employees. Employees today want to feel a sense of satisfaction in their jobs and will do a good job when they feel that the employer is fair and wants to see them succeed. Although this may mean only staying for five or ten years in a position,  employees can offer loyalty and make an important contribution during their time with the company. More companies today encourage employee feedback and offer employees an opportunity to lead in their area of expertise. This gives employees a greater sense of satisfaction and a sense of control over their job. Empowerment encourages employees to do their best work since companies are displaying a trust and expectation that they believe in their employees to do a good job.

RIGHT FIRST TIME (QUALITY AWARENESS)

The Total Quality Management is the popular concept views quality entirely from the point of the customer. The principles of TQM is based on "Fit for Purpose", the product should be suitable for the intended purpose, and *"Right First Time"*.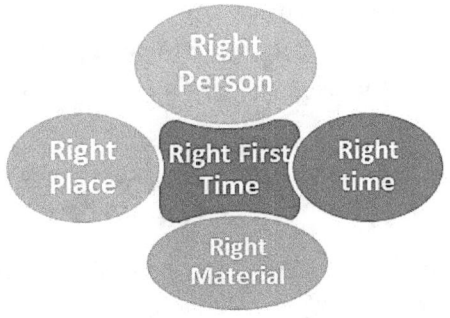

The right First Time concept states that the defects and problems have to be rectified at where it is happening or the discussion have to be made at the point of occurrence only. With a concept that, if a defect or problem is not solved at the very beginning of its development, it can cause major loss in the product, hence the RFT actions related to Quality Assurance will be taken right from Raw materials, assemblies, products and components, any defect found, it may be mended, if possible and will not affect the quality of product, or removed from the stage so that the defective session will never forwarded further in the production process,

MAINTENANCE & CLEANLINESS OF THE WORK PLACE

Workplace management is a series of activities for planning, designing, using and disposing items surrounding the workplace for the purpose of helping employees organize their daily tasks and optimize the use of resources and facilities. Regular maintenance of the workplace of essential to keep the work environment, machines and equipment's and workers in safe and reliable position providing positive atmosphere to work enrichment. It helps to eliminate workplace hazards. Lack of maintenance or inadequate maintenance can lead to dangerous situations, accidents and health problems.

The key aspects of workplace management are

✓ Plan – including collecting information, conducting risk assessment and deciding on control measures needed to control risk, such as training workers or keeping them informed.

✓ Make it safe - including obtaining the appropriate permits to work from the operating authority, securing safe access to and exit from work zone, 'power down', and securing the work area for the safety of maintenance workers.

✓ Work safely – including using only appropriate equipment; not only the correct tools, but also the right protective equipment and clothing.

✓ Work as planned – follow the agreed plan and the accepted system of work, taking no shortcuts.

✓ Check – make sure that the maintenance procedure has been successfully completed and that it has not created additional risks before signing off the job.

26 PRINCIPLES OF ERGONOMICS

Ergonomics derives from two Greek words, ergon, meaning work, and nomoi, meaning natural laws, to create a word that means the science of work and a person's relation to that work

Ergonomics is the study of the relationship between a person and their work environment. The objective is to adapt the workplace for the worker in order to decrease the risk of injury and improve the link between the worker and their environment

Principles of Ergonomics are,

- Keep everything in easy reach
- Work at Proper Heights
- Reduce Excessive force
- Work in good posture
- Reduce Excessive Repitition
- Minimize Direct Pressure
- Provide adjustibility and change of posture
- Provide clearence and access
- Maintain a comfortable environment
- Enhance clarity and understanding
- Improve Work Organization

Principle 1: Work in Natural postures

Our posture provides a good starting point for evaluating the tasks that you do. The best positions in which to work are those that keep the body "in neutral."

Maintain The "S-Curve" Of The Spine

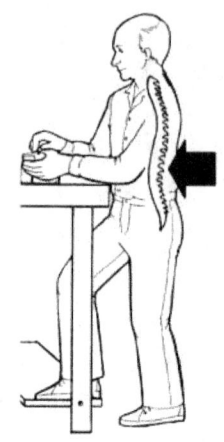

Your spinal column is shaped more or less like an "S." It is important to maintain the natural S-curve of the back, whether sitting or standing. The most important part of this "S" is in the lower back, which means that it is good to keep a slight "sway back,"

When standing, putting one foot up on a footrest helps to keep the spinal column in proper alignment.

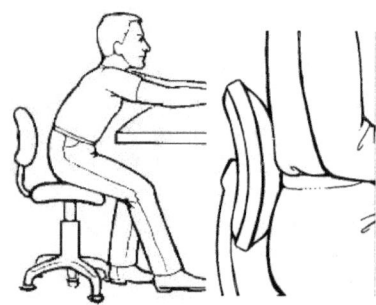

Working for long periods with your back in a "C-curve" can place strain on your back.

Good lumbar support is often helpful to maintain the proper curve in the small of your back.

The "Inverted V-curve" creates an even greater strain on your back. Even without lifting a load, bending over like this creates a great deal of pressure on the spine. One common improvement is to use a lifter or tilter. Or there may be other ways of making improvements depending upon the situation

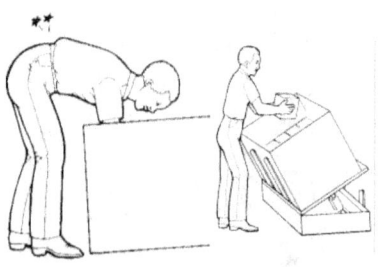

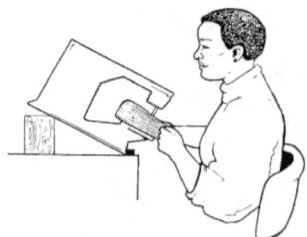

Keep the neck aligned

The neck bones are part of the spinal column and thus are subject to the same requirements of maintaining the S-curve. Prolonged twisted and bent postures of the neck can be as stressful as its equivalent for the lower back.

The best way to make changes is usually to adjust equipment so that your neck is in its neutral posture.

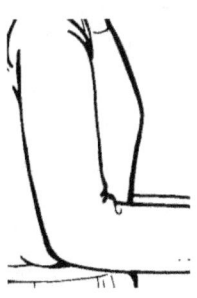

Keep elbows at sides

The neutral posture for your arms is to keep you elbows at your sides and your shoulders relaxed. This is pretty obvious once you think about it, but we don't always do it.

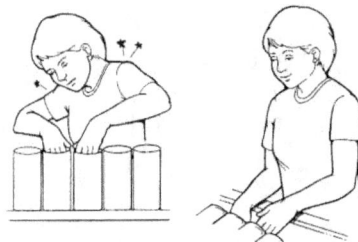

Here's an example of changing a workstation to get the arms in neutral. In the illustration at the left, the product is too high, and the employee is hunching her shoulders and winging out her elbows.

In the right-hand illustration, the product has been reoriented and the shoulders and elbows drop to their relaxed position.

Keep Wrists in Neutral

There are several good ways to think about wrist posture. One way is to keep the hand in the same plane as the forearm, as this person is doing here by using a wrist rest along with the computer mouse.

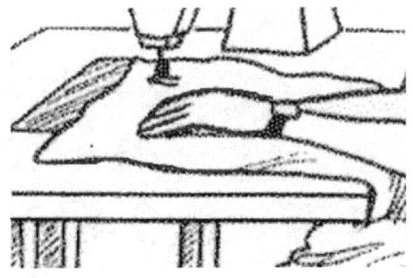

Principle 2: Reduce Excessive Force

Excessive force on your joints can create a potential for fatigue and injury. In practical terms, the action item is for you to identify specific instances of excessive force and think of ways to make improvements.

Pulling a heavy cart might create excessive force for your back.

To make improvements it might help to make sure the floor is in good repair, that the wheels on the

cart are sufficiently large, and that there are good grips on the cart. Or a power tagger might be needed.

Or another example of reducing force is to use a hoist for lifting heavy objects,.

Principle 3: Keep Everything in Easy Reach

The next principle deals with keeping things within easy reach. In many ways, this principle is redundant with posture, but it helps to evaluate a task from this specific perspective.

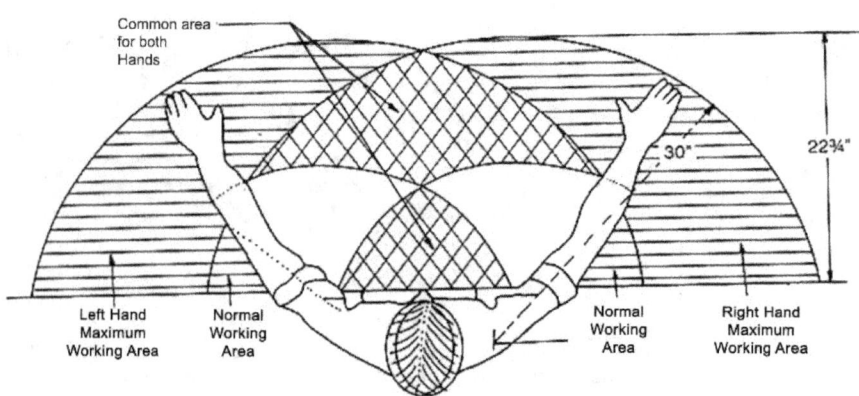

Much of the time, problems with reach are simply matters of rearranging your work area and moving things closer to you.

Often it is a matter of habit — you are unaware that you continually reach for something that could be easily moved closer.

Principle 4: Work at Proper Heights

Working at the right height is also a way to make things easier

Do most work at elbow height

A good rule of thumb is that most work should be done at about elbow height, whether sitting or standing.

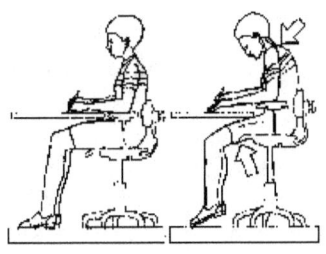

A real common example is working with a computer keyboard. But, there are many other types of tasks where the rule applies.

Principle 5: Reduce Excessive Motions

The next principle to think about is the number of motions you make throughout a day, whether with your fingers, your wrists, your arms, or your back. One of the simplest ways to reduce manual repetitions is to use power tools whenever possible. Another approach is to change

layouts of equipment to eliminate motions. In the example here, the box is moved closer and tilted, so that you can slide the products in, rather than having to pick them up each time.

Principle 6: Minimize Fatigue and Static Load

Holding the same position for a period of time is known as static load. It creates fatigue and discomfort and can interfere with work

In the workplace, having to hold parts and tools continually is an example of static load.

In this case, using a fixture eliminates the need to hold onto the part.

Having to hold your arms overhead for a few minutes is another classic example of static load, this time affecting the shoulder muscles. Sometimes you can change the orientation of the work area to prevent this, or sometimes you can add extenders to the tools.

Having to stand for a long time creates a static load on your legs. Simply having a footrest can permit you to reposition your legs and make it easier to stand

Principle 7: Minimize Pressure Points

Another thing to watch out for is excessive pressure points, sometimes called "contact stress."

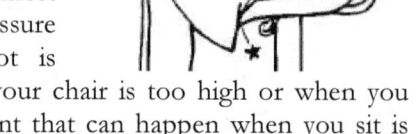

We've all had to sit on chairs that had cushioning and so understand almost everything we need to know about pressure points. A particularly vulnerable spot is behind your knees, which happens if your chair is too high or when you dangle your legs. Another pressure point that can happen when you sit is between your thigh and the bottom of a table.

A slightly more subtle kind of pressure point occurs when you stand on a hard surface, like concrete. Your heels and feet can begin to hurt and your whole legs can begin to tire. The answer is anti-fatigue matting or sometimes using special insoles in your shoes.

Principle 8: Provide Clearance

Having enough clearance is a concept that is easy to relate to.

Work areas need to be set up so that you have sufficient room for your head, your knees, and your feet. You obviously don't want to have to bump into things all the time, or have to work in contorted postures, or reach because there is no space for your knees or feet.

Being able to see is another version of this principle. Equipment should be built and tasks should be set up so that nothing blocks your view

Principle 09: Maintain a Comfortable Environment

This principle is more or less a catch-all that can mean different things depending upon the nature of the types of operations that you do

Lighting and Glare

One common problem is lighting.

In the computerized office, lighting has become a big issue, because the highly polished computer screen reflects every stray bit of light around.

Vibration

Vibration is another common problem that can benefit from evaluation. As an example, vibrating tools can be dampened

Principle 09: Reduce Fatigue Using Workplace Exercises

Neck and face, Shoulders & arms, Wrist & Hand, Back, Leg & ankles

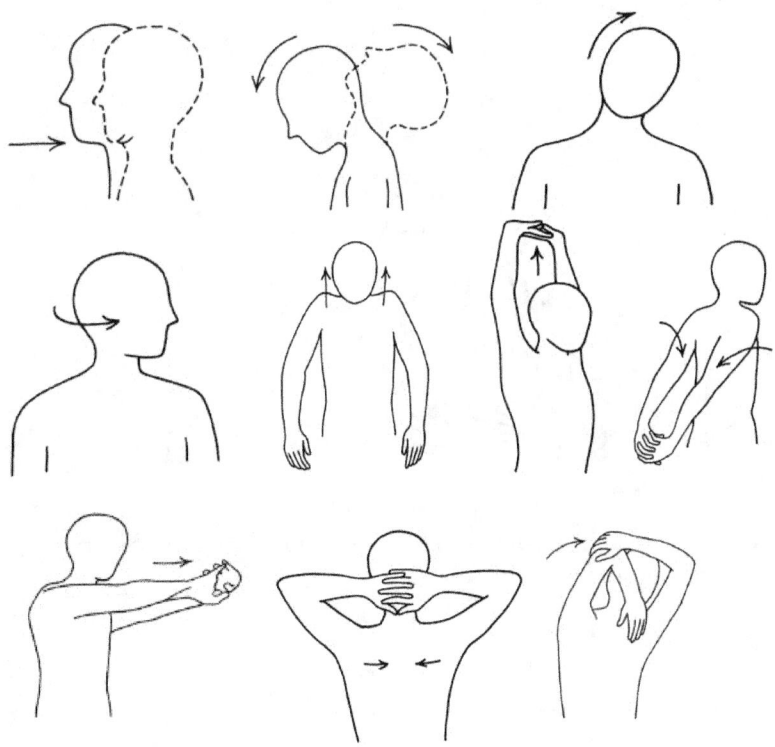

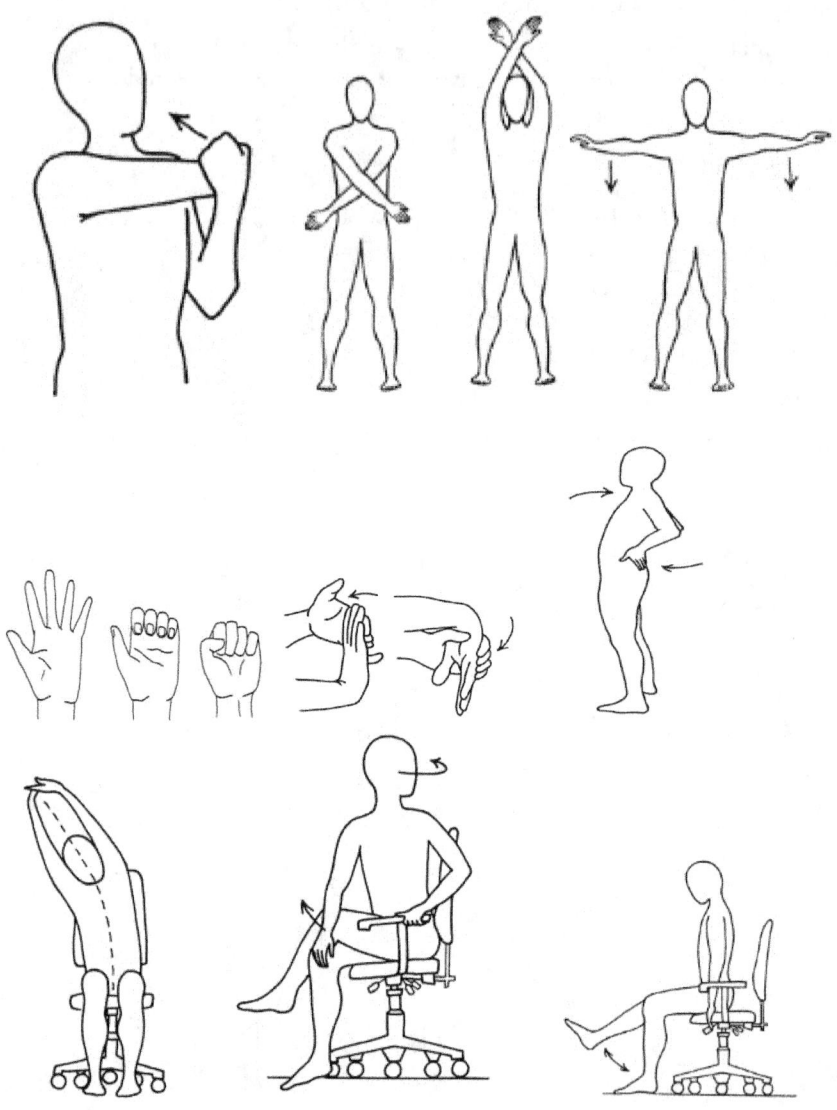

The session gives general awareness about the principles of ergonomics and the common ergonomic principles used.

27 IMPORTANCE & PRACTICES OF COMMUNICATION

Communication is the activity of conveying information through the exchange of thoughts, messages or information as by speech, visuals, signals, writing, or behavior. It is the meaningful exchange of information between two or group of living creatures. The world derived from the Latin word communicare means share.

Communication requires a sender, a message, and a recipient, although the receiver doesn't have to be present or aware of the sender's intent to communicate at the time of communication; thus communication can occur across vast distances in time and space. Communication requires that the communicating parties share an area of communicative commonality. The communication process is complete once the receiver has understood the message of the sender.

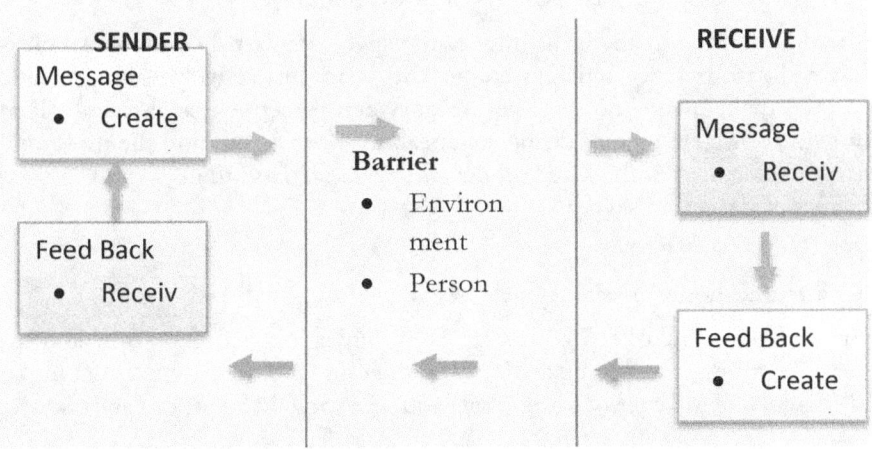

There are two types of communications happening in the apparel industry

1.   Verbal communication :- spoken or written mode

2.   Nonverbal communication :- gestures and other means

Important things to keep your eyes on while practicing the fine art of communication are:

Body Language

Do not shy away from the person with whom you are speaking. Be sure to maintain a relaxed, but not slouching posture, regardless whether you are the one speaking or listening. Other things that ensure your body is communicating your attentiveness to the conversation can include:

•   Making eye contact

•   Nodding occasionally to acknowledge a strong point in the conversation

•   Standing with hands clasped in front of you, never crossing your arms

•   Not displaying nervous ticks such as wringing hands, picking at your nails, or anything that the person communicating with you will view as a distraction from their conversation.

Speech and Attentiveness

When speaking, Speak on important matters directly and do not waste time with long drawn out stories that will cause your listener's mind to wander. Make sure you ask whether they understand, and be willing to further explain any of your points. Do not expect someone to just "know" what you are saying, even if it is crystal clear in your own mind.

In addition, one of the most important aspects of verbal communication is the ability to practice active listening. This is not just actively waiting to talk. Always make mental notes of key points when someone is speaking to. That way once you are given a chance to speak, you can respond to the most vital issues being dealt with. When others are speaking, try to think about the exact words that they are saying

Communication Consistency

Supervisors should keep consistent communication with employer and his team members, Do not be afraid to be the one who voices any concerns or difficulties. However, ensure that you are practicing open and honest communication with those who may depend on you. Be available and bold with tact.

Be sure to leave communication lines open to those who may need to address problems with, Discuss with the team to prevent the small issues that normally becomes the large.

Patience

During the communications with others always give them time to communicate their issues as well. Remaining focused on what they are trying to communicate will show them that you are indeed open to assisting with their issues. Many of people's communication lines tend to break down on the side where impatience is in a rush to get out of the conversation. Since you cannot control the other side, do yourself a favor and take a breath. The conversation you're involved in is important.

If you are confused as to what someone may be requesting, than repeat back to him or her what you think they said and ask if that is correct. Often this will inspire the speaker to be more in-depth about their needs, which will help you to understand them fully.

BARRIERS TO COMMUNICATION

When a communication occurs, it is important that the receiver decoded the same message that the sender send to him. In some cases it may happen that the receiver miss understands the speaker, may be in meaning or by means of action. There are many causes' affects the communication interpreting, the barriers may change or effect in it, some of the important barriers are as,

1. Environmental barriers: - are characteristic of the organization and its environmental setting. E.g.:- The receiver hears the message, but does not understand it. Due to inadequate attention paid to the message, the receiver is not really "listening."

2. Personal barriers: - arise from the nature of individuals and their interaction with others. E.g.:- some cultures believe in "don't speak unless spoken to" or "never question elders"

The collective issues happened due the common barriers of communication are,

1. Failure to listen

- Listening is a skill must be learned and practiced by the supervisor
- Often the message is in How it is been said then What it is

2. Status Difference
    - Newer employees listen to veteran employees
    - Bosses have status
    - Some may use status to manipulate and control others by withholding information

3. Psychological size
    - Closely related to status but has nothing to do with rank
    - People with power have physiological size making them either effective of intimidating

4. Noise
    - On average people have a 15 second attention span that can be directly affected by activities going around them
    - Meeting rooms are usually good for effective communication

5. Language
    - The 500most commonly used words in English have about 14,000 meanings (e.g. "RUN" a sprinter can run in a race, a women can get run in her home is troublesome, to score a run in baseball is different than a run in cricket)
    - Much of what we communicate depends on context, insinuation, local definition, common usage, dialect and even accent.

6. Feed Back
    - The communication cycle is not completed until you have received feedback about the message
    - Ask questions to ensure that you are being understood

7. Fear of criticism
    - Due to fear of criticism do not suppress words so that the meaning may be wrong.

8. Jumping of conclusions
    - Some personnel will make a pre judged decisions before making a conversation itself for example the supervisor should not make a blind decision to dispatch a tailor and speaks to him for his comments and whatever his reply takes the action, this communication method is pre judged and hence the pre judgment is the barrier

9. Filtering
   - New information's are passed through each person's set of filtering's that are based on that persons experience and training
10. Competing messages
   - Give only proper and sufficient amount of messages.

Communicating with senior Officials

The supervisor should be aware about the prospective / concerns of the senior manager to have a broader focus when communicating with senior management. Focus on the most critical things need to tell a senior manager. If the communication is through writing then the intent should be clear within first 2 to 4 lines and in verbal then it should be clear within the first minute (say 1 minute). Over communication is the major problems before going to talk with a senior official do the preparation

- Prepare a list of outlines of the points those you want to speak, take the notes and refer with those
- Always give a time bound, when asked unknown questions, to give answers those are unaware
- Don't sent any email or letters before verifying it twice
- Be an effective listener and establish eye contact with the speaker, focus on each points
- Always talk in a positive, clear and calm voice to the senior level, avoid harsh and critic words

Communicating with Operators

When communicating with operators a supervisor should always keep in mind that the operators are the "key" persons who have to do better Quality product in a maximum efficiency and the performance of the operators are the key measuring factor of a supervisor. Hence almost case should be taken with the operators of the industry. The below are the important things to be taken care,

- Be Motivate :- always appreciate the good works done by the operator
- Language: - Use simple and positive language, always use the local language of the operator to explain and communicate with the operator effectively so that the operator understands what the supervisors are explaining to him.
- Body language: - consider a smooth and pleasant gesture and body actions when communicating with operators in floor so as to convince them in their working. A pleasant speaker will always adapted by the operators.

- Give Privacy: - When dealing with an unfit operator who makes mistakes, lead them for a private workspace away from the primary job site. Your goal is to lead the employee away from other workers, customers and potentially harmful equipment or machinery. Gently encourage the employee to accompany you and your colleague; don't grab the person's hand or otherwise risk antagonizing him or her. And enquiry or advices have to be made there so as to make them more believe in the supervisor and Management so that they can be better handled.
- Prevent Violence: - a supervisor should communicate in a way that there should be no violence happen during the communication with the operators.
- Convey: - the management decisions to the operators properly and get the feedback from them is important.

Referrals

McMillan Publishing Co- Inside the Fashion Business.

Amubai Patel, Towards Zero Defects

Strong Elian- Fashion Merchandising

Hand Book of Textile Testing & Quality Control – Elliot B. Grover & D.S. Hamby.

Textile Testing – P. Angappan & R. Gopalakrishnan4.

Technology of clothing manufacture –BLatham& H.Carr

Apparel manufacturers hand book – Jacob Solinger(Sewing machine technical manuals)

Managing Quality in Apparel Industries – Pradeep V Metha & Satis K. Bhardwaj

Garment Engineering - Akhil JK- 2007 Pothybooks

Dr .N. Anbumani, "Knitting–Fundamentals, Machines, structures &Developments" New Age International publishers, Delhi

Social Accountability –Rajesh Chhabra

Seminar Textbook for sewing factory management Technicians- by Brother sewing Technology centre. Japan

Text Book on Product Management Skill and Technical Knowledge of industrial Sewing Machine for quality and Productivity Improvement by AOTS/Pegasus Japan20

Training Notes by Methods Work-study Training for ATDC by AEPC

http://en.wikipedia.org/wiki/Customstrade_Partnership_Against_Terrorism

http://www.wrapcompliance.org/en/certification-program

http://www.saasaccreditation.org/certbsci.htm

http://aepcdisha.wordpress.com/2012/10/12/compliance-code-guidelines-for-indian-garment-industry/

http://www.cbp.gov/xp/cgov/trade/cargo_security/ctpat/ctpat_portal/

http://www.onlineclothingstudy.com/2011/10/list-of-defects-found-in-garments.html

http://en.texsite.info/Printing_Defects

http://www.asiatextileinspections.com/

http://www.westminstercollege.edu/myriad/index.cfm?parent=2514&detail=4475&content=4798

http://www.preservearticles.com/2012051932603/5-main-importance-of-motivation-in-modern-organisations.html

http://www.managementstudyguide.com/team-motivation.htm

http://www.april1930s.com/html/machine_attachments.html.

http://visual.merriam-webster.com/arts-architecture/crafts/sewing

http://asq.org/learn-about-quality/cost-of- uality/overview/overview.html

Principles of Quality Costs: Principles, Implementation, and Use, Third Edition, ed. Jack Campanella, ASQ Quality Press, 1999, pages 3–5.

Training manuals and Training Note of Methods Work study training program, CITA Hong Kong Production Planning Training program etc. property of Akhil JK,

Akhil Jk

ABOUT THE AUTHOR

Akhil Jk , born in 1980 who has selected Textile as his subject of expertise in his first pace of life and undergone Engineering diploma studies from Central Polytechnic College, Thiruvananthapuram, Kerala, India. And further worked in leading apparel brands and Industries in reputed position. He latter continued his career as an Instructor in Apparel Training and Design Center and do as the state coordinator and South Indian Training of Trainer's Academy Head positions of ATDC. During the career and life he used to keep himself updated in the field.

Prior to this, he has written "Study of Woven Fabrics, and constantly updating his website www.fashionteacher.in , one of the reference websites in the fashion Learning